EARLY BUDDHIST PHILOSOPHY

in Light of the Four Noble Truths

Alfonso Verdu
Professor of Philosophy &
East Asian Studies
University of Kansas

University Press
of America™

University Press of America, Inc.™
4710 Auth Place, S.E., Washington D.C. 20023

Printed in the United States of America

ISBN: 0-8191-0189-3

Library of Congress Catalog Card Number: 79-66172

EARLY BUDDHIST PHILOSOPHY
in the
Light of the Four Noble Truths

Alfonso Verdu
University of Kansas

ACKNOWLEDGEMENTS

The composition of this work was made possible by a grant from the General Research Fund at the University of Kansas. Typing funds were provided by the Small Grants Subcommittee of the K.U. Research Administration. For their editorial assistance, the author wishes to express his gratitude to his graduate students Joseph VanZandt, David Duquette and Debra Nails. The author wishes to acknowledge the generous effort and help of Mrs. Connie Ducey (Department of Philosophy Secretary), and of Mrs. Pamela Dane and Nancy Kreighbaum (College of Liberal Arts and Sciences Word Processing Center) in bringing to completion the difficult setting of the final text, diacritics, notes, index and numerous charts.

Alfonso Verdu

University of Kansas

April 1979

EARLY BUDDHIST PHILOSOPHY
in the
Light of the Four Noble Truths

TABLE OF CONTENTS

Early Buddhist Philosophy

Introduction

Cattāri ariyasaccāni: dukkhaṃ ariyasaccaṃ
dukkhasamudayo ariyasaccaṃ
dukkhanirodho ariyasaccaṃ
dukkhanirodhagāminī paṭipadā ariyasaccaṃ.

There are Four Noble Truths:
The Noble Truth of Suffering
The Noble Truth of the Origination of Suffering
The Noble Truth of the Cessation of Suffering
The Noble Truth of the Path Leading to the Cessation of Suffering.

Dīghanikāya, II, 304

According to Buddhist tradition it is said that in the year 528 B.C., after having obtained final enlightenment under the bodhi-tree in Bodigayā, the Buddha Śākyamuni proceeded to Vārāṇaśī (Benares), where in a deer-park (presently called Sarnath), east of the city, he found five of his former companions in the practice of asceticism. These five ascetics had abandoned Siddhārtha Śākyamuni after the latter had forsaken the harsh practices of mortification and self-chastisement in favor of the mid-way of moderation as most conducive to the search of the ultimate truth. In the renewed presence of these five ascetics, Śākyamuni set "the wheel of the Dharma" (the Buddhist doctrine) into motion. So we are told in the Saṃyutta-Nikāya:

> Once the world-honored one was at Vārāṇaśī at the deer park called Ivipatana (presently Sarnath) he addressed the five monks in the following manner: There are two extremes not to be served by a wanderer (seeker of truth). One is the pursuit of desires and the pleasure which springs from desire . . . .the other is the pursuit of (self-inflicted) pain and hardship . . . .The Middle Way of the _Tathāgata_ (The Thus Come and Gone) avoids both of these two extremes. It is enlightened, it brings clear vision (of the Four Noble Truths) and it leads to peace and _Nirvāṇa_. . . .
> _And this is the Noble Truth of Sorrow._ Birth is sorrow, age is sorrow, disease is sorrow, death is sorrow; contact with the unpleasant is sorrow, separation from the pleasant is sorrow, every unfulfilled wish is sorrow. In short all the five _skandhas_ (components of individual existence) are sorrow.
> _And this is the Noble Truth of the Origin of Sorrow._ It originates from craving, which leads to rebirth, which brings delight and passion, and seeks pleasure now here, now there, the craving for sensual pleasure, the craving for continued life, the craving for power.
> _And this is the Noble Truth of the Halting of Sorrow._ It is the complete stopping of craving, so that no passion remains, abandoning it, being released from it, giving no place to it.
> _And this is the Noble Truth of the Way leading to the Halting of Sorrow._ It is the Noble Eightfold Path, namely, Right Views, Right Resolve, Right Speech, Right Conduct, Right Livelihood, Right Effort, Right Mindfulness, and Right Concentration.
> (_Saṃyutta-nikāya_ V, 421ff.)

This was the original Buddhist manifesto. It contains the roots of the whole, complex tree of Buddhist Religion and Philosophy. The Four Noble Truths are at the basis of all Buddhist efforts to explain the nature of existence, the structures of the psycho-cosmic reality of life, the Suffering that pervades these structures and the ultimate goal of absolute freedom. The whole History of Buddhist Thought, migrating from India into the vast regions of Southeast Asia and through China to Tibet, Korea, and Japan, represents the theoretico-practical dialectic of the Four Noble Truths. The variety of philosophical expression that has developed from the "sermon at the Deer Park" reached a vastness hardly equaled throughout the journey of the human mind upon the roads of history. Buddhist Philosophy, as a self-contained Totality of philosophical vision and spiritual freedom, has been previously presented by this author in his recent book The Philosophy of Buddhism: A "Totalistic" Synthesis. There, all the apparently self-overriding doctrines of the Buddhist schools of philosophy have been shown to integrate mutually from one into the other. In the present work, I concentrate on the roots of such a deployment of Buddhist philosophy as a totalistic theory and as a "totality" in itself. These roots, as said above, reside in the study of the Four Noble Truths and their immediate philosophical entailments as they were propounded by the early thinkers of Buddhism. Our aim is not to propound the theories of Hīnayāna scholasticism as this can be thought to stand against the Mahāyāna universalistic theories of esotericism, integrationism and totalism. Quite the contrary: for we are trying to look into the deep roots of the early doctrines, and this always remained essential not only to Buddhism per se, but also to its development as a historical ground of culture. It is only by superficial appearance that Hīnayāna scholasticism runs counter to the Universalism of the T'ien-t'ai and Hua-yen schools, and to the pragmatic and intuitive forms of Zen Buddhism. But Zen Buddhism could have never existed without Hīnayāna Indian scholasticism. To the extent that Hīnayāna scholastics disputed the issues of ontological impermanence as the root of the all pervading Suffering of existence, and attempted to unravel the mysteries surrounding human knowledge and action, to that extent were the meanings of Lin-chi's "shouting and beating" methods of instruction made open to the followers of Zen Buddhism.

In spite of its immense variety of doctrinal ramification, Buddhism is but one common vision of reality. The whole of Buddhism is mounted on the wheel of "Suffering." No "Suffering," no Buddhism. And the wheel of "Suffering" turns around the axis of causation, which is the most intricate of all philosophical issues confronted by the seeking human mind. Upon the universal fact of Ill and Sorrow and the origination that sets it into its ever turning motion resides the whole variegated effort of Buddhist thought. Its variegation is far from being an at-random occurence: the unity of the axis around which Buddhist thought turns is the same support around which it develops towards the most comprehensive coverage of this psycho-cosmic and embodied existence which houses Suffering. This is the reason why the Four Noble Truths enunciated by the Buddha at the very onset of his pravacana (evangelium) still are the Four Noble Truths of all of Buddhism. These Truths, as formulated in the Pali dialect in which they were originally committed to writing, have been briefly summarized in the Sanskrit through the following four simple terms:

1. Duḥkha = Suffering
2. Samudaya = Origin of Suffering
3. Nirodha = Cessation of Suffering
4. Mārga = The Path towards Cessation of Suffering

It is obvious that the formulation of the Four Noble Truths springs from the very roots of existence which is pervaded by ill and sorrow. The simple terms which express such basic truths of Buddhism will also head the three parts of the present work: In the first part we shall look into the constitutives of human world-conscious and world-inhabiting existence as carrying intrinsically the germs of "suffering." In the second part we shall delve into the aspects of causative origination that put such components of human existence to work. These aspects of causation, in their pluralistic fragmentation, will already bear the implicit directionality towards a totalistic notion of both origination (samudaya, samutpāda) and action (karma). And in the third part--dealing per modum unius with the third and fourth "Noble Truths"--we shall inquire into the original Buddhist conceptions of absoluteness as the basis for the extinction (nirodha) of "relative" and hence "suffering" existence.

All the basic and original sources for the Buddhist understanding of human existence in regard to the transcendental character of ultimate Truth, for its philosophical and scholastic formulations, and for the way of life which is conducive to the final realization of the Goal, are all to be traced back to the threefold scriptural Canon called the Tripiṭaka. The Tripiṭaka (literally meaning the "Three Baskets" which preserve the Scriptures) was orally extant and transmitted as early as ca. 320 B.C. In all probability, however, it was not committed to actual writing prior to the year 25 B.C. when it was compiled in Ceylon in a Sanskrit derivative called Pali. This language was the regional dialect of Ujjayinī, a Western Indian town that was the necessary sojourn of northern merchants and travelers heading for the South. Thus the Pali was given a similar role to the one played by the Latin in the early days of the Christian church. Although Sanskrit was the language of the Vedas and Upaniṣads in the Hindu set of scriptures, and was later adopted by many Buddhists, especially from the mid-Northern and Northwestern parts of India (the old Magadha and Gandhara regions), the ancient School of the Elders (the Sthaviras or Theravādins) fought strenuously to keep Pali as the sacred language of scriptural Buddhism. Commentaries also were written for the most part in the Pali, and attempts by Northerners to adopt the use of the Sanskrit was met by hard resistence in the Ceylonese stronghold of Hīnayāna founded as early as 246 B.C. by Mahendra, the son of Buddhist king Aśoka, ruler of the Magadha country west of Vārāṇaśī in the Ganges region.

The Tripiṭaka thus constitutes the threefold collection of "canonical" literature. The "first basket" contains the sayings of the Buddha himself and is called the Suttapiṭaka or "the collection of Sūtras" The Sūtras are the Scriptures per se, as they contain the sacred word on the Dharma or Buddhist Doctrine. However, the second and third part of the Tripiṭaka are also considered scriptural in that most of their works are also attributed, in a more or less direct manner, to the original teachings of the Buddha. The Second piṭaka (basket) is called the Vinayapiṭaka which contains the monastic rules of moderate asceticism as is to be observed by the followers of the Dharma as they joined the saṁgha (the congregation). And the third "basket" is the Abhidhammapiṭaka, the doctrinal and theoretical basis for early Buddhist philosophy. This Abhidhamma collection contains seven works as they are listed by the early Canon of the Theravādins. These seven works have been universally considered as the true and original works of the Abhidhamma (Skt. Abhidharma). The school of the Sarvāstivādins, however, considered their own Abhidharma as formed by seven different works. These works are not extant in the Pali or Sanskrit but are preserved in the Chinese versions of the more comprehensive (Hīnayāna and Mahāyāna) collection of the Chinese Tripiṭaka (available at present in the Japanese edition of the Taishō Daizōkyō). However, these seven Abhidharma works (as different from the Theravāda canon) are not attributed to the Buddha himself but to different early authors who favored the scholastic trends of the Sarvāstivādins.

The term Scripture (as "canonical" work) cannot be applied to a great number of classical commentaries which followed as interpretations of the Abhidharma canonical books. Nevertheless, these commentaries, usually called śāstras (treatises) or bhaśyas (commentaries), or saṃgrahas (compendiums) etc., are of the utmost importance for the study of the philosophical doctrines developed as explanation and interpretation of the scriptures. We shall have to refer very often to them and it is upon them that we shall rely most heavily.

Among these commentaries should be mentioned such works as the Aṭṭhasālinī (a commentary to the canonical work Dhamma-saṅghaṇi), and two Vibhāṣās (which became the doctrinal sources of the Vaibhāṣikas and Sarvāstivādins), the Abhidhammatthasaṅgaha of Anurudha (X cent A.D.?) and the most important and vastest exposition of the Hīnayāna philosophical doctrines which is the Abhidharmakośa of Vasubandhu (ca. 420-500 A.D.). Other essential texts are the celebrated Vimuttimagga ("Way of Emancipation") by Upatissa (IV cent. A.D.) and a further amplification of this latter work called the Visuddhimagga ("Way of Purification") written by Buddhagoṣa (V cent. A.D.). Among these important classics of early Buddhism, only the Abhidharmakośa of Vasubandhu was written in the Sanskrit, while the rest were compiled in the Pali. The Aṭṭhasālinī, the two Maggas and the Abhidhammatthasaṅgaha represented the doctrinal developments of the Theravādins. The two Vibhāṣās (extant only in the Chinese) were the main treatises of the Sarvāstivāda conceptions. The Abhidharmakośa of Vasubandhu--which relied heavily on the interpretation of the two Vibhāṣās--expounds both the doctrine of the Sarvāstivādins and that of their staunchest opponents, the *Sautrāntikas*. It is in this sense that the *Abhidharmakośa* constitutes one of the most important pillars for the study of *Hīnayāna* theories in their development up to the V century A.D. This large work (divided in nine parts) has served always as the basis for the Chinese and Japanese interpretation and study of the *Abhidharma*, and is usually referred to by its abreviated title as the *Chu-she* in Chinese or as the *Kusha* in Japanese. It is obvious that our work will rely primordially on this nearly inexhaustible source of *Hīnayāna* scholasticism. As for the *Vimuttimagga* and the *Visuddhimagga*, their main concern was the study of the methods of concentration conducive to the purified states of consciousness which are considered the preamble to *nirvāṇa*. Hence, they belong fundamentally in the explanation of the Fourth of the Noble Truths as this refers to the "Eightfold Path." Their philosophical relevance however is not negligible since large portions of these works contain a wealth of information on the psycho-cosmic conceptions that form the core of *Hīnayāna* metaphysics. Thus, such works will be taken quite often into explicit account.

As for the main schools of *Hīnayāna* scholasticism, some authors mention up to eighteen different groups. For the sake of clarity and in order to focus on the essentials, we shall rely fundamentally on the doctrines of the above mentioned three schools: the *Theravāda* on account of its early origins as the direct transmitter of the Buddha's tradition; the *Sarvāstivāda* on account of the prolific systematization of metaphysical casuistry which it produced; and the *Sautrāntika* school, which is practically known to us exclusively through the accounts of Vasubandhu in his *Kośa*. This later school is quite relevant in that it plays the role of a catalyst to the somewhat untamed analytic tendency and proliferous conceptualism of the *Sarvāstivādins*. On the whole, however, the *Sarvāstivāda* school will be the main object of our attention.

An explanation of the title of our main primary source, the *Abhidharmakośa*, will close our introductory chapter and will also provide us with the basis to delve into the philosophical entailments of the first of the Noble Truths, namely, *Duḥkha* (or Suffering).

The term *kośa* means something like the "scabbard" or "sheath" which preserves a sword, and from which the sword is drawn. Thus Vasubandhu (author of the *Abhidharmakośa*) refers to his work as "having been drawn from the sheath of the *Abhidharma*," i.e., as having been extracted from it. In this way Vasubandhu emphasizes the character of compendium and epitome of the doctrines of the *Abhidharma* that his *kośa* intends to be. Much too large a work to be a compendium! At any rate, *kośa* can be taken to mean also the ark or chest where a treasure is kept, hence the translation of *Abhidharmakośa* may be also given as "Thesaurus of Metaphysics."

In which sense, however, has the term *abhidharma* come to be rendered as "metaphysics?" Vasubandhu explains the term in the following manner: *prajñāmala sanucar abhidharmaḥ*: "the *abhidharma* is immaculate knowledge, with all its sequence,"[1] i.e., *abhidharma* is the exposition of the doctrinal tenets of Buddhism insofar as this is the sequence of transcendental knowledge (*prajñā*). Etymologically, the prefix *abhi* means "over," "next to," or also "beyond" or "above," whereas the term *dharma* carries a complexity of meanings throughout its pervading use in Buddhism. Derived from the root *dhr*, which means "to hold," "to carry," it originally was used to designate the "Law" in religious contexts meaning the Doctrine to be accepted by the mind and to be obeyed by the will. Thus the term *abhidharma* could justly be translated as the "Supreme Doctrine" or "Supreme Law." Vasubandhu, however, gives us more than one interpretation: he first conceives the *abhidharma* as the treatise (*śāstra*) designed to assist in the acquisition of the "immaculate" or untinged knowledge (*amalaprajñā*).[2] On the other hand, *abhidharma* is said to mean "whatever carries (*dhāraṇa*) a proper characteristic" (*svalakṣana*). In the words of Vasubandhu: "The *Abhidharma* is thus called not only because it envisages (*abhimuka*) the *dharma* that is the object of the supreme knowledge, namely, *nirvāṇa*, but also because it studies the characteristics of the *dharma-s*[3] (now in plural)," i.e. of those *primordial components or "factors of existence"* which are carriers (*dhāraṇī*) of both mental and physical determinations. Thus the notion of *dharma* as "primordial element," be it in the sense of absolute ontological validity (like *nirvāṇa* being the supreme *dharma*), or in the sense of basic, quasi-atomic "co-efficients" of relative and individual existence, becomes established. In both cases--whether relating to Absoluteness as such or to the relativity of individual being--the term *dharma* connotes the meaning of transcendental "holder" of the individual sentient being in its "suffering" status and of the *nirvāṇa* into which it extinguishes itself. "*Dharmas*" in plural, as elementary "factors of existence," are not in themselves the immediate object of sensorial knowledge. Only their interrelated conglomerates (*saṃcita*, *saṃghāta*) come to manifest themselves as the ever flowing stream of individual existence. In themselves, however, all the *dharmas* are meta-empirical, to be known only by inference, and thus they are the object of what generally can be called "metaphysics." Only in this sense is the rendering of the term *abhidharma* as "metaphysics" justified. With this preliminary notion of the supreme or absolute *Dharma* as the eternal goal of liberation from the warps of individual "suffering existence," and of *dharma-s* in plural as the ever transient and impermanent "holders" or "carriers" of such an existence, we are ready to enter our philosophical treatment of the first of the Noble Truths: *DUHKHA*.

P A R T I

DUḤKHA (Suffering) and the Buddhist Notion of Existence

Tattha katamaṃ dukkhaṃ ariyasaccaṃ?
Jāti pi dukkhā jarā pi dukkhā maraṇaṃ
pi dukkhaṃ sokaparidevadukkhadomanassupāyāsā
pi dukkhā appiyehi sampayogo dukkho piyehi
vippayogo dukkho yam p'icchaṃ na labhati
tam pi dukkhaṃ; sankhittena pancupādānakkhandhā
pi dukkhā.

What is the Noble Truth of Suffering?
Birth is suffering; old age is suffering;
death is suffering, sorrow, lamentation
grief and despair are suffering; association
with those one dislikes is suffering;
separation from those one likes is suffering;
not getting what one wishes is suffering;
in summary, the five *dharma*-aggregates of
attachment are suffering.

Dīgha-nikāya II, 304; *Vibhaṅga* 99.

Chapter 1

The Three Marks of Existence and Suffering

The Saṃyutta-nikāya (21-2) tells us: "All formations (of dharma-elements which constitute the individual stream of existence) are transient (anicca); all such formations are subject to suffering (dukkha); all things are without a self-substance (anatta) . . . .that which is transient is subject to suffering; and of that which is transient and subject to suffering and change one can rightly say: This am I; this is my Ego." Thus the three fundamental characteristics of individual existence according to Buddhism are established as anicca (Skt.: anitya), or impermanence, dukkha (Skt.: duḥkha) or suffering, and anatta (Skt.: anātman) or no-selfness, i.e. non-substantiality. The "three marks" are philosophically relevant in that they already point to the very root of suffering, namely, to the fact of radical transience and impermanence. Impermanence is expressed by the two marks which constitute the bipolar axis of the wheel of suffering. Anicca and anatta are these two "polar" marks. Anicca represents the transiency and impermanence of all the "objective" manifestations of being in the realm of relative existence, including all the corporeal reality which constitutes the embodiment and support (āśraya) of all mental operations. Anatta, however, represents the "subjective" side of impermanence as this mark points to the insubstantiality of what appears to be an absolute and permanent Ego; thus it signifies the total absence of a commonly postulated ontological basis to our mental and willing functions. In point of fact (anicca (impermanence) and anatta (non-substantiality) convert into one another in that the same impermanence afflicts both the flux of subjective consciousness which appears as the Ego and the external objects of our perceptions, feelings and volitive addictions. And by the same token, the same insubstantiality affects both the apparent, permanent Ego that seems to underly our conscious states as well as all the objects of the external appearing world that become the source for desire and action. The wheel of "Suffering" (dukkha) turns around this bipolar axis of world-impermanence (anicca) and Ego-insubstantiality (anatta).

Suffering (Skt.: duḥkha) therefore is rooted in the metaphysical characteristic of existence as radically impermanent and non-substantial. Thus "suffering" becomes an existential notion in the Heideggerian sense, namely, in that it is primordial and transcends all the aspects and manifestations of the individual conscious being. "Suffering" cannot be properly equated or identified with mere "pain." The *Sūtra* has made already a differentiation between the transcendental notion of *duḥkha* and such particular, concrete manifestations of pain as lamentation, grief, despair, etc. In a parallel manner to Heidegger's notion of *Angst* (anxiety) as this is related to the concrete manifestations of *Furcht* (fear), the Buddhist notion of *duḥkha* unlerlies all concrete modalities of conscious experience. *Angst*--according to Heidegger--is an original state of mind (*Urstimmung* or *Urgestimmheit*). This *Urstimmung* is ever present in all concrete modalities of "moodness" as an "existential" which cannot be identified with the particular emotion of being afraid of "something" (for *Angst* is fear of "nothing" in particular). Thus *duḥkha* is also an ever present and pervading trademark of individual existence which transcends into the highest states of delight and pleasure, whether it be physical or mental. In this sense, *duḥkha* (suffering) reaches even into the highest and most purified planes of individual existence, through which the self-manifesting, self-embodying manifestations of *Bodhisattvas* and *Buddhas*--as conceived in later *Mahāyāna* Buddhism--are drawn by the common goal of compassion (*karuṇā*) towards all sentient beings in the realms of karmic rebirth and retribution (*saṃsāra*). And "com-passion"--after all--is nothing but a "co-suffering," a self-less share the enlightened beings take in the retributive pains of the non-enlightened, for the sake of the emancipation of the latter.

As the characters of impermanence and insubstantiality ground the all-pervasive transcendentality of *duḥkha*, the very intrinsic character of the *dharmas* as factors of individual existence comes to the fore. This essential character is expressed in early Buddhism through the doctrine of "momentariness" (*kṣaṇikavāda*). "Impermanence" as non-substantiality and "non-substantiality" as impermanence are the only underlying common features that embed the streams of all conscious, individual existences. This trait of Buddhist philosophy strikingly compares to Hume's notion of impersonality in his accounting of conscious world-experience. The Ego and its world of experience exhibit only an appearance of permanence and fixity, and consists in nothing but in the serial stream of subjective-objective events. A Heraklitean notion of the panta rei is thus also applicable to the Hīnayāna conception of personality and world-continuity: it is no more than the apparent but false continuity of a motion picture being projected upon the screen; an illusion of continuing, self-standing reality takes place on the basis of discrete, momentary aggregations of a diversity of color-, shape-, and sound-manifolds as these are coordinated within the frames of instantaneously appearing single pictures. Thus individual existence, together with the whole realm of its world-object, is only the illusory outcome of momentary, "quantum-like" aggregates of dharma-elements simultaneously cooperating together on the basis of causative principles, and being successively projected from the potential future into the extinguished past through that indivisible and punctiform door of the present. We are nothing but temporal, down-the-line streams of such manifolds of momentary projections of "dharmic" factors: no permanent Ego underlies such a stream as the substantial support of experience. The Ego-consciousness of subjectivity partakes of this illusion of permanence which accompanies the rapid succession of discrete, blank flashes projected upon the screen. These blank flashes of consciousness serve as basis and support for the manifestation of objective manifolds such as the circumstantial world, epochs and persons involved in the "plot" of everyone's own motion picture. The question will arise: what determines the "plot" which particularly affects each individual stream of existence? The second Part of our book (dealing with the issues of causation) will confront these questions as they were answered by the early Buddhist thinkers of the Abhidharma. Now we shall proceed to the description and listings of such "co-efficients" of existence which henceforth are designated as dharma-s.

Chapter 2

The Doctrine of *dharmas*. Basic Divisions of *dharmas*.

From what we have said so far, the term *dharma* establishes itself as designating the basic, primordial constituents of the conscious stream of individual being, this considered as subject of world-conscious-experience. These elemental factors intervene in bringing about the fourfold aspect of total world-experience reality as psycho-physical (mental-material) and subjective-objective. The conception of the mind as a mere streaming river of sensations, perceptions and notions (a river where no permanent substratum or self "bathes twice") was staunchly advocated by the Western, British empiricist David Hume:

> "Pain and pleasure, grief and joy, passions and sensations succeed each other, and never they exist at the same time. It cannot, therefore, be from any of these impressions, or from any other, that the idea of self is derived . . . . For my part, when I enter most intimately into what I call *myself*, I always stumble on some particular perception or other, of heat or cold, light or shade, love or hatred, pain or pleasure. I never can catch *myself* at any time without a perception, and never can observe anything but the perception . . . . If anyone, upon serious and unprejudiced reflection, thinks he has a different notion of *himself*, I must confess I can reason no longer with him . . . . He may, perhaps, perceive something simple and continued, which he calls *himself*; *though I am certain there is no such principle* in me . . . . I may venture to affirm of the rest of mankind, that they are nothing but a bundle or collection of different perceptions, which succeed each other with an inconceivable rapidity, and are in perpetual flux and movement." (*A Treatise of Human Nature*, IV, Section 6: *Of Personal Identity*).

Regardless of the disputable nature of this tenet, no one in the West has better expressed the anatta and anicca priciples as established by early Buddhism. For nothing expresses more precisely the nature of the dharmas i.e., the elements of awareness as they associate with objective factors of sensations, perceptions, emotions, etc., than the lines quoted above. The "rapidity" of the flux is a clear connotation of the kṣaṇikavāda ("momentariness") theory whereby each set of dharmas constituting our present bundle of perceptions is as evanescent as the point of time which holds them for an instant and transfers them from the oncoming future over to the past.

The Sarvāstivādins considered all these evanescent elements (dharmāḥ) as really existing, either as potentials in the future or as actualized in their manifestation into the present on their way to the past. No Ego-substance or soul stretches throughout the three horizons or "epochs" of time and its flux of events. It is important, however, to note the real character of existence of such elements, and that in a transcendental manner all the dharmas are ultimately eternal in their potentiality; thus originates the name given to the Sarvāstivādins (Sarva asti = "every thing is"). The present existence of the dharmas is momentary inasmuch an they are manifested in association with one another; their evanescence is then restricted to their actualized manifestation in "bundles" or aggregations (saṃghāta) in the indivisible moment of the present. Thus the Sarvāstivādins seem to adjudicate the dharmas an ultimate, timeless, and transcendent though potential availability.[1] This tenet will make it easier for them to explain such vital notions as the retributive character of human--morally qualified--action through the karma-mechanism of retribution. This issue will be handled later in Part II dealing with causation. According to the Sarvāstivādins, the dharmas come from the future if the causal conditions are such that they are summoned into momentary manifestation (existence proper). As they flow into the past, they might retain certain characteristics which may enable them to re-manifest at a certain point in the future. Thus the three epochs (adhvan = the three "roads" or transitions of time, i.e. future, present and past)[2] are "real" for the Sarvāstivādins (hence the accusation leveled against them of advocating some sort of panrealism).

These "three roads" of time (triadhvanaḥ) are connected with each other: the future with the present, the present with the future and past, and the past with both the present and the future itself. This conception provided the Sarvāstivādins with a clear-cut basis for the explanation of the karmic cycle of retribution to be dealt with in the second Part of this work. Needless to say, the Sautrāntikas (the "true followers" of the sacred Sutras) did not adhere to this kind of quasi-phenomenalistic realism, and denied, together with many other notional entities propounded by the Sarvāstivādins, the true reality of the past and the future as really existing "roads" of time.

It is obvious that the Sautrāntikas advocated a purer form of phenomenalism, perhaps closer to the one propounded by Hume. Thus they provided for a transition (through the quasi-doketistic, almost Berkeleyan doctrine of the Mahāsaṁghikas) to the Buddhist idealism propounded by the Mahāyāna-Yogācāras (or Vijñānavādins). It will not be out of place to note here that Vasubandhu, the great expounder of both the Sarvāstivāda and Sautrāntika theories, inclined decisively in favor of the Sautrāntika standpoint. It is no wonder that later Vasubandhu would convert to the idealistic tenet of the Vijñānavāda (only consciousness) theory established and propounded by his own older brother Asaṅga. As a matter of fact, next to the Abhidharmakośa, the most relevant works of Vasubandhu were the Viṃśatikā-kārikā and the Triṃśikā-kārikā (the "Twenty Verses" and the "Thirty Verses") written in defense of the Vijñaptimātratā theory which claims that all elements of existence (dharma-s) are reducible to pure mental projections from the ultimate ground of consciousess. Needless to say, this change in the philosophical attitude represents a 180 degree turn from the "realistic phenomenalism" expounded by the Sarvāstivāda school. This turn signals the emergence of Buddhist idealism and monism which will reduce all the dharmas to mere mental contents of conscious experience as born and developed by an ultimate "mind-only" (vijñaptimātra), and as outwardly projected into the phantasmagoric (parikalpita) appearance of the world.

Nothing is further from this later monistic and idealistic attitude than the assertion of the Sarvāstivādins that "everything is," i.e., that all the dharmas have an essence and a givenness of their own which--in their potentiality--is ultimate and transcendent. Thus the *dharmas* are mostly conceived as *dravyas* (entitative essences in their own right) capable of coordinating with each other in order to travel from the *adhvan* (road) of the "future" into the *adhvan* of the "present" to be *deposited* into the *adhvan* of the "past." Only "aggregates" of *dharmas* and their actual *presentation* (*svalakṣaṇa*) are destroyed; their ultimate separate essences (*svabhāva*) cannot be destroyed.

The actual manifestation of existence--according to the *Sarvāstivādins*--is then based on "momentary co-emissions" (*kṣaṇikasaṃsarga*) of interrelated and interdependent *dharmas*. This correlated and interdependent co-discharge (*saṃsarga*) is effected by strict laws of causality to be expounded later on. The fountain of causation picks the *dharmas* from the depository of the "future," and discharges them like discrete, pluriform assemblages "gushing out" into the peripheral "present," only to travel back into the center where the "past" places them again into the discharging, motor-causes of re-manifestation.

This conception of "co-emission" (*saṃsarga*) or "discharge" (*utsarga*) strongly suggests the character of "unrest" and "turbulence" which affects the manifestation of the *dharmas*, and which constitutes the reality of conscious existence that we--and our world--are. Thus the *dharmas* are *saraṇa*[3] (in trouble!) engulfed into the turbulence and battle (*raṇa*) that existence is in its ever "gushing" ejection of "life-bundles." The term *raṇa* (turbulence) is directly connotative of *duḥkha* (suffering) which, in its transcendental and pervasive meaning, is also often translated as "unrest." This "unrest" of the *dharmas* is the source of suffering, and the mitigation and final disappearance of suffering can only be effected by the gradual bringing of the turbulent *dharmas* (*saraṇa*) to rest (*araṇa*). The *dharmas* affected by turbulence are also considered as impure, soiled by their causal links with evil passions. These "soiled" or impure *dharmas* are designated as *sāsrava* (tinged with passion), whereas the ones that are affected by *araṇa* (i.e.: rest, or the subsiding of turbulence through the practices of moral virtues and meditative practices prescribed by the Path) are designated as *anāsrava* (pure or unsoiled *dharmas*). The *sāsravadharmas* are predominant in lower stages of existence and the *anāsravadharmas* prevail in higher planes, or in the plane of human existence in the stage of the *śaikṣa* (novice, beginner in the Path), the *ārya* (saintly, morally "noble" person) and in the *arhat* (one who has reached the end of the Path through enlightenment).

The *sāsravadharmas* are objects of study in the first and second Parts of our book; that is, they belong to the understanding of the first Noble Truth of *Duḥkka* (suffering) and the second Truth of *Samudaya* (origin of suffering). The *anāsravadharmas* are brought forth as the result of following the Path (fourth Noble Truth). Any *dharma*-elements, which as absolute and eternal might constitute the Noble Truth of Cessation (*nirodha*), are placed beyond the *sāsrava-anāsrava* categories. These will be exounded in our third Part.

The second basic division of the *dharmas* is made according to the character of their manifestation. If their manifestations are correlative and interdependent with each other, if they are the constituents of the *kṣaṇika-saṃsarga* (momentary co-emission) and thus subjected to the forces of causation, then these *dharmas* are called *saṃskṛta* (conditioned); if they are eternally unchangeable, everpresent and indestructible, free from the impelling forces of origination and destruction, then they are called *asaṃskṛta* (non-conditioned).

Hence the *saṃskṛta-dharmas* (conditioned) are the objects of the First, Second and Fourth Noble Truths: of the First and the Second in that only the *saṃskṛta-dharmas* are the carriers of "suffering" (*duḥkha*) and the objects of "origination" (*samudaya*, *samutpāda*); of the Fourth in that they are also the objects of purification and of their transformation from *sāsrava* (soiled with passions) into *anāsrava* (pure and conducive to *nirvāṇa*). The *asaṃskṛta*, or "non-conditioned", *dharmas* are "absolute" factors which make possible the realization of the Third of the Noble Truths, i.e., *nirodha* (or the "act of extinction of suffering"). Of the three *asaṃskṛta-dharmas* advocated by the *Sarvāstivādins*, the first is the absolute medium for the worldly manifestation of the *saṃskṛta*-(conditioned) *dharmas*, namely space (*ākāśa*). The second *asaṃskṛta*- (non-conditioned) *dharmas* is the *apratisaṃkhyā-nirodha*, i.e., the state of obstruction or extinction of certain "conditioned" *dharmas* which is brought about without the intervention of "true knowledge" (*pratisaṃkyā*, *jñāna* or *parijñā*) but which takes place spontaneously because of the disappearance or non-occurrence of the causes which otherwise would have brought them into manifestation. The third and most relevant of the asaṃskṛta- (non-conditioned) dharmas consists in the state of perpetual extinction or obstruction of "conditioned" dharmas pertaining to an "individual stream of existence" (sentient being), extinction or obstruction which takes place through the intervention of acts of "true knowledge." This extinction or obstruction is called pratisaṃkhyā-nirodha, it takes place gradually, and it reaches its summit in the realization of parinirvāṇa, or total "cessation" of an individual stream of existence. Since these three non-conditioned dharmas relate directly to the third Noble Truth of Cessation (nirodha), they will be the object of our detailed study in the Third Part of this work.

As for the saṃskṛta- (conditioned) dharmas, the Abhidharmakośa designates them also as sahetuka (depending on causes) or savastuka (having a causal "basis" or vastu). As such "they are devoured (adyante) by the character of impermanence."[4] Being the constituents of the temporal flux of existence, they are also described as "travellers or wanderers on the roads (adhvan) of time."[5] Now we shall proceed to their classification and description as "carriers" (dhāraṇa) of individual, "suffering" existence. Thus the traditional classification of the Five Skandhas (pañcaskandaḥ) will follow.

Chapter 3

Saṃskṛta or Conditioned *dharmas*: the Five *Skandhas*.

In the passage of the *Saṃyutta-nikāya* above, reference is made to the three "marks" of existence, namely, *anicca* (impermanence), *dukkha* (suffering) and *anatta* (non-self). Subsequently the second *sūtra* of this *nikāya* tells us: Form (*rūpa*) is impermanent, sensation or feeling (*vedanā*) is impermanent, perception or notion (*saṃjñā*) is impermanent, (volitive) formations (*saṃskāras*) are impermanent, consciousness (*vijñāna*) is impermanent." The elements thus enumerated are the Five Divisions or Dharma-Aggregates of "suffering" and "attachment" (*duḥkha-pañcopādāna-skandāḥ*):

1. *Rūpa-skandha* = Division of materiality
2. *Vedanā-skandha* = Division of sensation and feeling
3. *Saṃjñā-skandha* = Division of perception and notion
4. *Saṃskāra-skandha* = Division of volitive and karmic "formations" or "forces"
5. *Vijñāna-skandha* = Division of consciousness or "subjective" discriminative awareness."

These constitute the *dharma*-aggregates which produce suffering through all sorts of craving (*tṛṣnātā sarva upajayati duḥkhaskandhāḥ*.[6] As expressed in the *Pali* by both of the *Suttas* and in the *Abhidhamma* they are as follows: *rūpa*, *vedanā*, *saññā*, *saṅkhāra* and *viññāṇa*. The term *skandha* (Pali: *khandha*) is usually translated as "aggregate." It literally means "heap" or "pile"; it also means the branching part of the stem, thus suggesting the meaning of the specific ramifications or divisions stemming from the same generic totality, in this case, the generic totality of the *saṃskṛta-dharmas* ("conditioned" factors or coefficients of individual conscious existence). Although the term "aggregate" seems to be in line with the doctrine that the *dharmas* manifest themselves in "groupings" or "heaps," these latter terms seem to connote the interactive coordination among clusters of qualitatively different "dharmic" elements as these offer the basis for sensation and perception. These "clusters" or "conglomerates" of *dharmas* are usually referred to as saṃghāta or saṃcita as they make up the perceptible compounds of materiality which further associate with the subjective factor of consciousness (vijñāna) and other mental functions accompanying such elements. Thus the term skandha (group, class, assortment) designates rather the result of "sorting" or "classifying" the different kinds of dharmas according to their specific characteristics (lakṣaṇa). Hence we prefer to translate the total term pañcopādānaskandhāḥ as the "Five Divisions of (dharma-) attachment." This is done with the understanding that such divisions, being related either to the subjects or to the objects of attachment (upādāna), will necessarily refer to five specific "classes" of dharmas as these provide the basis for craving and desire (tṛṣṇā). The five skandhas therefore will be thought of as being primordially sāsrava or "soiled with passions." And, as we shall see, even the passions themselves will be considered as dharmas in their own right, belonging in fact to the fourth of the Divisions (i.e., saṃskāras or "volitive forces"). This, however, will not preclude the presence of "purifying forces" within the "fourth Division" which will provide the capability to act towards the elimination of the sāsrava-dharmas ("soiled factors"), as will be expounded further below. With these presuppositions in mind let us now proceed further to the analysis and description of each one of the "dharma-heaps"" or "divisions":

1.- RŪPA-SKANDHA. Rūpa means both color (or also varṇa) and form or shape (also saṃsthāna). Hence this term comprehends in a generic way all the elements that belong to the Division of Materiality. Such are the elements constituting the bodily sense-organs and the physical objects of sensation and perception that appear as the surrounding world. In attending to the subclasses within the general division of materiality or rūpas, many authors proceed immediately to the enumeration of eleven different elements. In doing so, they either disregard or perfunctorily mention the fact that most canonical sources refer to rupaskandha as being distributed into four "primary elements" (bhūta) and eleven secondary or "derived matters" (bhautika, or also upādāyarūpa). Thus the Dhammasaṅghaṇi says: "How many rūpas are there all together? There are four (primary) great-elements and all the other (eleven) which derive from the four primary elements. Those and these are said to be all the rūpas."[7] The Abhidharmakośa follows suit in mentioning the "Four primary" or "great elements" (catvārimahābhūtāni) as the very origin of all the constituents of material manifestation: bhūtāni pṛthivīdhātur aptejovāyudhātavaḥ = the fundamental constituents (of matter) is the element (dhātu) of earth, as well as the elements of water, fire and air.[8] According to the kośa they are called "great," not in the Sāṃkhya sense of being "coarse" tangible elements as opposed to the "fine" ones (tanmātras), but on the contrary, they are called "great" because they are the primordial support of all the other eleven rūpas as "derived matters" (upādāyarūpa, bhautika).

These four "great elements" have often been misinterpreted as mere forces or qualities inherent to the eleven bhautika or "derived rūpas." Vasubandhu, however, considers each one of them as full-fledged dharmas in that each one of them is the "carrier" (dhāraṇa) of its own singular characteristic, and in that all four of them together (as combined) "carry" furthermore the eleven compounded matters that derive from them. Their four specific characters provide the primordial foundation for the four basic states of material things (solid, liquid, temperature and motion). Thus it should be noted that the headings of "earth," "water," "fire" and "air" are not to be considered in the literal sense, as though these basic elements of materiality should be taken as formal atoms of earth, water, etc. These latter should be regarded rather as gross conglomerations of atoms manifesting a predominance of the characters (lakṣaṇa) or activities (vṛtti) which are proper to each one of the four mahābhūtas. Hence the four mahābhūtas (great elements) should be considered as simple primordial dharmas of materiality, each one carrying its own specific kind of activity or energy and thus establishing the basis for each one of the fundamental states which can characterize or affect any of the appearing things in the material world. These activities and the physical state which they bring about can be correlated as follows:

1. Repulsion (khara), producing the state of "solidity" (khakkhaṭatva) = earth-element (pṛthivī)

2. Attraction or Cohesion (sneha), producing the state of "liquidity" or "fluidity" (dravatva) = water-element (āp)
3. Heat (uṣṇata), producing the degree of "temperature" (uṣṇatva) = fire-element (tejas)
4. Motion (īraṇakarman), producing the state of "lightness" (laghutva) and "mobility" (laghusamudīraṇatva) which is proper to all bodies in motion as well as the organisms expanding (vyūhana) by growth and development (vṛddhi). The states of "expansion" and "lightness"[9] are thus symbolized by the air-element (vāyu).

Given these fundamental four elements, the origin of the eleven "derivative" or secondary matters (bhautika or upādāyarūpas) is explained on the basis of the different ways in which these four "great elements" or energies combine and interact with one another. It should be strongly emphasized that all four elements are always present in the derivation of any of the eleven subsequent upādāyarūpas (derivative matters), and that the particular states described above as "solidity," "liquidity," "heat" and "motion" will manifest themselves (each one with the possible or necessary exclusion of the others) not on the basis of the absence of any of the four great elements, but only on account of the predominance of one upon the others. This predominance will occur only as due to the different interrelations and combinations among the four mahābhūtas. From all this, it follows that no one simple bhūta can exist separately on its own, and that all four must necessarily co-exist (sahabhū) with one another in order to form the "derivative matters" (bhautika). Thus, as there are no bhautikas without the bhūtas, so also there are no bhūtas outside the bhautikas.

The first five "derivative rūpas"--ensuing from the four mahābhūtas--constitute a very subtle matter[10] which is "mentally" translucent (accha)[11] and does not offer "resistance" (pratighāta) to the dharma of self-awareness or subject-consciousness (vijñāna-skandha) to be explained below. This kind of subtle derivative matter is called prasāda, which literally means "tranquility" or "equilibrium." Its similarity with the sattva-guṇa of the Hindu Sāṃkhyas is remarkable. Thus the rūpaprasāda originates as a derivative of a "tranquil" and well-balanced combination of the four "basic elements" (*mahābhūtas*). The idea seems to suggest that, in the production of this subtle "translucent" matter (*rūpaprasāda*), the four activities which characterize the four *mahābhūtas* neutralize one another into a perfect state of equilibrium. The result would yield a material basis for the constitution of the five sense-organs (*pañcendriyāṇi*) in their internal and subjective (*ādhyātmika*) essence. Thus the first five of the eleven *upādāya-rūpas* (derivative matters) are accounted for. *Rūpaprasāda*, therefore, designates some sort of quasi-aethereal and imperceptible matter whose state of "tranquility" would be far more subtle than any one of the four states (solid, liquid, hot, moving) manifested in the gross world on the basis of disproportion or unbalance in the interaction among the four *mahābhūtas*. *Rūpaprasāda* then would be more subtle than even the finest of the gaseous states characterized by extreme "lightness" (*laghutva*). Its *prasāda*- translucidity (*acchatva*) would allow the permeation of these five *prasāda-indriyāṇi* (sense-organs) by the subject-awareness seated in the *vijñāna-dharma* (fifth of the *skandhas*). Their being "not resistant" (*apratigha*) to the *dharma* of the subjective awareness (*vijñāna*) would make them suprasensitive (*atīndriya*) to the "grosser" resistance (*pratighāta*) offered to them by the other five derivative matters, i.e., the gross-matters or objects of sensation. These coarser matters derive from the four *mahābhūtas* according to the unbalanced combinations which would allow certain characteristics of the former to predominate upon the others. The absence of "tranquility" or "equilibrium" (*aprasāda*) among the four elements--always entering into the composition of these coarse and external (*bāhya*) matters--would bring about the different physical determinations which these latter exhibit, either as "colors and shapes" or as "sounds," or as "smells," or as "tastes," or as "tactile" objects of sensation. These five derivative *rūpas* are called the *viṣayas*, these being in summary the coarse matters which pose "resistance" (*pratighāta*) and thus "objection" (i.e., objectivity) to the five "subjective" *indriyas* or sense-organs, these latter being innerly constituted by the subtle and translucid *rūpaprasāda*.

Thus the previous considerations have already yielded ten of the previously announced eleven *upādāya-rūpas* (derivative matters) as follows:

ādhyātmika (inner and subjective)	Five sense-organs (*indriyas*) generically constituted by the subtle and "translucent" *rūpaprasāda* (i.e.: the four elements in the state of perfect equilibrium)	1. *cakṣur-indriya (sight organ)* 2. *śrotra-indriya* (auditory organ) 3. *ghrāṇa-indriya* (olfactory organ) 4. *jihvā-indriya* (taste organ) 5. *kāya-indriya* (touch organ)
bāhya (outer and objective)	Five coarse and "opaque" sense matters (*viṣa-yaḥ*) derived from the four elements in the state of unbalance	1. *rūpa-viṣaya* (visual matter) 2. *śabda-viṣaya* (sound-matter) 3. *gandha-viṣaya* (smell-matter) 4. *rasa-viṣaya* (taste-matter) 5. *spraṣṭavya-viṣaya* (tangible matter)

Let us elaborate somewhat further on the specific nature of each one of these ten derivative *rūpas*, since they are the ones which play a direct role in the constitution of sensorial experience.

From what we said above, the *rūpaprasāda* (tranquility-matter) establishes itself as the "support" or "point of reliance" for the *dharma* of mere subject-consciousness (*vijñāna*) in order for this to "sense" the external coarse world: *tadvijñānāśraya rūpaprasādas*.[12] If we were to represent graphically the symbols for each one of the "four great elements" (*catvārimahābhūtāni*), we would do it by the means of four circles each one headed by the capitals R (for Repulsion), A (for Attraction or Cohesion), H (for Heat) and M (for Motion), as follows:

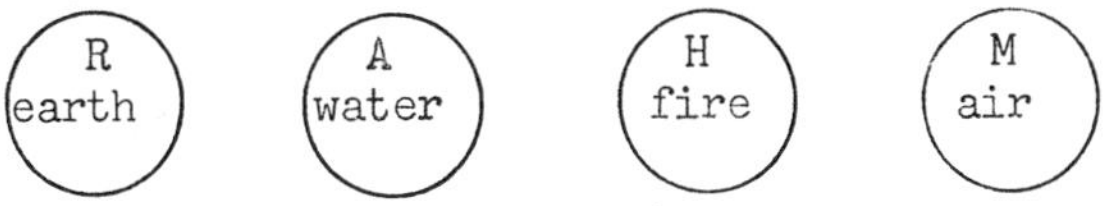

And if we were to depict the "tranquil" or "balanced" combination of these "four primal elements" as they form an atom of *rūpaprasāda* (subtle, sensitive matter) we could do it in such a manner as to combine the above four circles (representing the four elements) into a square-like position of balanced contiguity (nirantaratva).[13] Thus each one of the activities (vṛtti, kāritra) as exercised and "carried" by each one of them would cancel one another into a perfect state of equilibrium and "tranquility:"

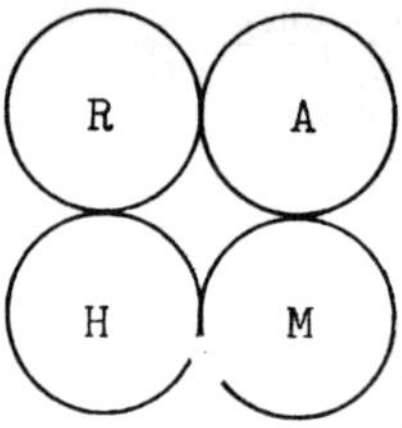

Huge conglomerations of such atoms (paramāṇu-saṃghāta or paramāṇusaṃcaya)[14] are said to pervade the living body throughout its life-span in order to form the five sensorial, subtle bases of the sense-organs or indriyas. Thus the "tetradic" atoms as depicted above would mass within its external recipients as made up of the coarser bhautika or "derivative matters" in order to form such externally and bodily manifested organs as the eyes, ears, nose, tongue and the rest of the body's surface which is endowed with tactile sensitivity. Let us keep in mind that the rūpaprasāda constitutes the inner (ādhyātmika) essence of each one of the sense-organs, essence which in itself is aethereal and not directly perceptible (anidarśana). Not even in its state of high conglomeration is such rūpaprasāda perceptible, i.e., it never becomes the object of its own sensitivity which perceives only--by contact with the vijñāna-dharma of consciousness--the "coarse" matters. According to the Abhidharma texts this kind of subtle "matter" does not have weight, cannot be cut, nor burnt away nor dismembered as can be done with the coarse formations of the body and its coarse organs. Hence, if a hand is amputated, the coarse matter of the hand continues to be until it corrupts, whereas the inner tactile sensitivity is no longer present in it by virtue of its immunity to coarse means of destruction, such as a knife or a flame, etc.[15] Although the pra-

sāda pervades the whole body with special accumulation in the parts of the external organs, no part of it can be separated from the rest, and all of it remains in close communication (as enlivening the total nervous system). In death, the *prasāda* disappears and disintegrates into its original atoms, without residuum.

Now the question arises: What makes the conglomerates of the subtle matter of sensorial sensitivity--as distributed into five different organs--become *specifically* destined to "register" *specifically* different kinds of "sense-matters" (*viṣaya*) such as colors and shapes for the eye, sounds for the ear, odors for the nose, etc? In other words, given the essentially identical basic constitution of the *prasāda*, what accounts for the exclusivity by which each organ is equipped to "sense" one particular kind of the *viṣaya*-stimuli? Most commentaries, including the *Vimmutimagga*, the *Visuddhimagga* and the *Abhidharmakośa*, seem to suggest that this exclusive distribution in the specific nature of sensitivity and stimulation proper to each one of the five senses is due to the way the conglomerates of the subtle *rūpaprasāda* spread within their own coarse encasements according to their different shapes and geometrical patterns. Thus, for instance, the sensory *prasāda* of the eye is arranged according to spherical, concentrical accumulations in the ball of the eye. According to the *Kośa*, these accumulations (*saṃcita*) are formed into the shape of pills "being translucid like pure glass so they do not obfuscate one another."[16] The disposition of *prasāda* in the interior of the two ear-holes "is like the stem of a blue-green bean," i.e., of tubular form, arranged through the *cochlea*, or "snail shaped" canal which looks also like "the leaf of birch."[17] The sensory matter of the nose (olfactory *prasāda*) is disposed in the form of a *kovilāra* (or *kovidāra*), i.e., the ebony-flower or flower of the jacaranda or *bauhinia variegata*[18] which shapes itself into the form of a cone; hence the shape itself of the *nāsāpuṭī* or nose. The sensory-matter of the taste-organ is spread upon the tongue in the manner of a "blue lotus"[19] or in the words of the *Kośa*, in the disposition of a "half-moon" (more or less the V or U form).[20] As for the sensory matter of the tactile *prasāda*, it is spread over the entire body as this is sensitive to the tangibles, excepting such parts "as the hair, fingernails, and teeth."[21] How these different form-arrangements finally account for the strict correspondences to the intrinsic nature of the five coarse matters or stimuli (viṣayaḥ) cannot be easily rationalized.

As for the "coarse" matters (as objective data or sense-stimuli) themselves, as said above, their differentiation and particular destination to each one of the sense-organs is determined by the unbalanced positions in which the four primaries can combine with one another, and by the subsequent overlappings, interpenetrations and varying intensities of their respective activities. Let us elaborate briefly on the variety of each one of these coarse, object-matters which manifest themselves only in correlation with the prasāda-sensory organs, and thereby provide sense-data for the raw sensorial experience of colors, sounds, smells, tastes and tactile impressions.

According to the Kośa, the visible matters (rūpāṇi) are colors and shapes. Color (varṇa) is fundamentally quadruple, namely, blue, red, yellow, and white.[22] Fascinating is the choice of basic atoms of color, since in point of fact they are quite close to what modern physics (and chemistry as it is applied to the art of color-photography) confirms to be the three essential and basic colors, namely, "cyan, magenta, and yellow." The mixture of cyan (blue) with yellow will provide green; magenta and cyan will yield purple, and so forth; and the perfect mixture of all these colors in perfect proportion will produce white, the all-synthesizing color established by the Kośa as the fourth. If we were to attempt to provide a pictorial way of illustrating the possible "unbalanced" compositions of the four basic mahābhūtas as they form the atoms of color we would do so in the following manner:

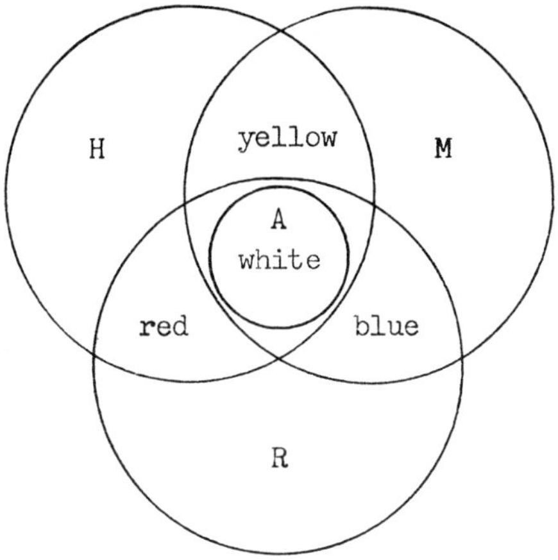

According to the Sarvāstivādins, shape or figure (saṃsthāna) is also a fundamental rūpa (or coarse rūpa-viṣaya) as object of vision. These basic shapes (or saṃsthānas) are eight, enumerated as follows: long, short, square, round, high, low, equal (symmetrical or proportionate) and unequal (asymmetrical or disproportionate). The Sarvāstivādins maintained that these fundamental shapes are real entities (dravya-dharmas), whereas the Sautrāntikas denied this separate existence of shape as an entity and relegated them to the level of figments or mental constructions (manasa).

As for the "sound matter," this is divided--according to its qualitative nature--into four fundamental groups: harmonious sound (sukhaśabda), disharmonious sound (asukhaśabda), sounds produced by "sentient beings" (sattvika-śabda) and sounds produced by "inanimate beings" (asattvika-śabda). Sounds produced by "sentient beings" are divided in their turn into "articulate voice-sounds" (speech, chant, etc.) and "inarticulate voice-sounds"; whereas sounds from "inanimate beings" are divided into two further groups, one group listing such sounds as the "wind-whistle," the "rustling of tree-leaves," and the "murmur of water" (these being predominantly "harmonious"), and the second group comprising all the other "noises" (being predominantly "disharmonious").[23] The atoms or quanta of sound as encompasing the potentials for the above mentioned auditive-matters, and as based on the four elements (R, A, H, M), can be illustrated in the following manner:

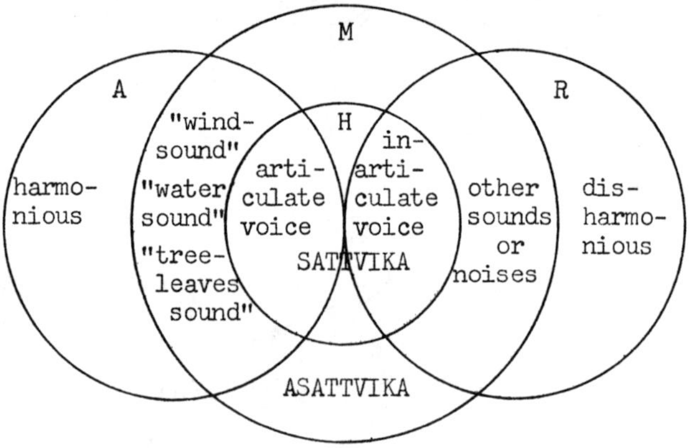

In their turn, the atoms of taste as taste-viṣayas (or stimuli of the taste-organ) contain, according to the Kośa, six flavor-potentials, namely sweet, acid, sour, salty, hot or spicy, bitter, and acrid.[24] On the basis of the four primary elements represented as above by the circles (R, A, H, and M), their unbalanced combination could be illustrated as follows:

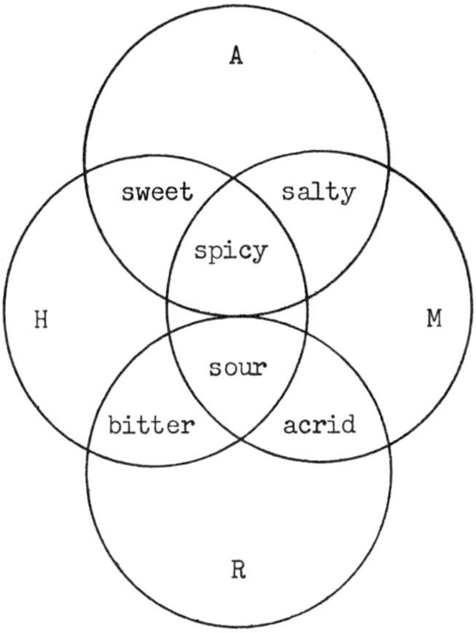

The odors are oversimplified by the reduction to merely four quite broad generalities: _sama_, _visama_, _utkaṭa_, _anutkaṭa_ or good odor, bad odor, intense odor, and weak odor, respectively.[25] According to the _Prakaraṇa_ they are further reduced to a mere three: good, bad and indifferent.[26] An attempt to illustrate such atoms of smell visually will not demand much effort:

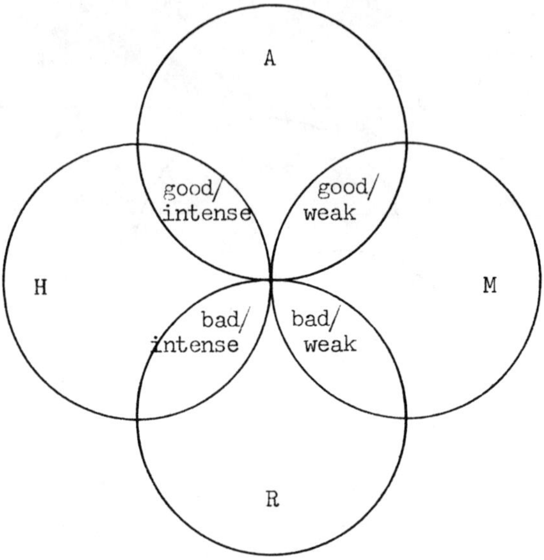

There is no doubt, however, that the most complex and in many ways the most interesting of all the viṣaya-matters (or coarse atoms) are the ones producing tactile impressions. The reason for this is as follows. Only the tactile-organ is capable of "sensing" directly and in immediate contiguity the states formally produced by the forces of "repulsion," "cohesion," "heat," and "motion" as these are "carried" by the sub-atoms of the four mahābhūtas, namely, the states of "solidity," "liquidity," "temperature," and "movement." Only the tactile-sense, as it spreads all over the body and concentrates more heavily in the tongue and the fingers and the palm of the hand, is capable of sensing such states directly and without intermediary. The vision of the liquidity of water by the eyes, or the "sight" of the solidity of iron, is only inferential and not direct. Vision may mislead judgement even in the apprehension of motion, just as it happens with the turning plate of a record player when forgotten and left on overnight just because "my sight" did not detect the turning motion. This is why I always touch the plate with my hand to verify that it is not turning. As for the air-element which represents motion--as wind--its "sound" is only inferentially conjectured through previous experience, whereas, its "touch" is direct and unmistakable. This is the reason why the four mahābhūtas are also called the pure "tangible entities" (sprastavyadravya) since they are capable of directly manifesting themselves to the organ of touch.[27]

However, as said above when explaining the perfectly balanced combination that brings about the derivation of the prasāda or "tranquil" rūpa, the four mahābhūtas cannot be experienced by "touch" unless they combine also with secondary tangible matters (kāyabhautikas or kāyopādāya-viṣayas). As mentioned earlier, the rūpa-prasādas (or sensitive "subtle" matter of the sense-organs) are in themselves as intangible as they are invisible, inodorous and untastable. They are never objects of sensory experience of any kind but only subjects of such an experience. This exclusion affects also the tangibility of the four primary elements (mahābhūtas). The tangibility of the four primary-elements can manifest itself objectively only in association with the other derivative tactile viṣaya-rūpas, which are counted in the number of seven:[28] soft, coarse, heavy, light, cold, hunger and thirst. These derivative "tactile matters" (kāyopādāya-viṣaya-rūpa) are then, as before, derived from the unbalanced combination of the four elements, just like in the cases of the rest of the secondary, "derived matters" (bhautika or upādāya-rūpa). As these seven classes of secondary tactile matters derive, then the possibility of the four mahābhūtas being outwardly experienced as pure tangibles (sparśavat) is actualized. The seven derived matters of tactile experience originate as a central nucleus around which--and as "outer" to which--the four fundamental states of the "solid," the "liquid," the "hot" and the "moving" manifest themselves as pure tangibles. Thus the whole number of tangibles, both "pure" and "derivative" are eleven in total: sprastavyam ekādaśātmikam ("the tanglibles are of eleven species").[29] A pictorial illustration of the way these eleven tangibles relate to one another is attempted in the following diagram:

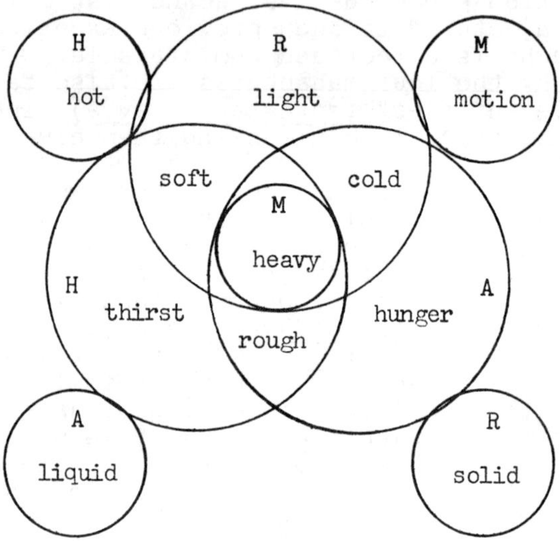

In this diagram the four primary elements as "pure" tangibles are depicted as externally manifested throughout their association with the seven "secondary tangibles" which are derived in their turn from the former. Thus the four primary elements posit the intermediary ground whereby they themselves come to manifestation in their own original and formal activities.

So much for the five <u>rūpaskandhas</u> of the sense-organs and their five objective stimuli. Now we have to proceed to a brief mention of the already announced <u>eleventh</u> and the <u>last but not least</u> of the <u>rūpas</u>. It is termed <u>avijñapti-rūpa</u>.

<u>Avijñapti</u> designates the negative form of the femenine <u>vijñapti</u>. <u>Vijñapti</u> is a term which literally

applies to the acts whereby our mental intentions, desires or volitions are intimated or externally manifested to somebody else, especially from inferior to superior. It is clear that the forms of expression of such desires and volitions are usually done not only through the use of the voice and speech (vāc, vacana), but also through external, physical motions of such bodily parts as arms and hands in the form of gesticulation. Thus two fundamental types of vijñaptis are mentioned as vāgvijñapti (or vācika-vijñapti, i.e., verbal intimation or expression) and kāyavijñapti (or kāyika-vijñapti, i.e., corporeal intimation or gesticulation).[30] On the other hand, in early Mahāyāna the term vijñapti came to mean also any act of human experience exercised and primordially posited by the superior mind-faculty (manas) as the seat of subjectivity (or Ego-awareness) and of the will. Such is the case of the use of this term in the compound vijñapti-mātratā (or "ideation-only") which is propounded as the central trait of Buddhist idealism in the Vijñānavāda or Yogācāra school founded by Asaṅga. Hence all contents of human experience would be vijñaptis and only vijñaptis, since according to idealism these contents--whether purely ideal or sensorial--are only projections externally intimated from within the subconscious bottom-recess of the mind which is designated as ālayavijñāna (or "storehouse of consciousness").

The term vijñapti, as used in the Hīnayāna texts, connotes as a matter of fact a trace of these two significations. On the one hand vijñapti is considered an external intimation or declaration of the willing intention, either in the verbal form, or through external, physical expression. However, vijñapti, as corporeal or physical manifestation, is not only taken in the sense of mere gesticular expression to another person (unlike the case of verbal intimation) but also as the outer and physical execution of the willing intention through the motion of the bodily limbs such as hands, etc. Thus the kāyika-vijñapti came to represent the very execution of a willing intention that in itself is purely mental, and which can be manifested externally through vacana (speech) as a mere verbal intimation. In the understanding of this expanded meaning of vijñapti (as both external expression and execution of the will) the correspondence and relationship of the two vijñaptis with acts of ethical validity and of moral nature becomes obvious. Thus the two vijñaptis become intimately related with the term that designates moral action, i.e., KARMA.[31] Accordingly, as there are two kinds of vijñapti, there are three kinds of moral action, the first being the mental intention per se which becomes either intimated by the vācika-vijñapti (or vāg-vijñapti) or executed by the kāyika-vijñapti. This purely mental and intentional act of the will which is previous to its intimation or execution, and which can also remain unintimated and unexecuted, is called mano-karma (mental moral action). Most codes of ethics and morality attribute an original moral value to our mental intentions, regardless of whether they are executed or not. Such is the case in Buddhism. In point of fact, the acts of mano-karma (mental action) are the ones which formally bear moral qualification per se. The evil intention which is not executed on the basis of precluding circumstances is not less evil than its execution itself. As mano-karma is expressed through the vācika-vijñapti (or vāg-vijñapti = verbal intimation) then it becomes vācika-karma or "verbal action"; the corporeal execution finally perpetrated through the kāyika-vijñapti (bodily intimation) becomes by the same token kāyika-karma (bodily action). Thus the two vijñaptis coincide de facto with the two external karmas, the vācika-(verbal) and the kāyika(corporeal) karma. However, the two connotations of vijñapti and karma are different in that the term vijñapti designates only the aspects of external expression of the mind, whereas the term karma denotes also the moral quality of such expressions as human acts.

This elaboration on the term vijñapti paves the way for a proper explanation of the meaning of the avijñapti-rūpa. As such this last of the rūpas etymologically entails its subliminal or subconscious nature as "non-manifested" in consciousness (a-vijñapti = not surfacing to consciousness, neither to the mind which performs the acts of mental karma, nor to the external senses). Hence the avijñapti is a rūpa (material factor) of the highest subtlety, even more subtle than the rūpa-prasādas which were described as constituents of the sensorial organs. Avijñapti is the most subtle of all the rūpas not only in that it does not offer resistance to the sense organs, but in that it does not even let itself be pervaded, and thus "contacted" (a-sparśanīya), by the dharma of consciousness (vijñāna). Thus it cannot be the direct object of sensorial, perceptional experience and hence its existence can be only inferred. Why is such a subtle, unmanifested (*avijñapti*) material factor postulated by the *Sarvāstivādins*? Its postulation is due to the character of potential retribution that all of human acts as KARMA (regardless of whether they are merely mental, or also verbal and corporeal) must bear in themselves. Hence *avijñapti-rūpa* is a subtle residuum left over by the two physical *vijñaptis*, verbal and corporeal. This residuum retains the moral quality of such *vijñaptis* (from whence it originates) as the passively accumulated "seeds" (*bījas*)--or "perfumes" (*vāsanāḥ*)--to re-fructify, re-germinate or re-exhalate--in future existences as "karmic" retribution.[32] Furthermore this residuum is physical in that it is also compounded by the four fundamental elements or "energies" (R, A, H, M). It could be explained by establishing that not all the physical energy invested in the intimations of the will by verbal expression and bodily execution comes to manifestation. Thus "non-manifest" (*a-vijñapti*) portions of this energy would be released in the form of extremely subtle and subconscious deposits emanating from the physical actions as such, and perhaps accumulating in some parts of the body such as the "heart-basis" (*hṛdaya-vastu*), i.e., the material seat of the mental organ (*vijñāna* as *manas*).[33]

At this point the extraordinary and far-reaching significance of the *avijñapti-rūpa* is obviously beyond our present capacity of explanation. The complete role of this *rūpa* in regard to the total mechanism of KARMA will be expounded in the Second Part of this work, where we shall deal with the issues of "origination" and "causation." For now, let us briefly define the *avijñapti-rūpa* as subtle, "non-manifest" residues released by the act of physical *karma* as enacted through the two *vijñaptis*, the "verbal" and the "corporeal." Such residues--which probably are thought to accumulate in the "heart-basis" (*hṛdaya-vastu*)--become the physical carriers of potentials ("seeds" or *bījas*) for future retribution, and thus they have to be transmitted from the "dying" individual to the conceptional matrix of its subsequent rebirth. It is to be emphasized that in spite of its extreme subtlety, the *avijñapti* is still of material nature, and thus derived from a highly balanced combination of the four primary *mahābhūtas*. It is therefore a *bhautika* or *upādāyarūpa* (derived or secondary matter): mahābhūtānyupādāya sā hyavijñaptir ucyate, i.e., "the avijñapti is said to derive from the (four) great elements."[34] Furthermore it is vyākṛtāpratighaṃrūpaṃ, i.e., a matter which is qualitatively defined (as bad or good = śubhāśubhaḥ), though "non-resistant" to the senses (apratigha) and thus anidarśana (non-perceptible).[35]

To finish our treatment of the rūpa-skandha (division of materiality) we should add a brief mention of other bodily organs which develop, not on the basis of the subtle matter (rūpa-prasāda) as this constitutes the five sense-faculties, but only on the basis of the coarse matters or viṣayas. Among these bodily organs there is the already mentioned "heart-basis" (hṛdaya-vastu) which is the corporeal heart as considered to be the material seat of the mind (manas). The intrinsic constitution of the mind has to be discussed later when we deal with the vijñāna-skandha (the fifth of the skandhas). As for other coarse organs we should mention the masculine (puṃindriya) and the feminine (strīndriya), and also the vāg-vijñaptīndriya and the kāya-vijñaptīndriya which are the organs of the external intimations of the will, namely, the vocal cords as well as the arms, hands, etc.

2.- VEDANĀ-SKANDHA.- Vedanā designates the original or "raw" feelings and sensations (raw or chaotic in the sense of being not yet integrated into organic manifolds such as the appearance of distinct and formal objects). These feelings and primal sensations come about as the immediate result of the contact (sparśa) between the five sensory organs (or prasādendriyāṇi) and their corresponding "sensorial-matters" (or viṣayas) as expounded above. Sparśa (contact) connotes a meaning of extraordinary importance in Buddhist psychology. Used in this extended sense (as it affects the functions of all the sense-organs) sparśa (contact) has a far broader meaning than when used only within the context of the tactile impressions resulting from the external contact of the hands and other parts of the body with the tactile-matters (spraṣṭavya-viṣayas). Sparśa, considered as the basis for the manifestation of all feelings and sensations, is more subtle than mere "touch" in that it constitutes the encounter, or better said, the "collision" (pratigha) of the conglomerates of gross atoms (paramāṇusaṃghāta) with the subtle, inner prasāda-element of the five organs. Hence the five sense organs are also termed as *sparśāyatanāṇi* (bases of "contact"). All sensations and feelings arise, then, ultimately on the basis of "contact." Vision, audition, smells and tastes are the outcome of this "contact" in the broadest and most subtle understanding of the term.[36] Sensory-matters such as atoms of light (the photons of modern physics) have to penetrate the sight organ and "collide" with, and thus also disturb to an extent, the inner equilibrium of the *prasāda*-element within the eye; thus vision (the experience of light and its colors) is established.

The number of specifically different "raw" or primordial sensations is usually given as nine. The primordial sensations or feelings (*vedanā*) are primarily classified as either pleasant (*sukhavedanā*) or unpleasant (*duḥkhavedanā*) or as indifferent (neither pleasant nor unpleasant = *asukhāduḥkhavedanā*). As a matter of fact these are the sensations *par excellence*, and Buddhist psychology considers them as originating simultaneously with the presentation of the sensorial-matters such as "perceived" colors, sounds, etc. The term *vedanā* seems to designate primarily these three primordial "feelings" and only secondarily is given to designate the raw, original sensations of color, sound, etc., and the other sense-data that are experienced by the senses. The *Abhidharmakośa* applies the term *vedanā* to such specific "sense-data" as the experience of color, sound, etc., only as these "present" themselves in association with the primary feelings (pleasant, unpleasant, neutral). Thus it seems that the early Buddhist philosophers considered the three "feelings" as some sort of "primary sensations," and the sensations of color, sound, etc., as only "presentations." This would entail that the feelings of pleasantness, unpleasantness and indifference are truly originated by *sparśa*, whereas such specific data as colors, sounds, smells, etc., are only "presented" by it. This is probably due to the fact that the distinct specifications of the sensorial data into five *viṣaya-ayatanāṇi* (or objective bases of sensation) are already formally given in the five sense-matters or *viṣayas* previous to their "encounter" or "collision" (*sampratigha*) with the five *indriyas* (eye, ears, nose, etc.). Hence such things as colors, sounds, smells, tastes and tangibles are not generated when they appear to the senses, but they are just "presented." *Sparśa* or "sensorial *contact" is the "condition" for their manifestation or "presentation." However, the feelings of pleasantness or unpleasantness, agreeability or disagreeability, pleasure or pain are "new" in that they do not pre-exist in regard to their experience and thus are totally original sensations that <u>come to be</u> through the function of "contact." "Contact" (<u>sparśa</u>), therefore, is not merely a condition for their manifestation, but is their immediate and generative cause (<u>kāraṇa</u>). This is the reason why most texts refer to <u>vedanā</u> as comprising primarily the three feelings of pleasure, pain, and/or indifference. These "feelings," as they are "generated" and "caused" by <u>sparśa</u> (contact), accompany the self-manifestation of the subsequent colors, sounds, etc., as these latter are just "made present" (not caused) by <u>sparśa</u> (contact).

It is obvious that these primary feelings are primitive and pre-reflexive in themselves. The primary feelings therefore seem to have nothing to do with the subsequent experience of reflexive attraction or repulsion that lays the basis for the acts of will. The three original <u>vedanās</u> are in this sense totally generic, unthematic and pre-reflexive, and as such they associate with the original presence of the specific raw sense-data previous to the formal discernment of full-fledged objects. It is obvious that these original feelings might persist in the further development of specific sense-data into perfected object-experience and grow into proper acts of will.

At any rate, the differentiation between "primary" and "secondary" sensation is not in the temporal priority of the first upon the second, but in the specifically different role played by <u>sparśa</u> (contact) in reference to their production: <u>sparśa</u> (contact) is the proper cause (<u>hetu</u>) of the three primordial feelings and only the "condition" (<u>pratyaya</u>) for the manifestation and "presentation" of the five classes of sensorial "matters."

Finally, it should be added that <u>sparśa</u> (contact) produces the three primary feelings also in the purely mental and non-sensuous form proper to the mind (<u>manas</u>, the "mental organ," to be explained below). Thus the total number of sensations are given as nine, namely, the three primary sensations of "pain, pleasure, and indifference" as these accompany the manifestation of five specific sense-data through "contact" with the five <u>prasādendriya</u>-s (sense-organs); and further, they accompany also the manifestation of non-sensuous objects (ālambana) to the mind (manas). Such are the words of the Kośa: "The vedanāskandha is the triple modality of sensing (anubhoga), namely, the sensations of pain, pleasure and indifference. Six further classes of sensations have to be distinguished: those which arise from the contact (sparśa) of the five material organs, the sight-organ, etc., with their own respective, material objects; and those feelings of "pleasure-displeasure-indifference" which originate from the contact of the mental organ (manas) with its non-sensuous, immaterial objects."[37]

3.- SAṂJÑĀ-SKANDHA.- This skandha represents the Division of formal perception of objects as organic and unitary manifolds of sensations. Thus it establishes the cognitive apprehension of full-fledged material objects. We do not experience just colors, smells and tastes, etc., but we see a good smelling and tasting apple, or orange, or any other object as a whole. The total perception of any external oject is the result of an organic integration of the raw sensations just discussed in the previous division (vedanā-skandha). Etymologically the term saṃ-jñā carries this connotation with the prefix saṃ-, which translates as the Greek syn- (like in syn-thesis) or the Latin con- or co- (like in com-prehensio, co-gnitio, etc.). Thus the term saṃ-jñā (with the verbal root jñā, like in the nouns jñāna, prajñā, etc.) reveals also the character of mental synthesis of "raw" sense-data that this cognitive function realizes. Hence saṃjñā (cognition) is a dharma which results from the synthesis of the raw sensations (vedanā) as these are integrated into an organic and sense-making "whole." Phenomenologically, it can be associated with the intentional and unitary morphé (or "eidetic form" as proposed by Edmund Husserl) as this informs the plural sense-materials (hylé) into a full-fledged noema or "phenomenal" object. Saṃjñā then seems to have--in phenomenological terms--a noematic character, as the organic and sense-making "presence" in consciousness of a distinct object. The noetic function (or noesis in phenomenological terminology) which generates saṃjñā is to be ascribed to the dharma of vijñāna, the last of the skandhas to be explained at the end of this section.[38] In the words of the Abhidharmakośa, saṃjñā is defined as nimittodgrahaṇātmika, i.e., as "the distinct apprehension and discerning of objective determinations" (*nimitta*, *pariccheda*).[39] In this quotation the term *udgrahaṇa* translates best as "apprehension," although sometimes it comes to mean also "abstraction," i.e., the function of the mind whereby mental notions and universal ideas are issued on the basis of "singling out" the distinctive or essential characters and formal traits of an external object. In other passages, however, the *Kośa* refers to *samjñā* as resulting from the function of the mind which is defined as *viṣayanimittagrahaṇa*,[40] or also as *viṣayaviśeṣarūpagraha*, terms which regard *saṃjñā* as the result of "com-prehending" and thus "syn-thesizing" (*saṃgrahaṇa*) the marks (*nimitta*) and differentiations (*viśeṣa*) among the sense-matters (*rūpa-viṣaya*) which have been "presented" by the sense-organs. Here, therefore, a more basic definition of *saṃjñā* is given as mere synthesis (*saṃgraha*) of raw sensorial materials. Both definitions of *saṃjñā* as resulting from *saṃgrahana* (comprehension) and *udgrahaṇa* (apprehension) point to functions of the mind (*manas*) which escape the limited capability of the five sensorial organs. Thus *samjñā* entails also the further function of abstraction, as the way towards the founding of the operations of thought and mental discourse (*vikalpa*). Since these functions belong to the last and most important of the *skandhas* they will have to be further discussed. It is important to note here that these two functions of *saṃgrahaṇa* and *udgrahaṇa* (as "comprehension" and "apprehension") whereby the *dharma* of *saṃjñā* (as content of perception) is originated pertain to the higher mental faculty which is called *manas* (mind), and that therefore *samjñā* can originate only on the basis of a "triple contact," i.e., the "contact" (*sparśa*) among the two *rūpas* of *prasāda* and *viṣaya* (i.e., "sense-organs" and "sense-matters") and the *dharma* of discriminative consciousness and subjective, pure awareness which is *vijñāna-skandha*.[41]

4.- SAṂSKĀRA-SKANDHA.- This is the division of what could be designated as "volitive forces" or also "volitive formations." This *skandha* comprises a vast spectrum of both mental and non-mental forces, some of them associated with the cognitive acts already defined as *vedanā* and *saṃjñā*, many of them representing either instinctive or subconscious proclivities which operate on the basis of various sources of "karmic" causation. Contrary to tradition, the *Dhammasaṅghaṇi* reduces the aggregates of *dharmas* to three main groups, thus including *vedanā* and *saṃjñā* within the division of the *saṃskāras* which are taken in general as "mental functions." In the traditional division of the Five Skandhas *vedanā* and *saṃjñā* are considered as *skandhas in their own right*, whereas *saṃskāras* are restricted to all such operations of the sentient being which belong--in a more or less direct way--*to the realm of volition*. Thus the most significant of the *saṃskāras is the* intentional act of the will, which, of course, is strictly associated with such cognitive acts, are performed by the senses and the mind (*manas*). This act of "willing intention" is termed *cetanā*. Hence *cetanā* is the *saṃskāra par excellence*, and as such is the foundation of *karma* ("human action") as morally imputable and "remunerable" through the "karmic" cycle of causation to be discussed later. *Cetanā*, however, though the most significant of the *saṃskāras*, is after all the first in a long list of 48 different functions, some of them directly associated with acts of consciousness (*caitasika-* or *cittasamprayukta-saṃskāras*) and thus characterized as carriers of "mental intentionality." They can be rendered also as "mental forces," the term "force" indicating here their ever underlying association with the will.

Of these *caitasika-* or *cittasamprayukta-saṃskāras* (or volitive functions *associated with acts of consciousness*), some of them are nothing but mere functions of *manas* (*vijñāna* as mind faculty) inasmuch as these are "commanded" by the will (*cetanā*); whereas others are innate propensities which "predispose" or incline the will towards the positing of certain actions. The first are cognitive functions ordered and directed by the will; the second, on the contrary, are inner proclivities which push and gravitate on the will. According to *Visuddhimagga*, the first are *karma-forming forces* (Pali: *abhisaṅkharaṇa-saṅkhāra*, Skt: *abhisaṃkaraṇa-saṃskāras*)[42] in that they are posited and commanded by the will and thus become the object of moral retribution: they are actively *karmic* and thus morally imputable as either evil (*akuśala*) or as good (*kuśala*) deeds. The second kind of "forces," i.e., those which "predispose" and "impel" the will, are *karma-formed-forces* (Pali: *abhisaṅkhata-saṅkhāra*, Skt.: *abhisaṃskṛta-saṃskāras*),[43] meaning that they are innate predispositions or propensities which are inherited as the reaction (or regermination) from previously accumulated "*karmic* seeds" (*bījas*) as "planted" by the will-posited acts (first class of forces). Most of these propensities (except those under the influence of the *anāsrava* or "pure" *dharmas* effected by the practice of the Path) are of soiled and impure character, producing an unwholesome gravitation on the will as inordinate passions (*anuśaya*) and evil tendencies (*paryavasthāna*). The first kind of forces have the will as their active or motive subject; the second kind have the will as their passive object. Thus the first kind of "karma-forming-forces"--as formal acts of *cetanā* (volition)--belong to the aspect of *karma* which will be called "*active karma*." The "karma-formed-forces," however, which weigh upon and predispose the will are to be considered as "fruits" of karmic retribution which will be designated as "*reactive-karma*" (*karmaphala* or *karma*-fruition). The intermediary "accumulations" (*āyūhana*) or "karmic seeds," which remain passively "stored" and "planted" within their carriers until the time for their "refructification" or retributive "fruition" arrives, are not counted here within the *saṃskāras*-division (fourth *skandha*). The reason for this exclusion resides in the fact that these passive accumulations either already constitute one of the *rūpas* (namely, the *avijñapti-rūpa*, the material accumulations ensuing from the two material acts, the vocal and the physical) which belongs to the first *skandha*; or else--as pure mental deposits--they are "stored" in the very mental faculty which issues purely mental acts, namely the *vijñāna-dharma* in its capacity of *manas* or *citta* (mind), a *dharma* which constitutes the fifth *skandha*. This role of the *vijñāna-dharma* as capable of "storing" the moral "perfumes" (*vāsanās*) exhalated from its own mental actions or willing intentions (for future "re-exhalation" or "fruition") will be explained later in our treatment of *karma* and causation (Second Part).

These *passively "stored"* accmulations of "karmic potentials" will also receive the designation of *saṃskāras* (forces) within a context other than the pentad of the *skandhas*. Thus *saṃskāras* will be a term applied also to the second "link" within the "twelvefold chain" of "interdependent origination" (*pratītyasamutpāda*) to be explained in Part II. This later application of the term *saṃskāras* is not to be counted as belonging to the fourth *skandha*. The *saṃskāras* that count as the fourth of the *skandhas* are active forces (will) and reactive functions (propensities) actually in operation, whereas the saṃskāras that count as the "second link" in the "interdependent chain of origination" designate all the passive potentials (mental and physical) which--as released by death--provide the basis for rebirth.

As examples of caitasika-saṃskāras (mental functions) that are "karma-forming" (abhisaṃkaraṇa-saṃskāras) the texts mention beyond cetanā--which is the proper act of will--such other will-commanded acts as smṛti (or memory), manasikāra (or attention, directed focus of the mind), vitarka (or searching, applied thought), vicāra (or sustained thought) and samādhi (or mental concentration). Among the innate, impure passions (anuśaya) that are "karma-formed" (abhisaṃskṛta-saṃskāras), and hence inherited from previous existences, such propensities as moha (stupidity), pramāda (carelessness), aśraddhā (perturbed mind), styāna (indolence, laziness), krodha (violent angry temperament), māyā (deceitfulness) mātsarya (envy), īrṣyā (jealousy), rāga (passionate love), dveṣa (hatred), māna (pride), etc., are listed. Good or wholesome propensities "formed" by former wholesome deeds are also listed as counteracting or abating the evil passions (anuśaya).

The second principal group of the saṃskāra-skandha comprise all other functions which are subliminal and non-mental (acaitasika) in that they are not directly associated with the conscious mind and its conscious acts (cittaviprayukta-saṃskāras). Here belong such vegetative functions as prāpti and aprāpti (acquisition and abandonment) of certain dharmas which either accrue to the individual life-serial (saṃtāna) or are rejected from it, mostly in the process of nourishment, metabolism and growth. Among these non-mental forces are also counted such functions whereby a similar nature is transmitted from "generators" to "generated" through the act of generation in living beings (nikāya-sabhāga or "community of nature"). This notion will reappear in our treatment of the issues of causation. Another non-mental force is listed as jīvita-saṃskāra, which is a vital energy that determines the span life to be covered by any living being from birth to death. Some of these forces (like the last one or jīvita) are also inherited from former karma and thus are also considered karma-abhisaṃskṛta (i.e., "formed by karma"). Others, however, are formed by universal aspects of causation that have nothing to do with individual retribution of past deeds: such as, for instance, the nikāya-sabhāga, which--as just mentioned--is a universal force that determines the identity of nature within living species. Such are also the forces of generation (jāti), subsistence (sthiti), decay (jarā) and destruction (anityatā). These forces which are exerted by universal and not individual karma-actions are merely designated as saṃskṛta-saṃskāras.[44] Other saṃskāras are also designated as "forces of convention, contrivence, application and expression"; such forces are said to intervene in the application of vocal phonemes (vyanjana-saṃskāra), or to impart meaning to sentences through the formation of grammatical forms (pada-kāya-saṃskāra). These last forces are collectively shared and thus they found the common use of language.

Finally, from the standpoint of moral quality the saṃskāras (vital forces) which are associated with mental and conscious activity (cittasaṃprayukta-saṃskāras) receive the following designations: mental acts ruled by the command or consent of the will (i.e., the karma-abhisaṃkaraṇa-saṃskāras or "karma-forming-forces") are qualified generically as vyākṛta or "morally defined," either as evil (akuśala, aśubha) or as good or wholesome (kuśala, śubha). The innate passions (anuśaya) and evil propensities (paryavasthāna), however, are "karma-formed" (abhisaṃskṛta-saṃskāra) and thus are the fruit of retribution (karmaphala). These forces are innate and thus carry in themselves no moral qualification or imputability. Only willful and deliberate acts of volition as "directed" or "consented" by the will are morally qualifiable and imputable. Hence innate propensities are called avyākṛta or "morally undefined" (neutral). However, the lower passions are designated as "evil," not because they themselves are ethically such, but because they impel or incline towards the positing of evil deeds. Thus only the consenting act of the will is moral evil per se and intrinsically; the passion itself in only evil per extrinsecam denominationem (as the Western scholastics would say), i.e., on the basis of both their origin (since they proceed as retribution from evil acts) and their natural entelecheia or directional gravitation (since they "predispose" the will). Consequently the evil passions and propensities are termed nivṛta-avyākṛta,[45] where nivṛta means "obscuring," "obfuscating," "covering" (and thus as "hindering," "impeding" the performance of meritorious deeds); and where avyākṛta means "morally undefined or neutral." However, the good or wholesome propensities which have been "formed" as the retribution from wholesome deeds are designated as anivṛta-avyākṛta[46], which consequently will mean: "morally undefined, though non-impeding, non-obscuring" the performance of wholesome karmic actions.

The analysis of the above expounded terminology will be of great assistance in the forthcoming study of the mechanism of the karma-cycle to be undertaken in Part II of this work. In order to bring together visually the correlations among the various terms which classify and subclassify the wide ranging realm of the saṃskāra-skandha, we offer the following chart:

- SAṂSKĀRA-SKANDHA
  - caitasika or citta-saṃprayukta-saṃskāras. Forces associated with mental acts or conscious forces intervening in the issuing of volition (cetanā)
    - karma-abhisaṃkaraṇa-saṃskāras ("karma-forming" or acts commanded and directed by the will.
      - "active karma" (kuśala = wholesome; akuśala = unwholesome)
    - karma-abhisaṃskṛta-saṃskāras ("karma-formed as passions (anuśaya) and innate propensities predisposing the will)
      - "reactive karma" (retributive fruition) as morally neutral but impure and offering hindrance (nivṛtāvyākṛta); fruition from unwholesome active karma
      - "reactive karma" (retributive fruition) as morally neutral but pure and not offering hindrance (anivṛtāvyākṛta); fruition from wholesome active karma
  - acaitasika or citta-viprayukta-saṃskāras (Non-conscious or subliminal forces)
    - karma-abhisaṃskṛta saṃskāras ("karma-formed")
      - "reactive karma" as retributive fruition from previous individual active karma; such as the forces of "life-momentum" (jīvita = life-span force, acquisition (prāpti), rejection (aprāpti), etc.
    - saṃskṛta-saṃskāras (effected by universal causes)
      - "non-retributive," depending on universal causes and not originated from individual active karma. Such is the force of nikāya-sabhāga (community of specific nature), the forces of origination of momentary dharmas (jāti), their momentary subsistence (sthiti), their decay (jarā, their extinction (anityatā), etc.
    - prayogābhisaṃskāras (contrivance forces)
      - "non-retributive" forces of usage, conventional contrivance and social communication such as "articulate sound-force" (vyanjana-kāya-saṃskāra), "wording force" (nāma-kāya-saṃskāra) and "sentence-forming force" (pada-kāya-saṃskāra).

VIJÑĀNA-SKANDHA. This is the fifth, and thus the last "but not least" of the skandhas. In its nature it is the most subtle and by the same token the most important of all the five skandhas. Our definition will be brief at this point; but its entailments extend not only to many of the concepts already mentioned above, but also to most of the concepts and structures to be explained hereafter. Vijñāna is the basic concept of Buddhist psychology and, by the same token, plays the most important role in Buddhist soteriology, since it is on its "purification" (visuddha) that the whole and strenuous road to deliverance is built. Vijñāna is the essential ground without which no vedanā (sensation) and saṃjñā (perception) can take place. No mental force as described in the saṃskāra-skandha can function without the dharma of vijñāna. As for the rūpas, they would have no psychological or cosmological role to play without vijñāna. Whereas the rūpas are conceived as entitative dharmas having a particle-like existence of their own (dravyaka-dharmas), vedanā (sensations), saṃjñā (perceptions) and cetanā (volitive acts) are not considered as dravyas (entitative elements) but as functional factors (kṛtyika-dharmas): they come to manifestation only through the interaction and "contact" (sparśa) between the rūpas (subtle and coarse, sense-organs, and sense-matters) and the fifth of the skandhas, namely the vijñāna. Thus the explanation of this most relevant of the skandhas will fill the remaining loopholes and gaps in the explanation of the preceding skandhas.

We have already dealt with the etymology of such terms as saṃjñā and jñāna. Saṃjñā, as perception, denotes the organic co-presence of an integrated manifold of sensations: saṃjñā is the result of a process of "reification" and "objectivation" whereby "things" (not merely colors and sounds, etc.) come to be experienced. The prefix saṃ- (co-) alludes to this process which is fundamentally a process of synthesis (viṣaya-viśeṣasaṃgrahaṇa = the "comprehension" of differentiated sense-data).[47] The operations which bring this "synthesis" about has been said to be of the "mind" (manas). An operation termed udgrahaṇa was mentioned at an earlier point[48] as meaning the "apprehension" of the essential traits of any perceived object. This operation intervenes also in the generation of saṃjñā (object-perception) as full-fledged perceptional, objective content. By focusing on the distinctive marks or determinations (pariccheda) of the objects, udgrahaṇa (apprehension) paves the way to the issuing of jñāna, which can be defined--within this context--as "abstract notion" (also termed mati). Udgrahaṇa is then in itself not only an "apprehending" function but also an "abstracting" one. This function was also attributed to the mind (manas) as its operation par excellence.

Manas is then refered to as a mental organ, capable of abstracting universalized notions from the experience of material, sensorial objects, and furthermore capable of "knowing" non-sensuous and purely mental objects that cannot by any means be apprehended by the sensorial faculties. According to the Abhidharmakośa, manas is nothing but the dharma of vijñāna as this sets itself into operation by its coming into "contact" with the external viṣayas (sense-matters) by supporting itself upon the inner and subtle matter of the five senses or indriyas (tadvijñānāśrayā rūpaprasādaś cakṣurādayaḥ . . .).[49]

In its original etymology the term vi-jñāna is especially significant. The prefix vi- plays the role of the Latin dis-, the German ent-, or the Greek dia-, such as in the verb dis-cernere, or in such Latin rooted English nouns as dis-tinction, dis -cernment, etc. As the prefix dis-entails some sort of separation (whether this be real or purely notional), the prefix vi- in the term vi-jñāna seems to connote the distinct sense of subjective awareness that accompanies and thus dis-tinguishes itself from every objectively appearing object of consciousness. According to Husserl, this awareness of the subjective polarity that necessarily accompanies all contents of experience constitutes also the very source of the activities which "discern" objects from objects. Thus vi-jñāna is the dharma of pure discriminative awareness whereby the empirical subject not only discerns objects from objects, but discerns any given objects from itself. The notion of vi-jñāna thus comes closest to what Husserl called "pure subjectivity." Vi-jñāna is hence also close to the Kantian conception of the "transcendental unity of apperception" which makes all the objective unification of sensorial manifolds possible. It is in this sense that *vi-jñāna* "dis-cerns" objects by exercising *saṃgrahaṇa* and *udgrahaṇa* (comprehension and apprehension) in order to experience or bring about *saṃ-jñā* (syn-thesis of manifolds). Obviously, in parity with Kant and Husserl, the early Buddhist thinkers, although acknowledging the presence of a continuing sense of "pure" subjectivity which provides the basis for the phenomenal manifestation of Self-ness, never admitted the substantial and transcendent existence of such Ego. In the admission of a *dharma* (or factor) or pure "subjective" awareness they exhibited themselves as ahead of Hume who seemed to deny even the phenomenal presence of this abiding polarity of Self-ness in the noetic functions of *dis*-cernment, as *dis*-tinct from the *dis*-cerned.[50] Hence *vi-jñāna* (the pure act of *dis-cerning* *dis*-tinguishes itself from its ever flowing companions, the *dis*-cerned (*vi-jñeya*).

Nothing is closer, then, to the Husserlian correlation of *noesis-noema* (discerning-discerned) than the Buddhist correlation *vijñāna-vijñeya*, expressed also (especially in the later Buddhist works of idealism) as *grāhaka-grāhya* (the grasping and the grasped).[51] Taking the above mentioned terms of *saṃ-jñā* and *jñāna* to signify respectively "concrete perception" and "abstract notion" as possible contents of the "discerned" and the "grasped" (*noema*), the phenomenological correlation between *vijñāna* as the pure subjective function of the *dis-cerning* and its objects (sensuous and non-sensuous) as the *dis-cerned* can be formulated in the following manner:

NOESIS (or the noetic functions)		NOEMA (or the noematic contents)
VI-JÑĀNA (*grāhaka*)	→	*VI-JÑEYA* (*grāhya*)
the "knowing" or *dis*-cerning (grasping)		the known or *dis*-cerned (grasped)

SAṂGRAHAṆA Com-prehension	→	*UDGRAHAṆA* Ap-prension and/or abstraction	*SAṂ-JÑĀ* perceptional or concrete	→	*JÑĀNA* eidetic or abstract

This distinction between the pure awareness of subjectivity as phenomenal unity of the discerning activities is further confirmed by the *Kośa* which also defines *vijñāna* as "the *vijñapti* (conscious intimation) which is *relative* to every object" and as "the *upalabdhi* (or naked apprehension) which accompanies every manifestation of the *viṣayas* or objective matters."[52] The term *upalabdhi* is especially significant in this context, since it is compounded of the prefix *upa-*, which means "next to" or "at this side of," and the feminine *labdhi* (from root *labh* = taking hold of) meaning "acquisition," "obtainment." In this sense, *vijñāna* is always "at this side of" and "next to" every consciously present object (*upalabdhi viṣayaṃ viṣayaṃ prati*)[53]; or in phenomenological terms, it is the subjective, intentional activity of "knowing" (*noesis*) which "grasps" and "takes hold" of the "object known" (*noema*).

Let us again emphasize that the *Hīnayāna* schools, by postulating *vijñāna* as a *dharma-dravya*, advocated the reality of the "knowing activity" without the commonly postulated existence of a permanent, substantial Ego as the transcendent substratum of such an activity. The awareness of continuing subjectivity is "serial" (*saṃtānaka*) and as such is still a part of the mere flux of "momentary emergences" (*kṣaṇikotsarga*), or "dharmic," quantum-like "flashes" which make up conscious experience.

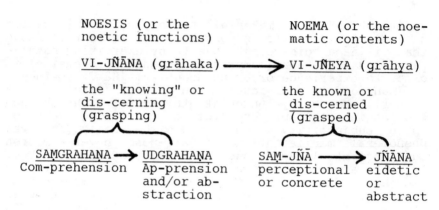

Chapter 4

Eighteen gotra-dhātus and three loka-dhātus

In view of the above, how does the term manas (as mind) refer to the term vi-jñāna as "discerning awareness"? According to the Kośa, there is no ontological distinction beween vijñāna and manas or "mind faculty," which is also termed citta: cittaṃ mano'tha vijñānam ekārtham, i.e., "thought--faculty, mind and dis-cerning awareness, all these designate one and the same thing."[54] Some differentiations of "karmic" relevance between the roles of citta and manas will be discussed later. Otherwise vijñāna differs from manas only in that vijñāna designates the dharma of mere awareness, prior to its operations and functions which take place only on the basis of vijñāna having as "supports" (āśraya) the sense-organs. Thus vijñāna becomes manas as soon as this contact (sparśa) with its "supports" is established. As manas (mind) arises through the contact of vijñāna with its supports (five sense organs), the subjective awareness that vijñāna itself is, will manifest itself according to the five specific natures of such "supports." Thus five sensorial levels of awareness will come about as a result of vijñāna pervading the prasāda-(subtle)-matter of the five sense-organs and thus coming into further "contact" with the external, sensorial, material objects. This five-fold spectrum of sensorial awareness will constitute five sensorial discriminative functions or five prasāda-vijñānas. However, as soon as the functions of saṃgrahaṇa (comprehension) and udgrahaṇa (abstraction) begin to take place, the pure mental and abstract awareness accompanying the knowledge of "mental and non-sensuous" objects manifests itself: this pure abstract awareness which discerns mental and abstract objects is called mano-vijñāna. Consequently, the givenness of five sensorial kinds of awareness (prasādavijñānas) plus the purely mental or abstract mano-vijñāna yield a total number of six cognitive faculties (i.e., the five prasādendriyas plus manas).

This yields further a six-fold division of objects corresponding to such a spectrum of subjective "discernments," namely, the sensorial objects of the five senses plus the abstract and non-sensuous objects as cognized by the *manas*-faculty.

Thus the so-called "eighteen *gotra-dhātus*" are established. They list the triple relation (through the "triple contact") between six faculties, six awarenesses and six kinds of objects.[55] *Dhātu* means basic element in a more generic manner than the term *dharma* does. Related to the term *gotra* (which means familiar relationship), the eighteen *dhātus* express the triple relationship between organ, its corresponding object, and the form which pure awareness (*vijñāna*) adopts as this relies on the organs in order to exercise its functions of "perceiving," "discerning" and "thinking." This "triple contact" and the six "family relationships" (among organ, consciousness and objects) which derived from it can be illustrated through the following diagram:

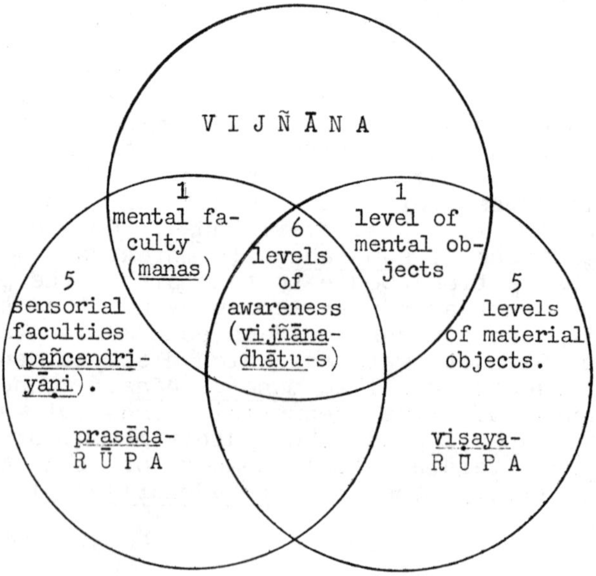

The three circles symbolize respectively the skandha of vijñāna (on the top), the five sense-organs as constituted by rūpaprasāda (on the left), and the five rūpa-viṣayas or "sense-matters" as these constitute external objects (on the right). The triple overlapping and contact (sparśa) among the three circles brings about further sections to symbolize the arising of the manas as mental, the sixth organ-faculty. This arising of the mental faculty (manas) is concomitant with the arising of sensorial objects (perceived as saṃjñā) and precedent to the arising of non-sensorial objects (dharmāḥ) which are perceived as jñāna-ālambana or non-sensuous, abstract, ideal objects. As vijñāna relies upon the five sense-organs to deploy itself in five different levels of sensorial awareness, any momentary dharma of vijñāna relies (as it appears in the present) on its own preceding and passing vijñāna-dharma in the serial flux, after this preceding vijñāna-dharma has already established contact with its non-sensuous object. Thus any preceding moment of vijñāna brings forth the mental-awareness of a given abstract object in the subsequent moment of its flux. This is the reason why the texts refer to mano-vijñāna (mental or non-sensuous awareness) as the subsequent vijñāna-moment that "carries" or "holds" (upalabdha) the outcome of such "contact." Hence any moment of the vijñāna-series (or flux) serves as manas-faculty for the subsequent moment which will carry its product, i.e., the manovijñāna or pure "mental awareness." In this way, any particular vijñāna-dharma, presently appearing in the flux, constitutes the manas or mental organ which further establishes contact with the non-sensuous, abstract or mental object to produce the subsequent moment of abstract or mental awareness (mano-vijñāna) in the following vijñāna-dharma within the serial flux. Thus in the words of the Kośa:

> Each momentary vijñāna-dharma which has just perished receives the name of manas (or manodhātu), in a similar way to a single man who is at the same time a son and a father, or one and the same vegetal unit which is fruit and seed.[56]

Thus each *vijñāna-dharma* within the flowing stream of moments is the *manas of* its subsequent *vijñāna-dharma* and the *mano-vijñāna* of its preceding *vijñāna-dharma*. There is then no entitative and real distinction among the *dharma* of *vijñāna* as such, the mental faculty termed as *manas*, and the mental awareness of non-sensuous objects which is called *mano-vijñāna*. The distinction resides only in the difference of the moments of the flux in which they either act (*manas*) or arise (*mano-vijñāna*).

As for the so-called "pure mental or non-sensuous objects"--which are the contents of *mano-vijñāna*--they are called *dharmāḥ* in the plural. The reason is that only coarser conglomerations of physical *rūpa*-atoms (*rūpasaṃcita*) can be the direct objects of the sensorial organs. All the *dharmas* as such, in their purely elementary reality, are objects of mental inference and thus they can only be cognized by manas. Of all the five *skandhas*, only the *rūpa-s* --in the state of conglomeration-- constitute the objects of sensorial knowledge, and this with one important exception, namely, the *avijñapti-rūpa* (the transmitter of passive accumulations of verbal and bodily *karma*) which being itself subliminal and "non-manifested" is also an exclusive object of mental cognition. And thus finally the three absolute, non-conditioned *asaṃskṛta-dharmas* (space and the two *nirodhas* which include the state of *nirvāṇa*) which *a fortiori* can be only the object of purely mental apprehension or elaboration.

As a final consideration in this chapter, mention should be made of the three *loka-dhātus* or planes of conscious activity and existence, as based in the interrelationship among the five *skandhas*. In this case the term *dhātu* translates as sphere (or plane) of both "psychological experience" and "individual existence." These three *loka-dhātus* (*loka* meaning cosmological plane and *dhātu* meaning psychological sphere) are listed as the *kāma-dhātu*, *rūpa-dhātu* and the *arūpa-dhātu* (or *ārūpya-dhātu*).

The *kāma-dhātu* is the sphere of conscious experience in which the individual existence is under the sway of the evil passions (*anuśayas*) and defilements (*kleśas*). Every single human being who is not following the Path of purification and emancipation is said to exist in the kāma-dhātu. This is the kind of existence in which the functions of the saṃskāras as "karma-formed" (i.e., as propensities) are in their full swing and thus dominate and motivate the exercise of sensorial and purely mental knowledge.

The rūpa-dhātu, however, constitutes the realm of conscious mental operations as they are based on vijñāna and its contact with both the "inner" or subjective (ādhyātmika) and the "outer" or objective (bāhya) rūpa-s, i.e., the "sense-organs" and the "sense-matters." If a person is able to control his disordinate appetites and bring about the inhibition of passions which rule the sphere of the kāma-dhātu, such a person is then said mystically or cognitively to ascend to the plane of "pure form" (rūpa-dhātu) in which consciousness is free from sordid and impure motivations. Thus the mind acquires great capabilities of deep and expanded pure knowledge (prajñā). In the free exercise of this detached and "passion-free" knowledge (araṇa-prajñā) the sentient being is still constricted and circumscribed by the limitations of both material and conceptual forms (as deriving from the conscious functions still rooted in the rūpa-skandha).

It must be taken into account that the term rūpa means "form," which is originally material. This justifies the application of such a term to the elements of materiality. Rūpa, however, applies also to all conceptual contents of thought as these are derived from the original "matters" via the "support" (āśraya) of the mental faculty (manas). Moreover, if a sentient being--who has already initiated his journey along the Path of purification--succeeds in reaching these states of "pure-form" in his life-time, he is said to be destined for "re-birth" in a future plane of existence where all impure saṃskāras are absent, and where he would be totally exempt from passion and turbulance (araṇa). Such a plane of existence as a realm of "birth of reward" is called the rūpa-loka, which is in itself further subdivided in different subrealms (mythically called heavens or devaloka, devakṣetra) in correspondence with the degree of mystical accomplishment in his former life in the kāma-loka. These cosmological sub-spheres of rewarded existence are called bhūmis (grounds, stages, étages).

As for the third sphere of the *arūpa-* (or *ārūpya-*) *dhātu*, this is constituted by the sole exercise of the *vijñāna-dharma* under the influence and command of pure *cetanā* or passionless (*anāsrava-*) acts of will focusing on the higher and most subtle spheres of consciousness and totally free from the obscuration (*nivṛtana*) produced by the impure, impeding, "karma-formed" forces (*nivṛtābhisaṃskṛta-saṃskāras*). Through this impulse of the purified will, the mind frees itself from the warps of "form" and "matter" (*rūpa*) and thus it ascends to the realms of self-expanding knowledge without bonds. Here the *dharma* of consciousness (*vijñāna* and the faculty that it seats, *manas*) operates on its own and flies expansively into the unlimited (*anantaka*, *ārūpya*), boundless regions of infinity (*anantya*). The cosmological level of these characteristics (freedom from "passion" and freedom from "form" = *araṇa*, *ārūpya*) which is the "birth of reward" for the persons obtaining such mental spheres through the practice of meditation and abstract concentration is called the *ārūpya-loka*. Its different substages (*bhūmis*) will be explained later in the Third Part.[57] These "formless" realms wich correspond to the highest degrees of attainment and meditative concentration are not yet *nirvāṇa*, since they still are commanded by the individual will (*cetanā*) and thus, albeit most purely motivated, they still are stages of karmic bondage. The individual will has to be tracelessly extinguished for ultimate knowledge and emancipation to come about.

In order to convey pictorially an idea of the interdependent coordination and interaction among the *dharmas* of the five *skandhas* as they constitute the three psychological (and by transference also cosmological) spheres and planes (*triloka-dhātus*), the following diagrams, it is hoped, will be of assistance.

First let us depict the *skandha* of *vedanā* (feelings and sensations) as resulting "functionally" from the immediate contact between two confronting poles of the *rūpa-skandha*, namely, the five *indriyas* (senses) and the five *viṣayas* (matters) in the following manner:

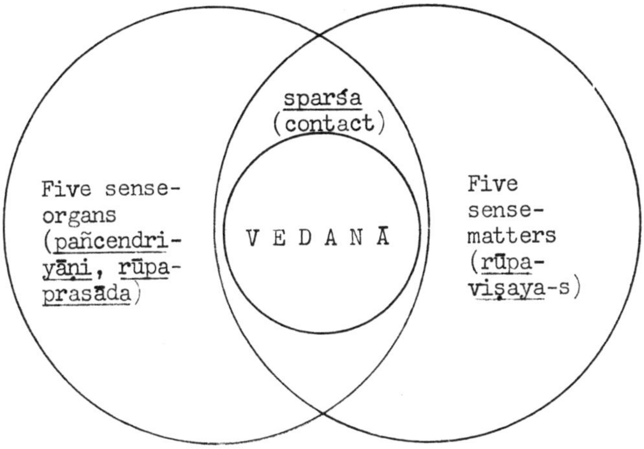

The *skandha* of *saṃjñā* (full-fledged, objective perception of unitary manifolds) has already been explained as requiring the intervention of the *manas'* function and thus has to be understood in terms of the "triple contact" among *vijñāna-dharma* and the above mentioned bipolar fields of the *rūpa-skandha*. By relying on *saṃjñā* and through the further exercise of the function of abstraction (*udgrahaṇa*) the *manas*--as said--"apprehends" purely notional objects as the contents of pure thought (*mati*, *jñāna*):

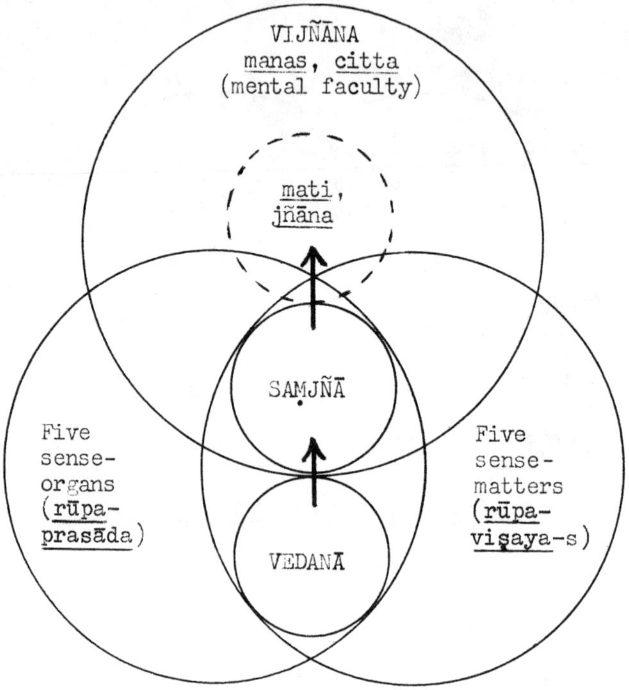

As we already know, there is an eleventh rūpa called avijñapti which is constituted by the cumulations deriving from verbal and bodily executions of the will. Hence it will be symbolized by a third small circle underneath the bipolar quintets of the prasādendriyas (sensorial organs) confronting their viṣayarūpas (sensorial matters). In this manner the complete realm of the rūpa-skandha becomes apparent as symbolized by a large second circle, in parity with the upper circle of the vijñāna-dharma:

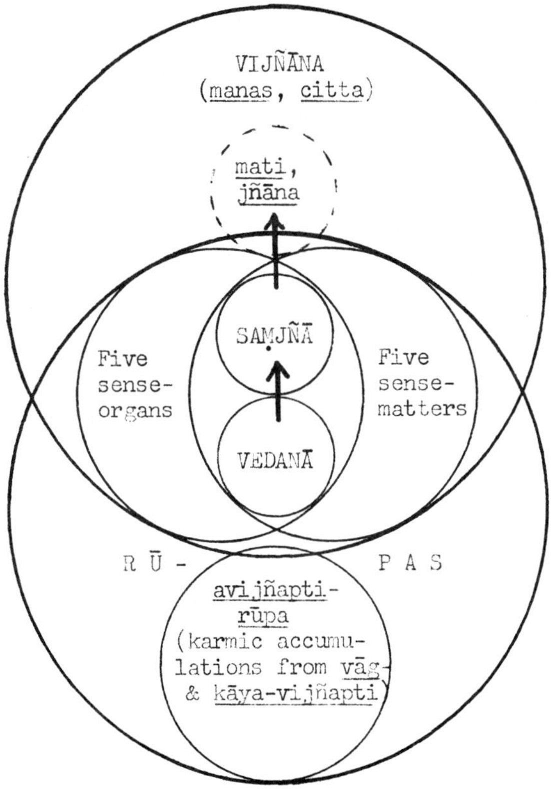

Avijñapti is, however, a *rūpa* which, being "formed" by external karmic action (*karmābhisaṃskṛta*), contains passively expectant *bījas* (seeds) of future fruition; a partial aspect of this fruition of re-fructification (as retribution) appears in the form of innate propensities and impure passions. Thus *avijñapti*, both from the standpoint of its causal origin (as it ensues from *cetanā* or acts of will), and from the standpoint of outcome (as "germinating" into innate passions and proclivities), immediately refers us to the fourth of the *skandhas*, namely the *saṃskāras*. As we know the *saṃskāras* comprise direct acts of the will as well as will-predisposing factors, and other vegetative, animal and subconscious forces. Hence three smaller subcircles will symbolize these three main subdivisions of the *saṃskāra-skandha*, namely *cetanā* (the acts of will or *saṃskāra par excellence*), the *caitasika* or *cittasaṃprayukta-saṃskāras* (as will-directed mental acts and will-predisposing factors) and *acaitasika* (or *cittaviprayukta-saṃskāras*) as subliminal, vegetative and biological forces.

Thus a third large circle emerges from underneath the *rūpa*-circle as symbolizing the realm of the *saṃskāra-skandha*. As the *vijñāna* circle overlaps with the *rūpa*-circle on account of its contact with the "sense-organs" and the "sense-matters" in order to elicit the three acts of *vedanā*, *saṃ-jñā* and *jñāna*, thus in a similar or parallel way, the circle of *saṃ͡skāras* overlaps with the *rūpa*-circle upon the *avijñapti-rūpa* which is both "product" and "producer" of *saṃskāras*. Thus the complete map of the correlation among the five *skandhas* and its derivative functions will appear in the following way:

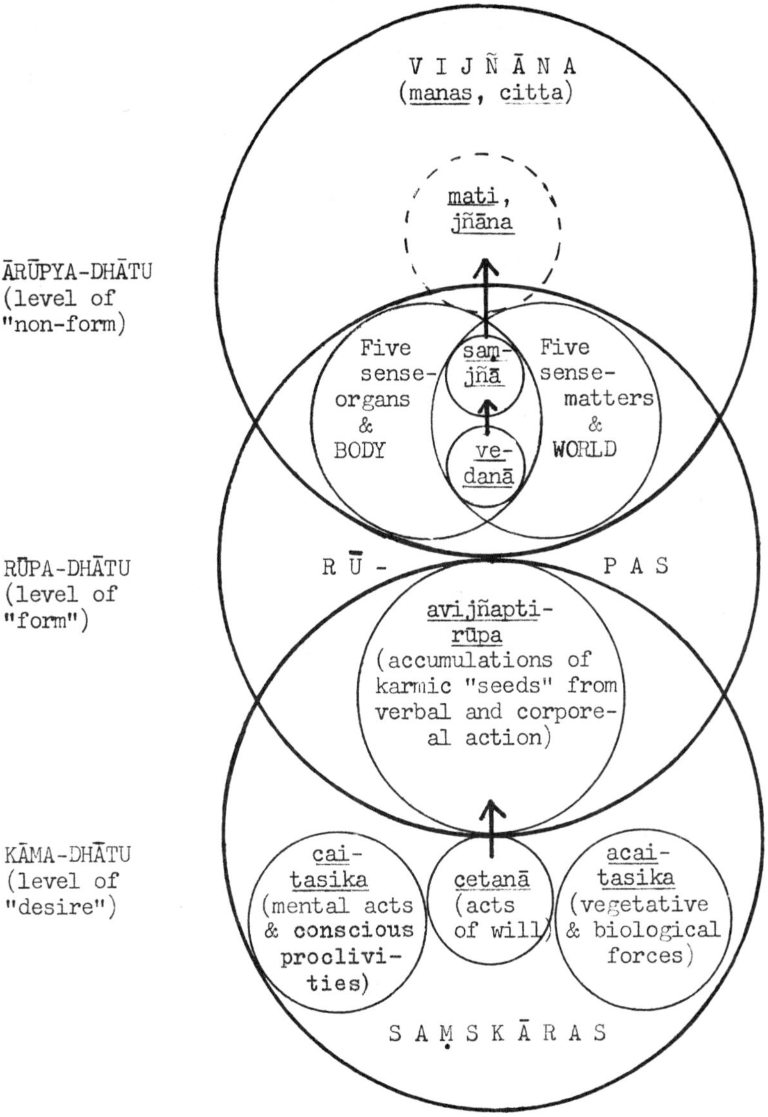
VIJÑĀNA
(manas, citta)
mati,
jñāna
ĀRŪPYA-DHĀTU
(level of
"non-form)
Five
sense-
organs
&
BODY
sam-
jñā
ve-
danā
Five
sense-
matters
&
WORLD
RŪPA-DHĀTU
(level of
"form")
RŪ-
PAS
avijñapti-
rūpa
(accumulations of
karmic "seeds" from
verbal and corpore-
al action)
KĀMA-DHĀTU
(level of
"desire")
cai-
tasika
(mental acts
& conscious
proclivi-
ties)
cetanā
(acts
of will)
acai-
tasika
(vegetative
& biological
forces)
SAṂSKĀRAS

In this diagram, the five *skandhas* appear situated as follows: The *rūpa-skandha* is located in the middle of the central large circle. The *vijñāna-skandha* is symbolized by the upper large circle. The *saṃskāra-skandha* is portrayed by the lower large circle. The two remaining *skandhas*, *vedanā-* and *saṃjñā-skandhas* are depicted as small circles in the lower section of the *vijñāna*-sphere and in the upper section of the *rūpa*-sphere as they are functional *dharmas* originating from the "triple contact." Given the structure of the map as formed by three main large superimposed circles, the three *loka-dhātus* become clearly manifest: The lower circle of the *saṃskāra-skandha*, as it overlaps with *rūpa*, expresses the constitutive elements of the *kāma-dhātu* or realm of desire. The second circle in the center, as it overlaps with both the *saṃskāras* and the *vijñāna*, brings to visual expression the composition of the *rūpa-dhātu* or "realm of form." The upper circle of *vijñāna*, as it overlaps with the *rūpa*-circle, depicts the level from which the *arūpa*-states are reached, i.e., from the lower section of the circle as entailing the elements of pure "form." The *arūpa-dhātu* *per se* is only depicted by the upper portion of the *vijñāna*-circle where the necessary elements of pure abstract thought are given as the proper conditions for the arrival at pure, blank and formless (*ārūpya-*) states of consciousness.

This diagram will be of assistance--we hope--not only in explaining the principles of causation and the karmic cycle to be expounded in the next Part of this work, but also in describing the mystical stages and planes of reward to be attained by the disciples and followers of the Path in the third Part.

It is to be understood that the lower large circle of the *saṃskāras* cannot be considered as dissociated from the circle of *vijñāna*. The separation in the diagram represents only an "exploded" visualization. *Vijñāna* and *rūpa* are two *dravyaka-dharmas* or "entitative factors" which can be conceived as separate, though correlated, entities in the flux-serial of existence. The *saṃskāras*, however, (similarly to *vedanā* and *saṃjñā*) are not "entitative" (*dravyaka*) but "functional" (*kṛtyika*) *dharmas* and thus cannot be understood either as separate or dissociated from the function of manas and manovijñāna (the caitasika or cittasaṃprayukta-saṃskāras, or forces associated with mental acts) or as independent from other causal principles (acaitasika- or cittaviprayukta-saṃskāras or subconscious, non-mentally associated, animal and biological forces). These causal principles are not accounted for through the mere exposition of the elements intervening in the constitution of the "suffering" existence. The five skandhas, the eighteen gotra-dhātus and the three loka-dhātus describe only the "build up" materials of the "serial-flux" of existence (bhāva-saṃtāna), not its causation. The elucidation of the causative principles behind the forming of both, the "varying" and the "fixed" patterns of the individual stream of existence, belongs to the Second Part of our work. This will dwell on the philosophical significance of the second Noble Truth, the Truth of the origin of suffering, namely DUHKHA-SAMUDAYA. Having learned the elements and factors of "unrest" and "suffering" let us proceed now to the explanation of the principles of causality which govern the "setting into motion" of such elements and factors as were conceived by early Buddhism.

PART II

DUḤKHA-SAMUDAYA (The Origin of Suffering) and the Notion of Causation

Katamañ ca bhikkhave dukkha-samudayaṃ ariya-saccaṃ? Yāyaṃ taṇhā ponobhavikā nandi-rāga-sahagatā tatra tatrābhinandinī, seyyathīdaṃ kāma-taṇhā bhava-taṇhā vibhava-taṇhā. . . . Yaṁ loke piya-rūpaṃ sāta-rūpaṃ, etth'esā taṇhā uppajjamānā uppajjati, ettha nivisamānā nivisati. . . . Idaṃ vuccati bhikkhave dukkha-samudayaṃ ariya-saccaṃ.

"What now, O monks, is the Noble Truth of the Origin of Suffering? It is that craving which gives rise to fresh rebirth and, bound up with lust and greed, now here, now there, finds ever fresh delight. It is the sensual craving, the craving for existence, and (even) the craving for self-anihilation. . . . Wherever in the world there are the delightful and pleasurable forms, there this craving arises, there it takes its root. . . . Such is said, O monks, to be the Noble Truth of the Origin of Suffering."

Saṃyutta-nikāya V, 421; Dīgha-nikāya II, 308; Vibhaṅga 101-3.

Chapter 1

Karma (human action) and the notion of "causation." The _hetu-pratyaya_ doctrine.

In a magistral manner, the _Majjhima-nikāya_ traces back to their causal origination all the elements of "suffering" which we have expounded in Part I.

> If, namely, when perceiving a visible form, a sound, odor, taste, bodily touch or an idea in the mind, the object is pleasant, one is attracted and if unpleasant, one is repelled. Thus, whatever kind of feeling (_vedanā_) one experiences--pleasant, unpleasant or indifferent--one approves of and cherishes the feeling and clings to it. And while doing so, lust originates; but lust of feelings means clinging to existence (_upādāna_); and on clinging to existence depends the _karma_-process (_kamma-bhava_); on the _karma_-process rebirth depends; and depending on rebirth are decay and death, sorrow, lamentation, pain, grief and despair. Thus arises the whole mass of suffering.

Hence the whole wheel of suffering turns around one causative and motive force pregnantly expressed by the word _KARMA_, i.e., "action." "Action" is primarily and fundamentally understood as "human action" in that this is morally imputable, and in this sense the term _karma_ has been frequently mentioned in the first Part. Now its genetic constitution and the structure of its dynamics must be explained. Although primordially referred to human action, the work _karma_ will expand into a number of derivative notions essentially pertaining to the overall structure of universal causation. For there is not only the ontological execution of moral retribution that has to be accounted for. In point of fact there is a whole universe in the state of constant process of manifestation, a process which is all of it "manifestation to consciousness." Thus _karma_, as a whole, has to offer a comprehensive account of the whole fact of universal origination of worldly existence, in both its amazing disparity in individual allotments and in the aspects of shared and commonly experienced universality. For there are the rich and the poor, the healthy and the sick, the beautiful and the ugly, the good and the evil ones who--in spite of their individual disparity--are given to experience the same earth, the same sun, and the same moon. Hence a clear-cut distinction will have to be drawn between individual karma as the causative activity which brings about such striking disparity of allotments (viśeṣabhāgya), and the further causative action which brings about the common sharing of specific sameness in biological nature and the oneness of cosmological ground (sabhāgatā, samānabhāgya).

All in all, karma is--as stated--human action as this is posited upon the command or consent of the will. As explained in the first Part, cetanā (the saṃskāra par excellence) designates the free, mentally and intentionally grounded exercise of the will. Thus cetanā formally constitutes the essence of karma. Let us repeat again that karma, as the central notion of causative action, has a far more wide-ranging meaning than has been assumed up to this point.

In any case, karma as human volitive action is considered by the above quoted texts of the Suttas as a principal and proximate cause of rebirth, and thus as the perpetuator of individual existence: to the extent that there is individual human action, to that extent there is birth and individual existence; no individual human action, no individual human existence. Thus the process of action is considered also as the process of "becoming" (karmabhava). That individual action is a causal conditio sine qua non of individual existence is obviously stated by the texts. That it is exclusively the only condition of existence, is a different story. As we shall see, pure and isolated individual action is causa necessaria sed non sufficiens of the whole universal fact of worldy and cosmic existence. Hence there needs to be some sort of "universal action" that transcends the merely individual action which primordially is designated as karma per se. In short, "individual karma," as primordial notion of causative action, will be distinguished from "universal karma," the conception of the latter deriving as a notional extrapolation from the former.

As far as individual action is concerned, *karma* is called *mano-karma* (mental action) in that any deliberate human action originates from and may be often confined to mere mental intention. Failure in the external fulfillment of the mental volitive intention will confine the action to its original, though already morally imputable, pure mental nature. However, insofar as the mental intention (*mano-karma*) is externally manifested to others through the act already mentioned above as *vāgvijñapti* (or *vācika-vijñapti* = verbal intimation), the human willing intention develops into an act of *vācika-karma* (verbal action). And if--and when--such intention is physically executed by means of the motive organs (*kāyikavijñapti-indriyāṇi*), the mental intention materializes and thus attains its target through an act of *kāyika-karma* (corporeal or bodily *karma*). This last kind of *karma* crowns the process whereby a morally imputable action is posited.

Now the point is: how does the moral quality of imputability of the action (in its three consecutive stages of actualization) further its causative force as a source of existence, i.e., as a process of becoming through rebirth? In the view of Buddhism, *karma*, as individual action, carries within itself the genetic mechanism whereby it will yield its own retribution, either as punishment or as reward.

Thus *karma*-causation widens its range far beyond the transient period of the time-consciousness of the present. It will, in fact, constitute the causal links between "remnants" (*upadhi*) from conscious states of the past and expectant conscious states of the future. "Past" and "future" refer here not only to "within-the-present-life" objects of memory and recollection, or oncoming objects of expectation. They emphatically refer to past and future lives. Thus the causative process of individual *karma* stretches throughout the continual cycle of worldly reembodiment which every conscious "individual stream" or personal flux of existence undergoes. This cycle of rebirth is not to be mistaken with a cycle of so called "reincarnation" or "transmigration." For in Buddhism there are no such entities as souls to transmigrate from body to body. The wheel of rebirth is in this sense based not in the transference of a soul from a body to another body, but from the transference of "karmic" remnants (*upadhi*) or karmic accumulations (*āyūhana*) from the disintegrative moment of death to a new womb of conception. The link that bridges the gap between death and rebirth in the ever turning wheel of existence is established solely by the karmic potentials which have been accumulated through the performance of _mano-_, _vācika-_ and _kāyika-karma_, i.e., through the positing of mental, verbal and corporeal action. The karmic potentials or karmic accumulations (_kamma-āyūhana_) establish then the "dormant" seeds of fructification in a future existence, an existence whose worldly status and circumstantial set-up will be determined by such fruition or re-germination. These intermediary "seeds" (_bīja_) which are accumulated by acts of the present, and preserved from acts of the past, provide the basis for the causation of future individual existence as based on the law of retribution which--according to Buddhism--keeps us journeying from birth to death and back to rebirth. But how does _karma_ as _individual_ action ground such a _universal_ "law of rebirth" as it affects all of us according to universally set patterns? How does the striking disparity of retributive allotments interlock with these "universally" set patterns that make the law of rebirth to be a "universal" one? In short, how does "individual" origination coordinate with "universal" causation? What are the universal forms of causality that intervene--or coordinate--with such a strictly individual harvesting of diversified fruits which are the effects of retribution?

Here the complex texture of the in itself fragmentary notion of causality according to the early schools of Buddhism comes to the fore. As Aristotle postulated four fundamental forms of causality (the efficient, the final, the formal, and the material)--which were extended to six by the medieval scholastics (with the addition of the exemplar and instrumental forms of causality)--the _Sarvāstivāda_ scholastics formulated their own principles of causality through the _hetu-pratyaya_ doctrine. According to this doctrine there are six forms of "proximate or generative" causation (_ṣaḍhetavaḥ_) and four forms of "remote or secondary" causation (_catvaraḥ-pratyayaḥ_). In view of these two sets of causal principles, the question arises: is the individual _karma_-causation a "primary and proximate" form of causality (_hetu_) or is it only a "secondary or subordinate" cause (_pratyaya_)? The answer will be that _karma_-causation, as ensuing from individual human action and whereby "karmic" retribution is effected, is a primary cause of individual existence and thus will be considered as one of the hetus.

However, the wide-ranging effect of the karma-causation (as individual action) cannot be understood unless it is expounded within the full context of the rest of the hetus and pratyayas. For although plural in number, and thus fragmentary, the laws of total causation as expressed by the Hīnayāna thinkers contain the roots for a unification of the source of causation. This unificaton and integration is attained later in the Mahāyāna developments of idealism and totalism.

As for the terms hetu and pratyaya, their use has been applied and interpreted throughout the Abhidhamma canonical works and their meanings newly reformulated by the commentarial literature such as the Vibhāṣās, the two Maggas and, above all, the Abhidharmakośa. In point of fact, the terms hetu and pratyaya mean originally very much the same, i.e., the "conditions" for something to come about, regardless of whether these conditions are generative per se or not. Conditions are understood as such factors as: if present, then the conditioned entity originates, and if not present, the conditioned does not originate. Thus the term "condition" aplies to such a factor (or manifold of factors) upon whose "occurence" and/or "concurrence" the existence or occurence of something else depends. In this sense "condition" entails the notion of "cause" in a very broad manner. In point of fact, the Paṭṭhāna (the last book of the Abhidhammapiṭaka, a vast and abstruse work never translated into a Western language) offers a long list of 24 modes of conditionality which are termed as paccaya (Skt. pratyaya). In this long enumeration the term hetu is at the very top of the list as the first and most important of the pratyayas. Thus hetu is understood as the "root-condition" or, in other words, the "proximate cause," the "condition (or pratyaya) par excellence." Hence the later commentators detached this "root- or principal condition" from the rest of the general list of pratyayas which they considered as concomitant conditions, and further divided into six the different forms through which the "root-condition" (as hetu) was conceived to operate. It is in this sense that the Abhidharmakośa handles the six hetus as "proximate or principal" causes and the four pratyayas as "remote or concomitant" causes.[1] A traditional example illustrating the difference between a proximate cause and the concurrent, subordinate or remote causes is that of a tree which originates from its seed as its hetu (generative cause) and grows on the basis of the soil, water, sun, etc., which are its pratyayas (concurrent conditions).

On the basis of the above, let us now proceed to a brief description of the six hetus and the four pratyayas. These brief definitions of these ten forms of causality will close this chapter, thus reserving for the following sections (Chapters two and three) the special treatment of those hetus which might be of the highest significance in understanding the range covered by such a central notion as KARMA, i.e., the "origin of suffering." Following the Abhidharmakośa in the main,[2] the six hetus and the four pratyayas are enumerated and can be defined as follows:

A) Ṣaḍ-hetavaḥ (Six root-conditions or proximate causes).

1. Kārana-hetu (Efficient or generative causality).

This is the hetu par excellence, "la raison d'être," corresponding in the main to the Aristotelian concept of "efficient" or "generative" (janaka) cause. Thus, for instance, the predominance of the element of fire in the sense-matters produces heat. In the sub-atomic primary rūpa-elements (or mahābhūtas) each one of the elements has an effectivity of its own, whereby it directly produces either the state of solidity, or liquidity, or heat, or motion. Each one of them is thus the kāraṇa-hetu of such immediate effects. On the level of the viṣaya-atoms, a sense-matter of light directly effects the vision of light in the sense-organ of sight. Thus each one of the viṣayas (sense-matters) is the kāraṇa-hetu of its corresponding perception in the sense-organs. These, of course, are the most elementary exemplifications of the generative causality which is termed kāraṇa-hetu. As we shall see later, the range of its effectivity will expand from the microcosmic activities of the dharmic elements to the macrocosmic causation of the universe itself. Hence kāraṇa-hetu will be the form of causality exercised by a "sovereign" or "all-ruling" action (universal or collective *KARMA*) to be expounded later in Chapter 3 of this Part.

The *Kośa* attributes also the designation of *kāraṇa-hetu* to the function of "non-hindrance" (*avighnabhāvāvasthāna*)[3] in virtue of which certain *dharmas* allow or even offer the medium for the manifestation or generation of their *dharmas*. Thus, for instance, space may be considered the *avighna-kāraṇa-hetu* (non-hindrance-cause) for the manifestation and deployment of all temporal, conditioned (*saṃskṛta*) *dharmas*.

2. *Sahabhū-hetu* (Mutual co-causality).

This is the "co-existence" causality whereby some elements might need to appear in combination with one another in order to exist and to operate. In the microcosmic level of *dharma*-elements this co-existence causality affects *all the* four primaries (*mahābhūta*) since they cannot exist except by supporting and combining with one another. Thus the four primary elements are the *sahabhū-hetu* of one another; even their specific functions as *kāraṇa-hetus* are, in point of fact, dependent on their "co-existence," that is, in their "causing one another" by equally "supporting" one another. Thus also the mental forces or *saṃskāras* (*caitasika*) like *cetanā*, *mati*, etc. coordinate with *vedanā* (sensation) and *saṃjñā* (perception) and support *one another* in order to co-exist, and thus they are also *sahabhū-hetu* of one another.[4] In this case the specific *kāraṇa*-(efficient) causality which is proper to each of the *dharma*-elements is conditioned and thus subsequent to their mutual *sahabhū*-(co-existence) causality.

3. *Sabhāga-hetu* (Homogenous causality).

This is the causality inducing uniformity and homogeneity between cause and its immediate effect. In general it will manifest itself as an aspect of the *kāraṇa-hetu* (efficient cause) in as much as any effects *are formally* similar in nature to their immediate, generative causes. The scholastic principle *omne agens agit sibi simile* (every agent enacts its own similar) *corresponds* perfectly to the Buddhist notion of *sabhāga-hetu*, the causality of "shared" (*bhāga*) nature. *It applies* to the successive and "down-the-line" transmission of similarity and continuity in specific nature (*sabhāgatā*) whereby horses generate horses and cats generate cats. In the microcosmic level of "dharmic" causation, the *sabhāga-hetu* is the causal function whereby a *dharma* of one species is always followed, down the momentary stream of "dharmic" co-emergences (*kṣaṇika-saṃsarga*), by *dharmas* of the same specific nature. Thus a *vijñāna-dharma* is followed by another *vijñāna-dharma*, a *rūpa-dharma* by a *rūpa-dharma* of its own sub-group, a *viṣaya-rūpa* by another *viṣaya-rūpa*, a *prasāda-rūpa* by another *prasāda-rūpa*, etc.

The homogeneous streams of specifically (not individually) identical *dharmas* are termed *naiṣyandika-srotas*[5] (homogeneous down-flow-stream), a term which applies also--in the macrocosmic level--to the "down-the-line" stream of beings of one particular species generating beings of the same specific nature. Thus the effect of the *sabhāga-hetu* is termed *niṣyanda-phala* (homogeneous "down-flow" fruition or effect.)

4. *Saṃprayuktaka-hetu* (Association causality).

This is the causality of "association-by-reliance." This form of causality is similar to the *sahabhū-hetu* in that both exert their effects in the horizontal manner of simultaneous coordination and not in the vertical way of successive generation (like the *sabāgha-hetu*). The difference, however, between the *sahabhū-hetu* and the *saṃprayuktaka-hetu* lies in the fact that the former applies to the equal parity among elements in effecting their own co-existence; whereas in the present causality some elements appear in "association" or "conjunction" (*saṃprayukta*) with one another by reason of their "common reliance" (*saṃāśraya*) of all of them upon another.[6] Thus an act of visual awareness (*cakṣurvijñāna*) appears "in association" with certain sensations (*vedanā*) of pleasure or displeasure, with a certain object of visual perception (*samjñā*) like the vision of an apple, and with certain acts of volition (*cetanā*) like desiring or deciding to eat it or not. However the association of all these elements (*cakṣurvijñāna*, *vedanā*, *saṃjñā*, and *cetanā*) takes place on the basis of *their common reliance or support* upon the organ of sight (*cakṣur-indriya*). *Saṃprayuktaka-hetu* is thus also the kind of causality that associates *mano-vijñāna* (or an act of mental awareness)-- as explained above-- with an intellectual sensation of pleasure or displeasure, with certain non-sensuous or abstract objects of thought (through *jñāna* or *mati* = abstract notion), and with any volitions which might accompany such acts of "mental awareness" (i.e., *mano-vijñāna*). This "association" (*saṃprayukta*) takes place *only by the common reliance* of all these purely mental elements of abstract cognition upon the mental organ which has been termed *manas* (see above, p.55).

Saṃprayuktaka-hetu, then, can be said fundamentally to be the form of causality which interrelates the elements of the eighteen *gotra-dhātus*, where the *vijñānas* or six sorts of "awareness" arise in association with their corresponding objects (*viṣayas*, *ālambanas* through *vedanā*, *samjñā*, and *cetanā*) by reason of their respectively "common reliance" upon the six faculties or *indriyas* (which include, of course, the mental faculty or *manas*). It is through the association and kinship effected by the *saṃprayuktaka-hetu* that the eighteen *gotra-dhātus* form six tripartite "families" of *dharma*-associates (See above p.55f.)

5. *Sarvatraga-hetu* (All-pervading causality).

Literally this means the "all-pervading" or "all-underlying" cause. It formally refers to *avidyā* or "ignorance" as a primordial, general and universal condition of causation. Causation is *KARMA*, and *KARMA* takes place only on the basis of ignorance. When ignorance is dispelled then the *visaṃyoga* or total "disjunction" from the warps of causation takes place. *Nirvāṇa*, which is attained through the *visaṃyoga* (the disjunction) of all the *dharmas* from the causes that bring them to manifestation, is only the fruit of absolute knowledge *as this dispels Ignorance*. In the *Kośa* this *sarvatraga-hetu* is often associated with the works of the *sabhāga-hetu* inasmuch as our state of Ignorance is the ultimate ground by which we are destined--through the *karma*-accumulations that Ignorance conditions--for rebirth within a particular species (*sabhāgatā*) of sentient[7] beings in different planes of existence (*bhūmi-lokas*).

6. *Vipāka-hetu* (Maturation or "heterogeneous" causality).

This is the "maturation" (*vipāka*) causation that takes a morally imputable act (*karma*) to produce a fruit in a future life as its retribution. Hence this causality constitutes the kind of "agent-effect" relationship attributed to individual *karma per se*. Often this causality is also designated as "heterogeneous causation" (in the Chinese texts wu-teng-liu yin) so as to contrast it with the sabhāga-hetu. For as the sabhāga-hetu determines that all proximate effects be of the same nature as their immediate causes, the vipāka-hetu projects the effects of individual karma upon the distant future and determines that these effects be of a totally disparate nature than the remote cause which produced them. So the act of robbery might result in being reborn in a hell or into a deformed body, or cause me to lose my hands by accident or disease, etc. Thus vipāka-hetu designates the form of causality that sets the whole mechanism of "karmic" retribution into motion. The next chapter will be exclusively dedicated to the further study of this kind of causality.

B) Catvaraḥ pratyayaḥ (Four concomitant conditions or subordinate causes).

1. Hetu-pratyaya (Causal conditions).

The last five of the mentioned hetus, (2-6), being as they are intrinsically hetus (principal causes), can be also, from some extrinsic point of view pratyayas (subordinate causes) as they might concur with the kāraṇa-hetu in the effecting of something.[8] In point of fact all the hetus can play the role of pratyaya in different respects from those in which they are hetus. Such, for instance, is the case with the four primary elements whose respective kāraṇa-activities are conditioned by the sahabhū-hetu (con-causality) in virtue of which they "co-exist." Hence the sahabhū-hetu (mutual co-causality) operates intrinsically as hetu in that it brings about the coexistence of the four mahābhūtas, whereas it acts as a pratyaya inasmuch as it conditions the kāraṇa-activities of each one of them separately. Let us keep in mind that no mahābhūta can operate solely on its own unless it coexists with its inseparable three other companions (See above p.23)

2. Samanantara-pratyaya (Immediate-sameness condition).

This term would translate as the "condition of equality and immediacy." It refers to the conditions which coordinate with the above mentioned sabhāga-hetu (homogeneous causality). It is by virtue of the sabhāga-hetu that dharmas of one species are always followed by dharmas of the same specific resemblance in the "down-flow" of the personal stream (naiṣyandika-saṃtāna). Thus a dharma of one species begets a subsequent dharma of the same species. But by begetting the subsequent dharma, the said dharma disappears. In point of fact any dharma begets the following one by disappearing. Hence the sabhāga-hetu (homogeneous causality) operates in connection with the force of evanescence (anityatā) of a dharma at a given moment. But by the same token, the force of origination (jāti) of the subsequent dharma is the condition (pratyaya) for the antecedent dharma to exert its sabhāga-causality (i.e., the transmission of specific sameness) on the subsequent. Hence the sabhāga-hetu is exerted from an antecedent into a subsequent dharma, whereas the samanantara-pratyaya is exerted by a subsequent dharma in respect to its immediate antecedent. Such is the case with the resemblance between parent and child. The parent is the proximate cause of his resemblance in the child. The child, however, is the condition for a "resemblance" of the parent to be transmitted."

3. Ālambana-pratyaya (Object-as-support condition).

This is the "object-support" condition. Such is the subordinate causality exercised by the viṣayas (sense-matters) upon the rūpa-prasādas or indriyas (sense-organs). In this sense, as the vijñāna-dharma is the kāraṇa-hetu (efficient cause) for the generation of visual consciousness (cakṣur-vijñāna) in the sight-organ (cakṣur-indriya), the rūpa-viṣayas or "sense-matters" are the ālambana-pratyaya (as "objective support") for the same visual consciousness. Thus also the pure vijñāna (as mind: manas) is the kāraṇa-hetu of the mano-vijñāna (mental awareness), whereas any "non-sensuous" object of cognition (as manasa-ālambana, or mental object) is the ālambana-pratyaya of such mano-vijñāna or mental awareness.

4. Adhipati-pratyaya (The dominant or ruling conditions).

This term indicates certain concomitant mental factors or influences which "dominate" or "control" other subordinate elements. The Abhidhammatthasaṅgaha enumerates four of these "dominant" (adhipati) factors which might rule and direct the conscious act of apperception: intention, effort, directed thought, and investigation. The *Kośa*, however, refers to *adhipati-pratyaya* in quite a universal fashion, namely, as a *pratyaya*-aspect of the macro-cosmic function of *kāraṇa-hetu* (generative, efficient cause), inasmuch as this form of causality acts also as the causal condition (*pratyaya*) for the coming into effect of a *karma*-fruition (*phala*) which is "all ruling" and "sovereign" (*adhipati*), i.e., universally shared by all sentient beings. A detailed account of this "universal fruition" (*adhipati-phala*) will be offered in Chapter 3 when dealing with the nature of "universal *karma*" as opposed to "individual *karma*."

Now let us proceed to a more detailed elucidation of three of the above mentioned *hetus*, namely, the *vipāka-hetu*--as this represents the proper causality exerted by "individual *karma*"--and the *sabhāga*- and *kāraṇa-hetus* as these are the forms of causality exerted by a universal force of world-causation, a force which has been designated tentatively as *"universal KARMA."*

Chapter 2

The Vipāka-hetu ("Maturation-causality") and the Cycle of Individual Karma. The Twelve Nidānas.

The term vipāka-hetu translates as "maturation-cause" and thus formally refers to the causation which--as already stated--is proper to the individual positing of karma as morally determined and imputable volitive action. The etymology of the term vipāka (from the prefix vi- meaning "dis-" and the noun pāka meaning "maturing" of a fruit) already suggests the character of "heterogeneity" which characterizes this form of causality. The "fruit" of karma-actions, as brought into effect by the vipāka-hetu is entitatively "dis-similar" (visadṛśa) from the actions (karma) which deposited its "seed." This is the reason why this kind of causality is also termed "heterogeneous causation." However, the opposition of the vipāka- to the sabhāga-hetu (as "homogeneous" causation) is only relative and extends itself to the mere entitative constitution of the fruit or effect. In fact, the sabhāga-hetu still underlies the doings of the vipāka-hetu in that regardless of how disparate the effects might be from their original "karmic" causes (like being born blind for having committed acts of cruelty, or acts of thievery, or acts of lust, etc.) there is still the homogeneous extension of the quality as good or evil throughout the whole causative process. That is, good or "meritorious" acts will always ripen into good or "rewarding" fruitions, whereas evil or "demeritorious" acts will always ripen into evil or "punishing" effects. At any rate, on the causal basis of the vipāka-hetu these karma-effects are supposed to crystallize into the diversity of future mental and bodily endowments and worldly allotments (bhāgya) which are in stock for us. In this sense, by virtue of the vipāka-hetu each individual "stream of existence" (bhāva-saṃtāna) lays down--by morally imputable action--the groundwork of its own future status in lives to come.

The "maturation-process" (vipāka-pariṇāma) of individual karma--as exerted and ruled by the vipāka-hetu--consists in a complete cycle of cause-effect relationships which entails three fundamental moments:

A) Active karma; or karma proper (cetayitvā-karman)
B) Passive karma; or "accumulation" of "karmic potentials" (karmavāsanās, or karmabījas)
C) Re-active karma; or karma-fruition (karma-phala)

It is obvious that the terms "active," "passive," and "re-active" karma are to be taken as conventional manners of conveying the meaning of these three aspects of the "maturation"-process. The expression active karma is literally redundant in that the noun karma itself already means "action." Hence the term "passive karma," if taken literally, would imply a verbal contradiction since karma, meaning "action," cannot be strictly understood as passive. Karma, therefore has to be understood in its broadest sense as comprising all the aspects of the karmic process of retribution effected by the vipāka-hetu. This notion of karma, as the total process unleashed by human action, is perfectly in keeping with te Kośa's definition: "What is Karma? It is volition and whatever is produced by volition (cetanā tatkṛtaṃ ca tat)."[10] The whole process whereby a tree produces seeds--which are stored in a state of passive potentiality or "suspended activation" as provision for their "maturation" and "reactivation" into a new tree and new fruits--can be understood as a process of active causation throughout. This "active" process includes also this period of "passively" expectant "storage of seeds" as the further potentials of germination. Let us then proceed with the use of such conventional terms as "active karma," "passive karma" and "re-active karma" as they are meant to convey the three aspects of such a similar process effected by the vipāka-hetu.

"Active karma" is formally constituted by the acts already designated as cetanā, whether these acts be merely mental (manokarma) such as intentional and mental volitions with no external intimation or execution, or be they physical, either as "verbal action" (vācika-karma), or as "corporal execution" (kāyika-karma). "Active karma" is therefore karma per se, the act deliberately posited or consented by the will, the acts which as such will be morally "determined" or "defined" (vyakṛta) either as "good or wholesome" (kuśala) or as "evil or unwholesome" (akuśala). It should be taken into account that only mano-karma (mental act) is the formal constituent of cetanā as pure mental decision, and that it alone carries the moral quality proper to karma as a law of retribution. Thus manokarma, which in this case is synonymous with cetanā as "mental volitive intention," is the conditio sine qua non of the extended morality of vācika- and kāyika-karma (verbal and corporeal action). Also to be kept in mind is that, while physical karma (verbal and corporeal) cannot occur without the mental (since the former are only responsive to the command of the latter), the mental can be performed without the physical whenever this latter is impeded or obstructed by extrinsic circumstances. Thus mental karma is as imputable as its external execution.

With the second aspect of the karmic or vipāka- (maturation-) process, i.e., "passive karma," the far-reaching and, for that matter, the most mysterious and hidden mechanism of the vipāka-causation begins to operate. Passive karma has been designated also through the compounds karmavāsanās and karmabījas (karmic "perfumes" and "seeds"). Both terms are used by the Abhidharmakośa in reference to the vipāka- (maturation-) process of karmic retribution. The first term vāsanā means the "impregnation" or "suffusion" of some substance when penetrated by another. Thus it translates also as "perfume." Hence the term vāsanā refers to the moral perfumes produced by moral actions as such perfumes "impregnate" or "suffuse" certain organs which are susceptible of "suffusion" and "perfumation." Vāsanā (perfume) is an analogy used to designate the accumulation of karmic potentialities which, as perfumes, will "re-exhalate" into future effects.

The second compound, i.e., karmabījas, conveys perhaps a less metaphorical sort of analogy and a more stringent connotation of the karmic potentials. For seeds (bījas) are such that can be "stored" in the state of "suspended" activation for future "germination." However the implications of the use of both analogies, "perfumes" and "seeds," are much the same in that no "suffusion" can take place without something being "suffused" or "perfumed" and that no storage of seeds can be effected without a carrier, recipient or depository for such seeds being available. Thus the concept of passive karma entails the existence of karmic carriers or depositories. Such carriers have been clearly defined by the Sarvāstivādins as being of two different natures in open divergence with the Sautrāntikas who accepted only one kind and one receiver of karmic "suffusions" (vāsanās). No wonder the term vāsanās would be more popular among the Sautrāntikas, whereas the term bījas (seeds) were of more frequent use among the Sarvāstivādins.

As just mentioned, the members of the Sarvāstivāda school propounded the separate existence of two different carriers of the karmic bījas or "seeds," this of course due to the dichotomic and irreducible character that separates the purely mental karma (mano-karma) from the physical karma intimated and executed through the bodily organs. As for the accumulation of seeds deriving from physical karma (i.e., verbal and corporeal) it has already been designated as avijñapti-rūpa, the last and most subtle of the eleven material skandhas. The vijñapti, then, is itself material, i.e., the vāgvijñapti (or verbal act) and the kāya-vijñapti (or corporeal act). As already stated, these two physical vijñaptis (or "intimations") are the constitutives of vācika- and kāyika-karma.[11] Following an ontological principle well formulated also by the Western medieval scholastics, namely that "effects must be proportionate to their causes" (effectus proportionantur causis) the Sarvāstivādins propounded that material acts of karma (as vācika- and kāyika-karma) yield material "seeds" for future material fructification, whereas purely mental karma issues "perfumes" or "suffusions" (vāsanāḥ) of strictly mental nature. Therefore, as the avijñapti-rūpa was meant to be formed by accumulations of material karmic potentials, the mental organ itself (manas, citta), as seated in the vijñāna-dharma and as issuer of mental intentions, was also to be considered as the very recipient of its own moral "perfumes." It was stated above that both terms manas and citta convey the same meaning of "mind" as mental faculty. In most contexts both terms are used indiscriminately as perfect synonyms. Vasubandhu, however, in expressing the opinion of the Sarvāstivādins, gives a different connotation to these terms as designating two different roles of the mind-faculty. Manas is commonly used in the sense of acting, eliciting mind, whereas citta is rather used as designating the passive, or cumulative mind. The mind does not only actively "mean" things and produce notions; it also "stores" them as mental impressions or "memories." In this sense, a certain parallelism arises in reference to the notions of *manas* and *citta* on the one hand, and the Western scholastic distinction (based on Aristotelian psychology) between the "active" and the "passive" intellects on the other hand. Hence, as there is a *species expressa* (expressed concept) which is the mental act elicited by the "active" intellect, so there is also a *species impressa* (impressed concept) which is received and "stored" by the "passive" intellect. Of course, the Western scholastics did not mean to postulate two different and separate intellects. Through the expressions "active" and "passive" they rather meant two different roles of one and the same intellect. In a similar way *manas* and *citta* refer to one and the same mental faculty that is *both* "agent" and "patient," or using the Buddhist analogies, the "seeder" and the "seeded," the "perfumer" and the "perfumed." According to Vasubandhu:

> (*Vijñāna*) is named *manas* in that it is *actively* mindful (*manute*) and it is called *citta* in that it *accumulates* (*cinoti*) both *goodness* and evil.

Or also:

> . . . *vijñāna* is named *citta* in that it becomes *variegated* (*citra*) by pure and foul (mental) elements.[12]

Thus the mental faculty is such that it "suffuses" itself with the moral "perfumes" of its own moral intentions. In this sense the passive, cumulative character that is proper to *manas* (as *citta*) plays a far more extensive role than the one attributed by the medieval Western scholastics to their notion of the "passive" intellect. For the *citta* (beyond accumulating "memories") provides also the depository for the "mental seeds" as these constitute the mental basis for the maturation-process exercised by the *vipāka-hetu* in regard to future retribution. This "maturation" or "germination" (re-exhalation in the case of *vāsanās* = perfumes) is meant to take place not only within this life, but also and more emphatically in future lives.[13]

The use of the term *bījas* (seeds) is rather common in the *Kośa*. Its use extended later to such idealistic works as the Vijñaptimātratā-siddhi, thus becoming (together with the term vāsanā = suffusion, permeation, or perfume) the common way for the Vijñānavādins (Buddhist idealists) to designate the "passively" stored "karmic accumulations." In canonical and earlier texts of the Abhidhamma these "karmic accumulations" are termed sometimes as (Pali) kamma-āyūhana or also as katattā-kamma ("stored-up" karma).[14] In the Kośa, the bījas (or karmic "seeds") are nāma-rūpa, i.e., "both mental amd material." They are also classified as kuśalākuśala or śubhāśubha (good, evil: pure and soiled). Thus the karmic "seeds" or "perfumes" are considered as vyākṛta, a term frequently used (and already mentioned) to designate their "definition" or "determination" (good or bad) according to the moral acts from which they proceed. This is in contrast with the "karma-results or fruitions" (such as passions and propensities, anuśaya) which are always considered as morally neutral in themselves (avyākṛta) since they are merely inherited as the result of a germination which is beyond the control of the will; and thus they do not constitute formal imputability. Only the consenting to them involves imputability. "Consent" to the passions, however, is already an act of cetanā which takes us anew to the very beginning of the karmic process. The "karma-results" are "obfuscating" = nivṛta; or also kleśācchādita = "veiled by defilement")[15] in the case of the anuśaya or evil propensities, even if they are morally "undefined" in themselves, and thus they offer "hindrance" (āvaraṇa) to the performance of wholesome deeds. "Good" or "wholesome" inclinations which are the karma-results of "wholesome" deeds are contrarily anivṛta, i.e., "non-hindering," "non-obfuscating."

On the basis of these distinctions the Kośa further designates the bījas ("seeds") from the viewpoint of their origin, i.e., according to the nature of the act of will which "sows" them:[16]

A) Aśubha-bījas or impure seeds. These are called also anuśayabījas in that they are accumulated by acts of will under the sway of the evil passions.

B) Śubha-bījas or pure seeds. These are subdivided in two sorts:

a) aupapattika-bījas or "seeds" which originate from deeds posited under the influence of wholesome propensities.

b) prāyogika-bījas or "seeds" which are deposited by the wholesome effort of the will as performed against the inclination of the evil anuśayas (or passions).

As for the use of the term vāsanās, Vasubandhu is more sparse in the Kośa than he is in his later idealistic work the Triṃśikākārikā (as commented upon by the Vijñaptimātratā-siddhi. In the Kośa the vāsanās (perfumes) seem to be referred almost exclusively to the karmic impregnations accumulated in the citta. Such is the case when Vasubandhu interprets the meaning of the frequent compound bhāvanā-mārga (or "path of meditation or contemplation"), in which the feminine noun bhāvanā is understood as an active "permeation" or "suffusion," contrary to vāsanā which is taken as the passive result of this active "suffusion" or "perfumation." The first term relates to the act of "perfuming," the second refers to the "perfumed." Through the practice of the bhāvanā-mārga, the acts of contemplation and meditation "perfume" (bhāvanati) the mind (citta) with good "perfumes" (vāsanās), "similarly to the scent of the sesamum-grains which remains in them by reason of the flowers wich perfume them" (puṣpagandhamayīkaraṇāt).[17] As we shall see later, the term bhāvanā will also acquire a universalistic connotation, especially in such idealistic works as the Vijñaptimātratā-siddhi (Dharmapāla's commentary to Vasubandhu's Triṃśikākārikā or "Thirty Verses on the Theory of Ideation Only"). Then bhāvanā will come to mean the universal "impregnation" or "perfuming" suffused by universal KARMA into all living beings in order to bring forth the universal or "common" (sabhāga, "shared") aspects of existence such as the "world-receptacle" or universe in which all of us live, etc.

From what has been explained it becomes clear that the main "stumbling block" for the *Sarvāstivādins* in their conception of "passive *karma*" lies in their irreducible, dualistic and total segregation of the nature which is proper to purely mental acts and the nature which is proper to materially expressed or executed acts. The *Sarvāstivādins* panrealism and pluralism in regard to the existence of the momentary *dharmas*, and their radical distinction between the *rūpa-dharmas* (material factors) on the one hand and the *vijñānadharma* and its associates (mental factors = *caitta* or *saṃprayuktakasaṃskāras*) on the other hand, explains this dualism. Such a rigorous distinction between the mental and the material compels them to the total dissociation between two different carriers of "karmic seeds," corresponding to the total and unabridged distinction between the *nāmabījas* (mental seeds) and *rūpa-bījas* (material seeds); hence their postulation of the *avijñapti* as a separate *rūpa* (material factor) which provides the basis for the accumulation of "material seeds." *Avijñapti-rūpa* stands therefore in sharp contrast with the nature of *manas* (mind) as *citta* which accumulates the mental seeds deriving from its purely mental intentions and volitions. How the re-fructifications ensuing from two such disparate "depositories" of karmic impregnations coordinate and cooperate with one another in order to bring about a unitary "retribution" in a future life remains a mystery never solved by the *Sarvāstivādins*.

This is the reason why their opponents, the *Sautrāntikas*, did not accept the existence of an extra *rūpa* called *avijñapti*, but adhered to the unitary doctrine that makes *karma* to be of one kind, all of it originating from the *will*, and all of it "impregnating" the whole "undercurrent" (*bhavaṅgasrotas*) or sub-conscious stream underlying the flux of personal consciousness (*saṃtāna*). It is opportune to note here the more markedly phenomenalistic tendencies of the *Sautrāntikas* who, together with the quasi-idealistic trends of the *Mahāsaṃghikas*, paved the way for the advent of Buddhist idealism. It is no wonder that Vasubandhu, already very inclined towards the theories of the *Sautrāntikas*, converted--as it is claimed--to the idealism propounded by his brother Asaṅga. The Buddhist idealists are to be credited with the final fusion of the two separate carriers of the karmic seeds. i.e., the *citta* and the *avijñaptirūpa* of the

Sarvāstivādins, into a common "store" of passive karma. Thus Buddhist idealism will advocate the givenness of a common store of purely mental character wherein the seeds germinate as a purely mental projection of the retributive inheritance of individual karma and from which the projection of the whole external and commonly shared world takes place. This "common depository" was given the name of ālaya-vijñāna, i.e., the "storehouse of consciousnes,"[18] a notion which became central to the development of Mahāyāna Buddhist philosophy and which is pervasive throughout the philosophical and even religious literature of the "great Vehicle" in China, Tibet, and Japan.

Thus far, much has been said about the nature of "passive karma," the central notion involved in the process of the vipāka-hetu or maturation causality. However, a word is still to be said for the further elucidation of the third, and in itself, formal aspect of the maturation-process, i.e., the act of "maturation" itself whereby passive karma "reacts" and yields its fruits. Little can be said for the hidden and mysterious mechanism which connects the acts of "individual karma" with its distant and disparate effects in the future. The material heterogeneity between the maturation causes (vipāka-hetu) and their final effects (vikāpa-phala) opens a mysterious gap in the Hīnayāna context, a gap that escapes all possibility of logical explanation. This process of transformation of the "seeds" into its heterogeneous fruits is designated as bījasaṃtati-pariṇāmaviśeṣa, i.e., "metamorphosis of the streamlike seeds."[19] What is the mysterious, still unexplained force that is at work in the "maturation-causality" (vipāka-hetu) as to yield such fruits of the most heterogeneous nature? How does the "undercurrent" of karma, be it called avijñapti (non-manifested factors) or bhavaṅgasrotas (sub-conscious stream of the "perfumes"),[20] determine itself into such disparate fruits of retribution? There is an indefinite number of thinkable possibilities of retribution for qualitatively and formally identical acts of the will. Wealth itself might be as much the result of evil karma as disease or poverty; and vice-versa. An act of lust may result for one individual in being born deformed, and for another in being born from wretched parents or in squalid poverty. What is the hidden aspect of this "maturation" causation (vipāka-hetu) which predetermines to one retribution in the first instance and to the other in the second? Can the *vipāka-hetu* explain itself without the intervention of other supra-individual forces which transcend the individuality of the karmic process of retribution? These issues will join other questions which ensue from the universal character of "world-fruition." For world-fruition is also the fruition of *karma*. But what is the ultimate meaning and entailment of the word *karma* as "action"? In Chapter 3 these issues will be further expounded--if not totally answered.

One thing remains certain in regard to the nature of the *vipāka-phala* as "maturation-fruition" or "reactive *karma*," and this is that it bifurcates into two totally different levels of fruition: one is the subjective and inner (*ādhyātmika-phala*) referring to the inherited passions (*anuśaya*), the other is the objective or external (*bāhya-phala*) referring to the allotment (*bhāgya*) of worldly and bodily circumstances. The first "inner" aspect (as passions and propensities) is not "determinative," but "predisposing." Thus the will can counteract the inclinations which past *karma* imposes upon our psychological nature and thus perform acts of merit. The second or "outer" aspect of the fructification (*bāhya-phala*) is totally predetermined and the will can "accomodate" to it, but do nothing else about changing it. We could offer a diagramatic illustration of the total mechanism of the three main aspects of the *karma*-maturation (*vipāka-hetu*) in the following manner:

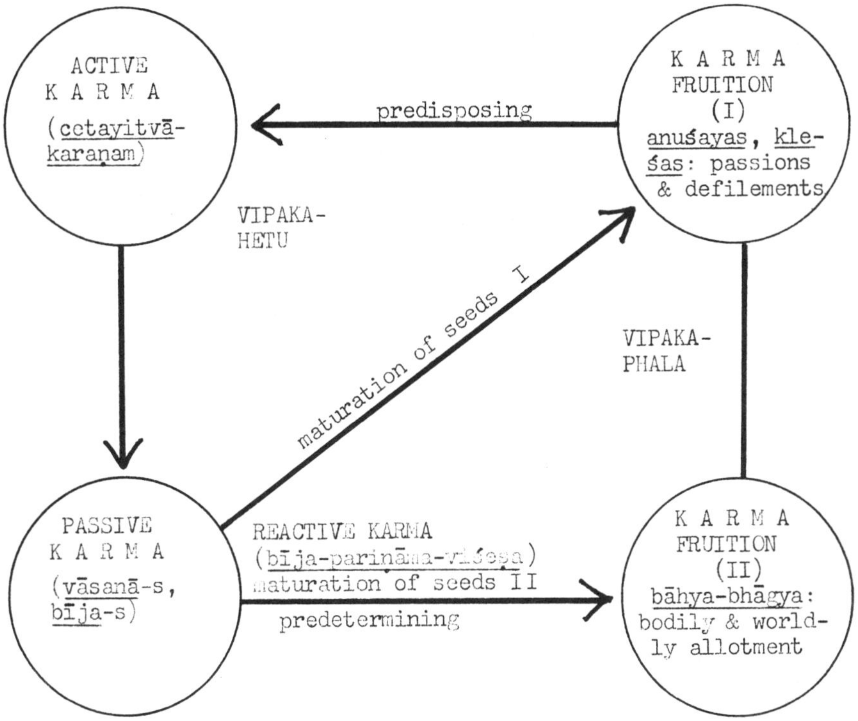
ACTIVE
K A R M A
(cetayitvā-
karaṇam)
predisposing
K A R M A
FRUITION
(I)
anuśayas, kle-
śas: passions
& defilements
VIPAKA-
HETU
maturation of seeds I
VIPAKA-
PHALA
PASSIVE
K A R M A
(vāsanā-s,
bīja-s)
REACTIVE KARMA
(bīja-pariṇāma-viśeṣa)
maturation of seeds II
predetermining
K A R M A
FRUITION
(II)
bāhya-bhāgya:
bodily & world-
ly allotment

As envisioned by the above chart, the *vipāka-hetu* covers--strictly speaking--the process of "active *karma*" through "passive *karma*" to the "maturation" *per se* of the "seeds." The results yielded from this process of maturation are designated as *vipāka-phala* (maturation-fruition) and they should be distinguished from the process of maturation itself which is "reactive." Thus the whole process of the karmic-mechanism of retribution consists of the process proper from "active" *karma* to "passive" to "reactive," and the yielded products (*vipāka-phala*) of this reaction. In a broader sense, however, "reactive *karma*" can be envisioned as comprising both the maturation itself (*vipāka*) and the products or "fruitions" (*vipāka-phala*) yielded or born (*vipākaja*) from this maturation.

At any rate, the three moments of the total karmic cycle of retribution appears as a three-spoked wheel which turns around the motive force of the *vipāka-hetu*:

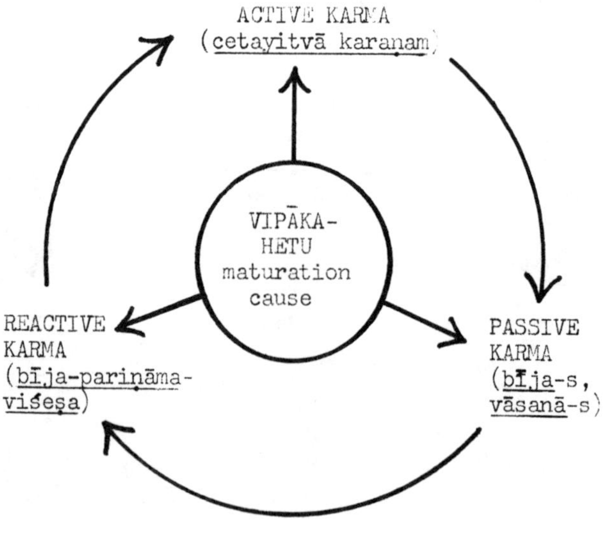

All of these three fundamental links in the circular motion condition one another in that each of them both _pre-supposes_ and _pre-posits_ the two others in their cycle from the past to the present to the future. "Active _karma_" represents the acting state of the present, "passive _karma_" represents the potential forces stored from the past, and "reactive _karma_" depicts the future assemblage of a new platform for a renewed staging of "active _karma_." Two ever revolving events take place in invariable sequence between the three links of the maturation process: _death_ and _rebirth_. Death inserts itself at one point between the links of "active" and "passive" _karma_; rebirth bridges the links of "passive" and "reactive" _karma_. Furthermore, "passive" _karma_ can be considered as splitting into two complementary stages, the stage in which it is in the process of "being formed" or "being accumulated" as the direct deposits immediately following the execution of "active" _karma_, and the stage in which it is _already "formed"_ (_abhi-saṃskṛta-bījas_). These two stages of passive _karma_ are separated by "death," where the "forming" of passive _karma_ (or the "seeding" of the "seeds") stops. The _already_ accumulated and thus "formed" hoard of _bījas_ (seeds) is thereby released from the dying body as the basis for the chain of "reaction" which begins with "rebirth."

Similarly to "passive _karma_," "reactive _karma_ comprises also two stages, namely, the stage of the "maturation-process" whereby the _bījas_ go through the metamorphosis (_bīja-saṃtati-pariṇāmaviśeṣa_)[21] which renders them into "full-fledged fruition" and this "full-fledged-fruition," as such (_vipāka-phala_). Re-birth is the link which bridges these two stages of the "reactive" process. Thus the above three-linked circuit of karmic retribution can be developed further into a more detailed cycle now exhibiting seven totally co-dependent links:

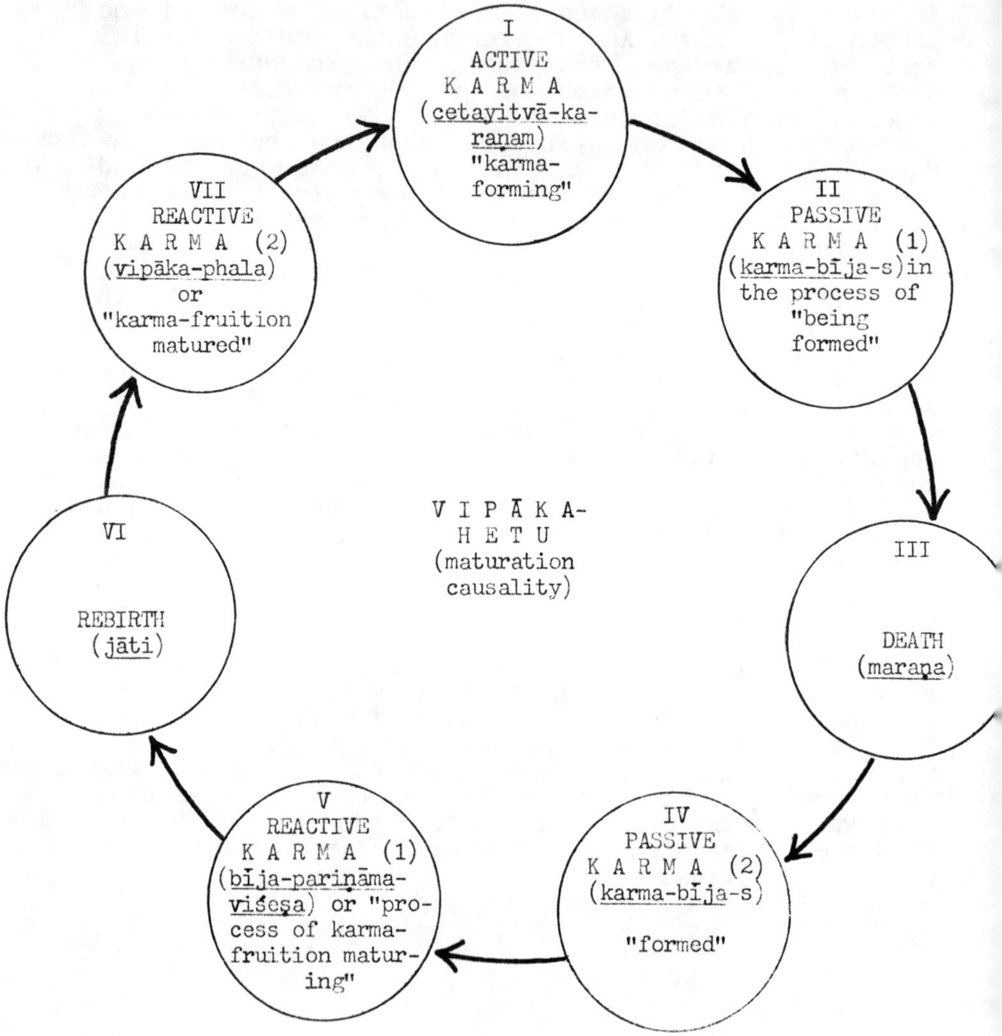
I
ACTIVE
K A R M A
(cetayitvā-karaṇam)
"karma-forming"
II
PASSIVE
K A R M A (1)
(karma-bīja-s)in the process of "being formed"
III
DEATH
(maraṇa)
IV
PASSIVE
K A R M A (2)
(karma-bīja-s)
"formed"
V
REACTIVE
K A R M A (1)
(bīja-pariṇāma-viśeṣa) or "process of karma-fruition maturing"
VI
REBIRTH
(jāti)
VII
REACTIVE
K A R M A (2)
(vipāka-phala)
or
"karma-fruition matured"
V I P Ā K A-
H E T U
(maturation
causality)

Each of the links depends on the preceding one in order to appear or operate. Since the total process is circular, the result is that each link depends on all the other ones, as all of them depend on each particular one. This principle of interdependency (*samutpāda*, *samutpanna*) establishes a notion of total co-origination of existence-links as these are originated and coordinated by the form of causality which has occupied us throughout this chapter, i.e., the *vipāka-hetu*. *Vipāka-hetu* (maturation causality) is then the motor of interdependency and co-arisal of the links which form the ever turning wheel of individual origination and existence. In spite of the temporal flux in which the links succeed one another, the closed circularity of the process establishes a simultaneous co-presence of all the links in each one and of each one in all. This is due to the perpetual and underlying act of causal conditioning whereby each one of the links depends on the whole circular series *at the same time*. This principle of "interdependent co-arisal" of all the succesive, temporally flowing links of the chain of individual existence is called *pratītya-samutpāda* (literally: dependent co-origination), a traditional doctrine of individual existence-causation that is primarily based on the *karma*-causality as exercised by the *vipāka*-process of maturation.[22] This *pratītya-samutpāda* doctrine, attributed to the direct teachings of the Buddha in the canonical *Suttas* and celebrated throughout the whole literature of Buddhism in both its *Hīnayāna* and *Mahāyāna* forms, lays down the basis for the no less celebrated *maṇḍala*-illustrations of the *bhavacakra* (wheel of existence) exhibiting a total of twelve links. These twelve links are graphically depicted as forming a circle (*maṇḍala*) that resembles a clock. And in point of fact *it is a clock* in which each hour tolls together with--and because of--the still resounding echo of all the others. This twelve hours, termed as the twelve *nidānas* ("causal factor," "link," originally meaning a "rope" dragging something), further expand upon the seven essential links formulated above in our preliminary exposition of the *pratītya-samutpāda* doctrine.

The commentarial classics of early Buddhism, including the two *Maggas*, the *Vibhāṣās* and the *Abhidharmakośa* offer long and detailed expositions of the twelve *nidānas*. Their formulation is traced back to the *nikāyas* of the *Sutta-piṭaka*.[23] Thus for instance the *Majjhima-* and *Saṃyutta-nikāyas*:

> Craving arises from sensation, sensation from contact-impression, contact-impression from the six organs, the six organs from form-matter, form-matter from consciousness, consciousness from karmic accumulation, and karmic accumulation from ignorance. . . . Or to repeat (in the order of origination):
>
> 1. Ignorance conditions karmic accumulations (*avijjā-paccayā saṅkhārā*).
> 2. Karmic accumulations condition consciousness (*saṅkhāra-paccayā viññāṇaṃ*).
> 3. Consciousness conditions mentality and corporeality (*viññāna-paccayā nāmarūpaṃ*).
> 4. Mentality and corporeality condition the six bases (or faculties) (*nāma-rūpapaccayā saḷāyatanaṃ*)
> 5. The six bases or organs condition contact-impression (*saḷāyatanapaccayā phasso*).
> 6. Contact-impression conditions sensation or feeling (*phassa-paccayā-vedanā*).
> 7. Sensation or feeling conditions craving (*vedanā-paccayā taṇhā*).
> 8. Craving conditions attachment (*taṇhā-paccayā-upādānaṃ*).
> 9. Attachment conditions the process of *karma* or becoming (*upādāna-paccayā-kammabhavo*).
> 10. The process of *karma* and becoming conditions rebirth (*kammabhava-paccayā jāti*).
> 11. Re-birth conditions old age and death (*jāti-paccayā jarāmaraṇaṃ*).
> 12. Old age and death produce all the sorrow lamentation, pain, grief, and despair (*jarāmaraṇaṃ soka-parideva-dukkhadomanas-supāyāsā sambhavanti*).

Arranged as the hours of the clock of existence, the twelve *nidānas*, ever wound up by the maturation-process of *karma*, would run as follows:

BHAVA-CAKRA (wheel of existence). "Interdependent co-origination" (pratītya-samutpāda) as based on the vipāka-hetu (maturation-cause).

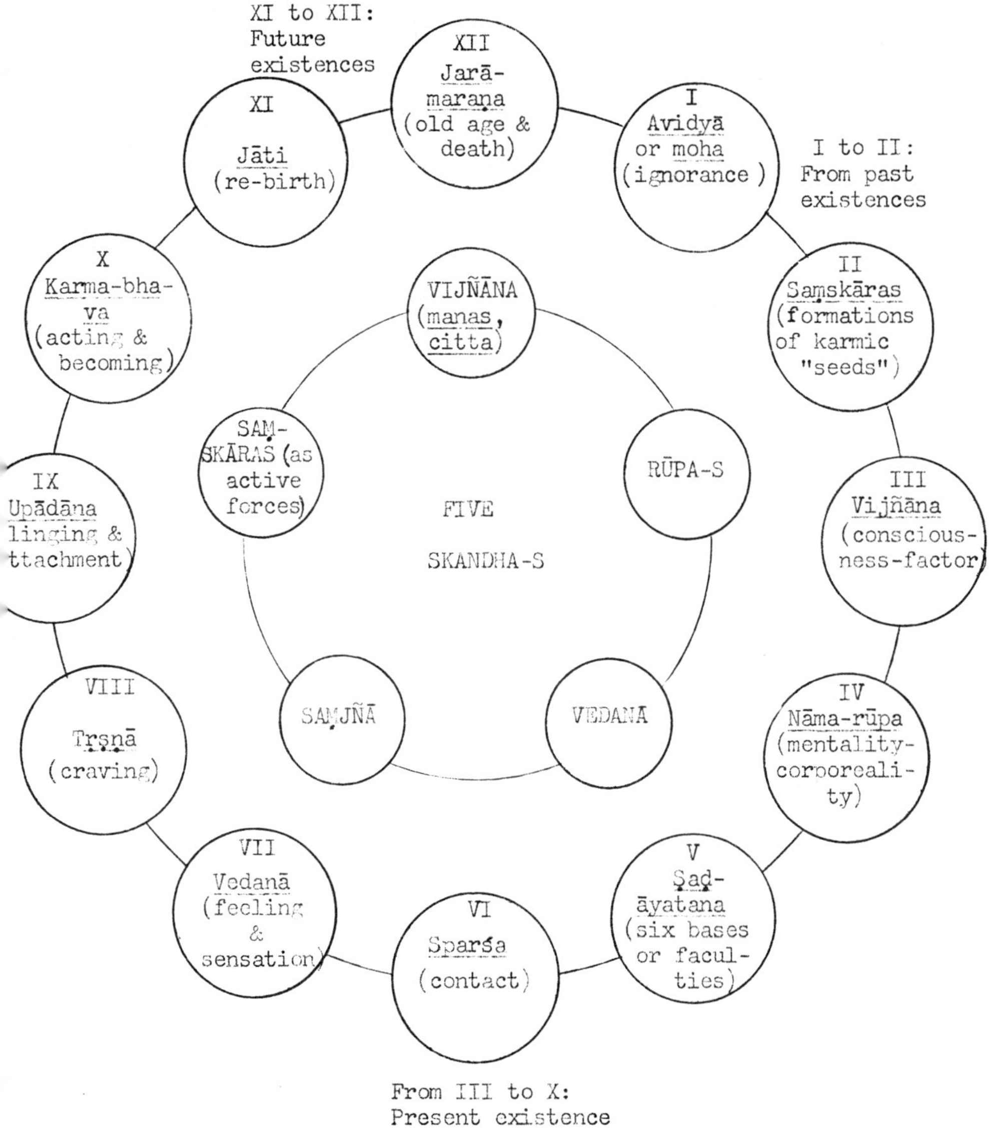

The "hours" of the bhavacakra (wheel of existence) represent the circular sequence of the plot of life projected by the vipāka-causality upon the illusory substantiality of the Ego and the World. Projected upon this empty screen of "non-substantiality" (anātman), the self-recycling plot of individual life--with its sequel of suffering and impermanence (duḥkha, anitya)--unfolds itself from birth to death and from death to rebirth. Both the action of cetanā-karma (active karma) and its inevitable re-action (vipāka-pariṇāma) constitute the "throw and bounce" motion that sets forth the projection of each one of the twelve "episodes of the plot" and their unending reiteration. Thus the bhavacakra may compare to a nightmarish motion picture which--though projecting a continuing variation of circumstances--keeps rerunning itself from end to beginning and throughout to the end. As a closed circuit of mutually conditioning factors, each one of the links in the chain of episodes is at the same time causal subsequent and precedent to the rest of the links.

Hence--as we said--although the clock means to represent a temporal succession in the arisal of the mutually conditioning episodes, in point of fact there is supratemporal interinclusion of each one of the links with the others. The twelve nidānas condition one another, both in the ever rotating order of their succession and in the perfect co-simultaneity of their mutual conditioning. Thus each one of the links is cause and at the same time effect of all the others. In this context, the term pratītya-samutpāda refers to ech one of the twelve nidānas (links) as being the cause of all the others, whereas the term pratītya-samutpanna expresses the fact of each one of the nidānas being the effect of all the others (hetur atra samutpādaḥ samutpannaḥ phalam matam).[24] Let us explain briefly the meaning involved in each one of the twelve successive links, and subsequently explain the mode of their co-simultaneity, their co-arisal, and their interinclusion:

1) Avidyā. (Ignorance). Ignorance, also portrayed as a pervading cause of existence (sarvatraga-hetu), is in itself not a generative cause; it is, however, the necessary, underlying condition of all the arisal of causation, both individual and universal. Avidyā is the primary and most original of all the

"root-conditions" (hetavaḥ). Hence it has to be presented as the first link of the revolving chain of dependent co-origination (pratītya-samutpāda). Generative causation, as ever re-germinating seeds of action, cannot set itself into motion except from within the vacuum of ignorance. Thus avidyā, besides constituting the "point of departure," pervades with its presence the whole journey of existence and underlies each one of its milestones.

2) Saṃskāras. (Karmic accumulations or potentials). As suggested (p. 44) the saṃskāras which represent the second link of the bhavacakra do not exactly correspond with the notion of saṃskāras as the fourth of the five skandhas. In the skandhas the saṃskāras (volitive forces) are understood as both the producers of karmic-potentials (designatd as "perfumes" or "seeds," i.e., passive karma), and also as the passions (anuśayas) and forces, both of mental and of non-mental nature, arising as "fruition" of such karmic potentials. In the fourth skandha the term saṃskāras referred to "karma-forming" and "karma-formed" functions and activities. Now, however, the term saṃskāras refers precisely to the intermediary, passive and dormant state of karmic potentials per se and thus it designates the "seeds" (bījas) themselves (or "passive karma) as already "formed" from past lives (karmābhisaṃskṛta-bījas). In short: the saṃskāras as fourth skandha refer to actual functions of "active" and "reactive" karma; the saṃskāras as second link of the pratītya-samutpāda process exclusively refer to "passive" karma. These karmic potentials or "seed-accumulations" constitute the origins of reactivity which are primordial in the order of individual existence in that they are the generative source of rebirth. Thus they establish the basis for conception in the womb or matrix chosen by their own reactivity or maturation. According to the Sarvāstivādins, the transmission of such "karmic seeds" and "potentials" is effected by the coupled concurrence of their two carriers: the citta and the avijñapti-rūpa.

3) Vijñāna. (Consciousness). Vijñāna, or the dharma-element of subjective awareness, although still inoperative due to the lack of concurrent causes (sahabhū and saṃprayuktaka-hetus) such as the sense-organs and objects, enters into the maternal womb in

its function of passive carrier (*citta*) of all the purely mental karmic potentials. Its presence in the womb of conception is then, according to the *Sarvāstivādins*, simultaneous with the *avijñapti-rūpa* which, as we know, is the transmitter of the karmic potentials of material nature. Thus both *citta* and the subconscious *avijñapti-rūpa*, as carriers of the passive *saṃskāras* or potentials released by death, have to be co-present at the very outset of the new conception. Thus the mention of *vijñāna* as the third link of the *pratītya-samutpāda* process must be understood not from a functional but from an entitative standpoint, inasmuch as *vijñāna*--as *citta*--serves here, together with the sub-conscious *avijñapti-rūpa*, as basis for the formation of the six organs or faculties of cognition.

4) *Nāma-rūpa*. (Mentality and corporeality). In this link the factors intervening in the forthcoming formation of mental and sensorial organs enter the matrix of conception. Hence the four "primordial elements" begin the constitution of *rūpa-prasāda*-atoms (subtle matter) and tangible *viṣaya*-atoms of solidity (gross matter), etc., which collect around the *dharmas* of *vijñāna* and *avijñapti-rūpa* in order to provide the basis for the arising of the mental organ (*manas*) and the five sensorial faculties (*indriyas*).

5) *Ṣaḍ-āyatana*. (Six bases or organs of cognition). On the basis of the elements of mentality and corporeality mentioned above the proper organic constitution of the six faculties of cognition (*manas* and five sense-organs) takes place. In keeping with our explanation in Part I, *vijñāna* is formally instituted as *manas* (mental faculty) by its pervasion of the subtle and translucent (*accha*) *prasāda-rūpas* of the five sense-organs. However, since "contact" with the external objects is not yet established, the pervasion of the *prasāda-rūpas* by *vijñāna* remains inoperative. The new arising mental faculty (or *manas*) cannot bear actual mental awareness (*mano-vijñāna*) unless contact with its proper non-sensuous objects is established. "Contact" (*sparśa*), however, cannot take place unless actual birth and the release of the new existence from its matrix is accomplished.

6) *Sparśa*. (Contact). "Contact" designates, as a matter of fact, the actual event of birth as delivery from the maternal womb. But the notion of rebirth in a wider sense (as usually employed in the meaning of the karmic cycle) has to be understood as connoting the initial conception in the maternal womb, rather than the actual delivery from it. *Sparśa* points to this moment of delivery from the matrix and the release of the new existent into the external world. This "release" constitutes by the same token the "clash" (*saṃpratigha*)[25] with the external objects which sets into function all the six organs constituted in the previous link.

7) *Vedanā*. (Sensation). *Sparśa* or contact unleashes the whole process of object-perception which is primordially based on *vedanā* or raw sensation. Thus *vedanā* implicitly includes the formation of *saṃjñā* (full-fledged perception of objects) and the coming about of the further functions of the mind such as the ones already studied in Part I as *saṃgrahaṇa* and *udgrahaṇa* ("comprehension" and "apprehension").[26] In this way the external world-environment "allotted" (*bāhyabhāgya*) to the new existence by the karmic potentials of materiality (*avijñapti*) comes to "fruition."

8) *Tṛṣṇā*. (Craving). The cognitive presence of objects, as accompanied by their primordial sensations of agreeability, unpleasantness, etc., unleashes the reaction of the *anuśayabījas*, i.e., the seeds of innate propensities previously stored as *saṃskāras*, which now germinate into predisposing passions in their full swing. Emotional attraction and repulsion, sympathies and phobias develop, and the will becomes inclined to the appropriation of such objects of attraction and to the rejection of such objects of repulsion. Thus the temperamental, psychological "allotment" (*ādhyātmika-bhāgya*) as rooted in the mental *saṃskāras* (*mano-karma-bījas*) stored up in the *citta* comes also to full "fruition."

9) *Upādāna*. (Clinging or attachment). On the basis of all the karmic potentials or *saṃskāras* coming now to full fruition, the will attaches itself to objects of the alloted world-environment as impelled by

the force of the innate propensities and "inherited" (*karma*-formed) passions.

10) *Karmabhava*. ("Becoming" or "karma-process-existence" as perpetuation of the will to act). This link has been variously and sometimes obscurely interpreted. *Karma-bhava* represents the acts that perpetuate the cycle of "becoming." These are the proper acts of the will (*cetanā-karma*) which constitute the continuing exercise of active *karma* with its immediate sequel, namely, the continuing "forming" of further karmic deposits (*vāsanās*) that were considered in the second link as already "formed." This link represents the process of both "*karma*-performing" and "*karma*-forming," in that any "performed" act of the present increases the stock of "formed" karmic potentials (*saṃskāras* in the passive sense, *bījas*, *vāsanās*) to be transmitted as residues from the *past* into *future* fruitions. In short, as the second *nidāna* is the link of the "passive karma-formed" (*karma-abhisaṃskṛta-bījas*), this tenth *nidāna* is the link of the "*active karma-positing*" and the "*passive karma-forming*" as a present process of "seeding" and "perfuming." Here, then, belong the proper acts of the will as conditioned by the previous links of "craving" and "clinging." Often, however, the becoming of other individuals through the equally *karmic* act of sexual procreation is also mentioned here. Some Tibetan representations of the twelve *nidānas* exhibit this link as a pregnant woman, thus including "conception" as resulting from a proper act of *karma*, and also as a bridge to the following *nidāna* which is "rebirth."

11) *Jāti*. (Birth) The *nidāna* of future "re-birth" is given here without the expected intermediary of "death." Death in the present existence is self-understood as the final milestone in the preceding *nidāna* of "becoming," in the same manner as birth in the present life was implicitly meant by the sixth of the *nidānas* (*sparśa* or "contact"). The reason is that the karmic significance of birth does not lie in the fact that it represents the beginning of the present life-existence, but in that it represents the beginning (and hence also the end) of innumerable future existences--innumerable, that is, unless the practice of the Path does put an end to the cycle by short-circuiting it with a supreme act of knowledge. Hence

the eleventh and twelfth *nidānas* are the hours of the future, the hours which reiterate themselves again and again as the film of existence is rerun anew. Hence the implicit interinclusion of the I to X *nidānas* comes to the fore. For birth and death, as self-reiterating events of the future, imply the continuing undercurrent of *nidānas* I and II and the successive reiteration of *nidānas* III to X.

12) *Jarā-maraṇa*. (Old age and death). This last of the *nidānas* summarizes the common destination of future existence by rebirth, which is to travel again through the stage of "becoming," and through the process of decay (*jarā*) unto death, at which point the "*karma*-formed" accumulations of passive *saṃskāras* are ready to restart the cycle all over again. Thus the last of the *nidānas* is paradoxically far from the last. The proximally impending death of the present existence is not even mentioned in the X link--wherein it belongs--because the present-life's death has no proper significance. The significance of death, like the significance of birth, lies in the fact that it has to take place "again and again," until the hidden, self-winding mechanism of the *vipāka-hetu* (*karma* maturation causality)--as pivoted on Ignorance--is destroyed, and the clock of existence stops at its last and eternal moment of *nirvāṇa*.

In order to visualize or envisage the sequence of the twelve *nidānas* in correspondance with the seven links of the *vipāka-hetu* as we interpreted them in page 92 , and with the three "roads" (*adhvanaḥ*) of time (past, present and future), we have the following chart:

PASSIVE *karma* as "formed."	I. II.	Ignorance Karmic deposits	TOTAL PAST
REACTIVE *karma*-process I: Karmic deposits or "seeds" maturing.	III. IV. V.	Conception-consciousness Mentality and corporeality factors Six faculties	TOTAL PRESENT (including: within-this-life past; within-this-life present; within-this-life future)
REACTIVE *karma*-process II: external worldly allotment (*bāhya-bhāgya*).	VI. VII.	Contact (with actual *birth*) Sensation and perception of external world	
REACTIVE *karma*-process III: inner temperamental allotment (*anuśayas*).	VIII. IX.	Craving Clinging	
ACTIVE *karma* (as "performing") PASSIVE *karma* as "forming").	X.	Acting, *karma*-forming (with actual death)	
TOTAL interinclusion of active, passive and reactive *karma*.	XI. XII.	Re-birth (with reiteration from II to X) Death	TOTAL FUTURE

In order to see further into the meta-temporal interinclusion, simultaneity and co-presence of all the *nidānas* (marked with Romans from I to XII) throughout the three *adhvanaḥ* (future, present, past) this chart might be of assistance:

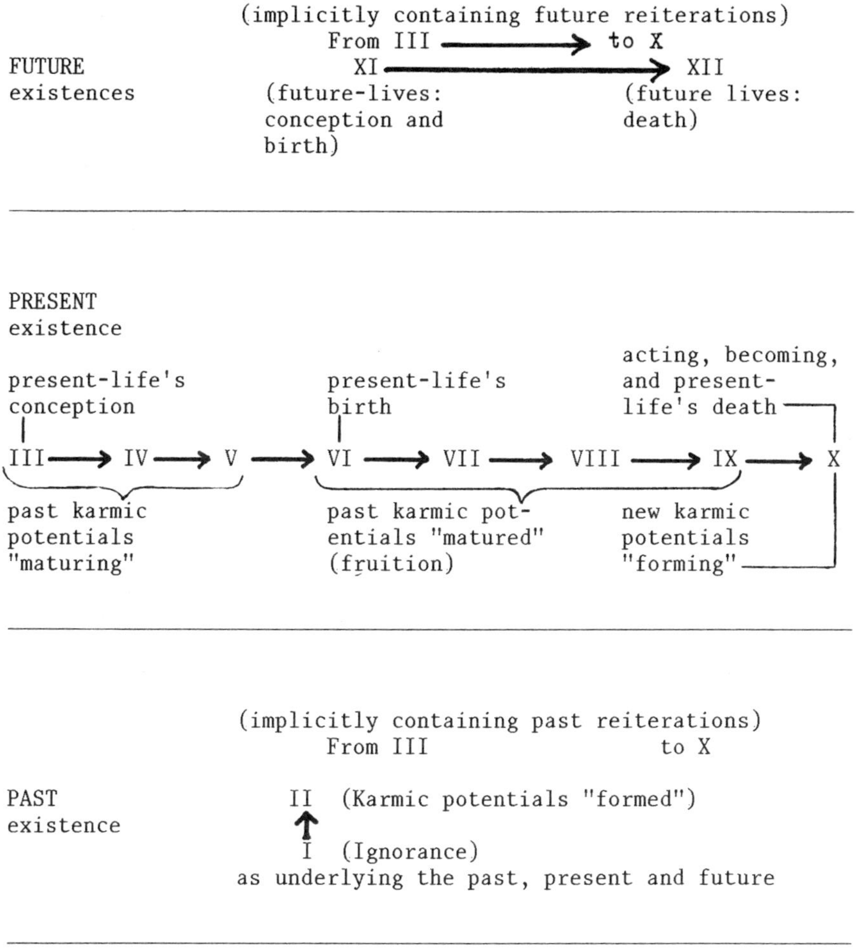

This exposition of the *pratītya-samutpāda* (interdependent co-origination) doctrine, as based on the conception of the individual *karma*-process and its "maturation" causality (*vipāka-hetu*), brings to a close our second Chapter on the nature of causation. Causation has been envisioned so far from the point of view of the individual's contribution to its own existence through the process designated as individual *karma*. In the *vipāka-hetu* (or maturation-causality) which lies at the bottom of the individual karmic process of causation a great and deep mystery opens up to the philosopher. Where lies the ultimate ground for the heterogeneity of the fruition that ensues from the *vipāka-hetu*? Where is the missing link that bridges any human act and its karmic imprint (as "seed" or "perfume," i.e., as passive *saṃskāras*) to the selecting of one among the indefinite number of possibilities of maturation? This maturation as such, which strictly speaking takes place in the moment of conception and development of the embryo, carries as retribution such concomitants as the internal, mental and temperamental constitution, as well as the external bodily endowment and worldly allotment. The spectrum of possilities that the maturing seeds might select in their fructification is virtually infinite. But *karma* is not conceived as an at-random lottery. It is supposed to work strictly according to organic laws rigorously established and automatically working. How can these laws be formulated and spelled out? The transformation of the seed (or *vāsanā*) into its retributive effects has been designated as *bījasaṃtatipariṇāmaviśeṣa*[27] which liberally translates as "the metamorphosis of the serial flow of seeds." This "metamorphosis" takes place in the possible transformation of an imprint relinquished by an act of thievery into being born from wretched parents, or being born without hands, or even being born as an animal or as a demon in hell, etc. The causal factors which conduct and direct *ad litteram* the process of maturation of the seed or imprint into such variety of fruitions remain shrouded in mystery. The *Hīnayāna* Buddhists are not unaware of this mystery. It will not be the only philosophical issue to remain covered by the veil of mystery. Our exposition of the universal and shared Force which propels the life of the Universe as such, with its objectively fixed natural laws, its organic constitution, and its determination into living genuses and species will also disclose the bottomless ground of a great mystery to all philosophies: Why is there such a thing as causation at all? Why is there universal Ignorance? or in Hinduistic terms, why is there *māyā* (illusion) and *upadhi* (limiting "adjunct") to the infinite Brahman?

The present mystery of the "metamorphosis" into "heterogeneity" as entailed by the doings of the *vipāka-hetu* was well expressed by the philosopher and

Bodhisattva Vasubandhu himself. As it is related by the Abhidharmakośa:

> Here the force to produce a vipākaphala (a maturation-fruition) which is produced by a vipāka-hetu (a maturation cause) disappears after having produced the vipāka (the maturation itself). . . . But why does not another similar vipāka arise from the vipāka, as from a fruit's seed-grain another seed-grain? . . . But how? It arises from a special change which is produced by a special maturation. . . . This much I have expounded as I understand it. The causes, being the influence (bhāvanā) of different actions through different forces, having reached this state, produce this (other) result--this is the domain of the Buddhas alone. Again it has been said: "Action (karma), the impregnation or perfuming of it (bhāvanā), the manifestation of it (vṛttilabha), the result of it (phala) no one else than the Buddha necessarily and thoroughly knows.[28]

This is the mystery of the vipāka-hetu which the Buddha, reaching wisdom and omniscience, can allegedly disclose and come to know for himself. Can he explain it to us? Will the Buddha also be able to unravel the mysteries lurking in the attempt to philosophize on the nature of a universally shared aspect of KARMA? Will the Buddhist philosophers, as Buddhism expands its frontiers in search of further doctrinal embodiments, be able to explain these mysteries in the name of the Buddhas? The development of Buddhist idealism and totalism in China, as they assimilate the traditional Taoist intuitionism and Confucianism, will produce dialectical notions of karma which will be all-emcompassing and self-explained. For the moment, in our study of the philosophers of early Buddhism we can look into the groping attempts to confront--vis a vis--these mysteries of causation. At this point the issues which they pose are as relevant as the possible answers, which only the further history of Buddhism in its growth towards inclusivism and totality will be able to afford.

Let us now proceed to the explanation of the *sabhāga*- and *kāraṇa-hetus* as they represent the forms of a KARMA-force which is shared by individual existence, but which, by the same token, has to transcend individuality.

Chapter 3

The sabhāga- and kāraṇa-hetu-s ("homogeneous" and "efficient" forms of causality). The notion of Universal Karma and Universe-causation.

1. Sabhaga-hetu

The vipāka-hetu (maturation-cause) has been expounded as the form of causality which is at work throughout the process of individual karma. Through it human action produces its own retribution within the continuing cycle of birth and death. This causal process was also designated as asamāna or asabhāga ("heterogeneous") in that the karmic effects--as fruition of past deeds--do not bear resemblance to their original causes. The intrinsic nature of this causality, as producing fruitions (phala, effects) of the most disparate nature, remains shrouded in mystery. The philosophical search has been unable to discover the intrinsic detail and operation of such karmic mechanism. At any rate, the retributive role of this "maturation causality" (vipāka-hetu) resides precisely in its heterogeneity. For "retribution," as effected by the vipāka-hetu, is the source of diversification among sentient beings due to the disparate allotments ensuing from their individually different merits and demerits.

However, the vast diversity of allotments which set asunder all sentient beings can only happen on the basis of a common background of shared nature and shared world. Even the twelve nidānas, which exhibit the process of maturation and diversification from one kind of existence into another, move around upon the pivots of uniform and shared patterns. All the diverse aspects of the karmically inherited variations are set on the self-iterating succession of the nidānas. In the rerunning of our life-existence only the episodical circumstances of the journey change, not its essential milestones. The lives of a bum, or of a scientist, or of a monk, go round the clock sharing not only a common participation in the development of sensorial and mental experience, in perceiving, craving and clinging, but also in the sharing of a common human nature and in the inhabiting of a common world. The diversification produced by the vipāka-hetu in its retributive role can take place only upon common--generically and specifically--preset forms of sentient existence, "streaming down" (*niṣyandana*) on the riverbeds of this commonly shared universe. This common and universal aspect, upon which the diversification operated by the *vipāka-hetu* takes place, splits into two different planes of shared participaton. One can be considered as a *vertical*, "down-flow" participation of community; the other can be considered rather as a *horizontal* one. This first accounts for the fact of "down-the-line" uniformity which is proper of genetic and biological life-processes. Its proximate motive force is the act of generation whereby parents generate children, and whereby any generated individuals resemble their generators. It is in this sense that apples produce apples, horses produce horses, and humans produce humans. As for the second kind of communal participation, this is based in the *horizontal* share of a world which is already there for us to inhabit, and which stands there to sustain the temporal flux which is the mark of generated life, as this flows down along its ready-made riverbeds. It is on such world-platforms that so many species of plants, so many species of animals, and so many ethnic classes of humans are generated. They all grow, mature, reproduce and die under the common influence of one sun, and within one atmosphere, and upon the common soil which they share.

As briefly stated in the above summary in Chapter 1,[29] the *sabhāga-hetu* or "homogeneous causation" covers all ranges of immediate or proximate causality which produces the above mentioned "down-flow" of uniformity proper to life-generation. In point of fact, the *sabhāga-hetu* lies originally at the base of the "momentariness" theory (*kṣaṇika-vāda*), according to which any *dharma* of one nature is causally followed by another *dharma* of the same specific nature. Thus a momentary flash of *vijñāna* is followed by another *vijñāna*, a *saṃjñā*-moment (perception, notion, imagination) is followed by another *saṃjñā*, a *cetanā* by another *cetanā*, a *viṣaya* by another *viṣaya*, etc. In this respect the *sabāgha-hetu* plays a pervasive role in bringing about the aspects of sameness and uniformity within the discrete succession of *dharma*-aggregates that we are. Hence the illusion of a permanently abiding and substantial ego is produced; the self-stretching and temporally extending states of mind are due to the *sabhāgatā* (community of nature) of the flash-like succession of *dharmas* sharing identical essences (*dharmatā*). Thus the discrete and quantum-like succession of momentary *dharmas* can be said to constitute a "life-continuum" (*naiṣyandika-saṃtāna*) which provides for a true, though relative, basis for what is called "empirical personality."

Naturally, as already said, the range of the "homogeneous" causation (*sabhāga-hetu*) greatly transcends the microcosmic and sub-empirical realm of the *dharmas*. It also transcends vastly the confined realm of our own embodied individuality as this appears in the macrocosmic manifestation of our "dharmic life-continuum." Hence *sabhāga-hetu* is the form of causality responsible for the universality of the *niṣyanda-phala*, i.e., the "down-flow fruition" of specific sameness (*samāna*) which provides continuity to the "vertical" succession of human and animal life. *Niṣyanda-phala* ("down-the-stream fruition") is the by-product of the *sabhāga-hetu* as this effects universality in the sharing of living genuses and species. The *Kośa* says: *niṣyando hetusadṛśaḥ*, or "the fruit which resembles its cause is called the *streaming-fruit*."[30] The *sabhāga-hetu* is therefore a sort of formal cause, whereby one specific form of life is transmitted from generators to generated. This specific form constitutes, according to the *Sarvāstivādins*, a real *dharma* on its own right which, like the modern notion of genes, accompanies the transmission of the karmic individual "seeds" (*bījas*) as these--via their carriers--enter the maternal womb of generation. This *dharma*-force which transmits specific sameness is called *nikāya-sabhāga* ("community of nature"). The *Sarvāstivādins* list it among the "non-mental, sub-liminal forces" (*citta-viprayukta-saṃskāras*) cited in the fourth of the *skandhas*.[31] In point of fact, the *nikāya-sabhāga* is in itself a sort of karmic "seed," similar in its potentiality to the individual "seeds" accumulated by individual *karma* (either in the form of *avijñapti-rūpa* or in the form of mental "perfumes" or *vāsanās* in the *citta*) except that the *nikāya-sabhāga* (or "community of nature," sometimes termed *sabhāgatā* in the abstract form), as a seed which determines the specific resemblance between generator and generated, is not directly planted by individual *karma*, but by a universal one. The deposits of individual *karma* contain "seeds" predetermining a "retributive" birth by assignation to a certain genetic group, but the formal and proximate embodiment within such a genetic group is done by virtue of the nikāya-sabhāga "seed." This "seed" is planted in the karmic carriers by a form of karma-process which transcends the one ensuing from individual action. This universal KARMA is depicted as a "mysterious" force" (adṛṣṭa-bala) which pervades and dominates the whole variety of the streaming life, and controls its fixed formations as genuses and species. This force, which in its mysteriousness is labled as adṛṣṭam and apūrvam (non-seen and unsurpassed), is given the name of bhāvanā or also adhipati-bala, meaning respectively the "universal impregnation," or the "all-ruling," "all-controlling" (ādhipata) FORCE. Its fruits are adhipati-phala, i.e., the "all-ruling, all-controlling fruition" of such effects as the preset patterns of generic (abhinna) and specific (bhinna) modes and forms of living existence. According to Vasubandhu:

> "Sabhāgatā is the principle which causes resemblance among the sentient beings. . . . There are two kinds of sabhāgatā (common nature), one is abhinna (generic) and the other is bhinna (particular or specific). The first accounts for a common similitude among all the sentient beings (sattva-sabhāgatā), the second accounts for the plurality and diversity of specific divisions.[32]

Therefore--contrary to Stcherbatsky's opinion that the sabhāga-hetu effects only homogeneity within the material and mineral world--this form of causality is essential and proper to "life-by-generation." As far as it produces the human species it is called puruṣa-sabhāgatā (personal, rational nature). Other kinds of sabhāgatā produce similitude among other sentient beings, not only inferior to humans, like animals, but also superior, such as devas and the conscious beings of the higher realms of "form" and "non-form" (rūpa- and arūpa-lokas). Its effect, the adhipati-phala (all-ruling effect), is a fruit which, according to Vasubandhu, is shared by the sentient beings in common "on account of the collective share of the acts which concur to their creation."[33] These acts, however, as collectively shared by the beings of each species, proceed from the maturing of such "seeds" as the nikāya-sabhāga-bījas ("community of nature" seeds) which in themselves are not individual seeds (anādhāraṇa-bījas) but common and univeral seeds (saādhāraṇa-bījas). Although these universal or "common seeds" are remotely assigned to us by individual karma, however they are proximately produced, set and planted by the Universal Force (adhipati-karma or adhipati-bala) which, as a universally shared élan vital, pervades, impregnates and underlies the actions of all individual sentient beings.

It is in this sense that the sabhāga-hetu, or the "homogeneous" form of causality, is said also to be the adhipati-pratyaya, i.e., the "all-ruling," or "supreme" condition[34] for the coming about of universally shared communities of nature in the generative succession of living beings. Thus the sabhāga-hetu, being in itself a form of proximate causality (hetu), becomes also a pratyaya (subordinate condition), namely, it becomes adhipati-pratyaya (the all-ruling condition) in that such a form of causality is applied by the universal KARMA-FORCE for the pre-setting of a diversification of universal genuses and species. Thus the sabhāga-hetu becomes the instrumental "condition" whereby universal KARMA provides universally shared "channels" (specific natures) for the fruition of the individual karmic retribution.[35]

In short, this new kind of karma, which is universally shared as an all-pervading form of ACTION or FORCE (adhipati-bala), exercises the mode of causality which is sabhāga-hetu in order to generate universally shared "seeds" (sa-ādhāraṇa-bījas) of specific sameness (bhinna-sāmānya). But by the same token such a cause (namely sabhāga-hetu) is made into the necessary and "all-ruling" condition (adhipati-pratyaya) for the germination of a fruition which is also "all-ruling" and "supreme" (adhipati)

All this has been said about the common share of nature by generation (sabhāgatā or nikāyasāmānya) in the vertical line of a fruition d'écoulement ("down-flow" fruition) in that it follows the works of sabhāga-hetu, and is also called adhipati-phala ("all-ruling" fruition) in that this sabhāga-hetu is used or applied by a universal FORCE (adhipati-karma, adhipati-bala) to produce effects which are "sovereign," "all-ruling" and "supreme" (adhipati).

It should be emphasized that the hetus are forms of causality to be distinguished from the source of action which exercises them; and the source of action is always the will, whether it be individual will or universal WILL. The very sources of action (as wills or "WILL") determine also the final scope of the use of such forms of causality and thus render them into instrumental conditions (pratyaya). It is in this sense that the sabhāga-hetu (homogeneous cause) is also an adhipati-pratyaya (all-ruling condition) in virtue of the instrumental application of such a form of causality by an adhipati-bala (all-ruling FORCE). This "all-ruling FORCE" has been also designated as "universal KARMA," a form of karma which is collectively shared by all sentient beings; but which--in a mysterious way--transcends also the confined realm of individuality.

2. Kāraṇa-hetu

The sabhāga-hetu is not the only mode of causality which universal KARMA applies as a condition (pratyaya) for the fruition of universally shared aspects of existence. The collective sharing of common biological natures which flow "down the river" of life-generation (niṣyanda-phala) is not--as already suggested--the only aspect of existence shared in common by sentient beings. They also share the "horizontal," ever standing availability of a ready-made "world-receptacle" (bhājana-loka) which serves as the "support" and "container" of the living beings. Such is our share of the one Universe under this Sun, this Moon, upon these continents in the common breathing of one atmosphere, etc. It is the Ganges river which is always there for us to go and bathe in, generation after generation. This "horizontal," universally shared aspects of existence constitute the external world. Thus, as the Universal "all-ruling" KARMA (adhipati-bala) gives us an intrinsic nature, (ādhyātmika-bhāva) which is the inner principle of our biological similarities (ādhyātmika-sabhāgatā), this very same universal KARMA provides us with the external stage of life which is there for us to set foot upon and inhabit. This is a world of non-living entities which are "outer" (bāhya) to us and thus become the extrinsic aspects of a vastly classified nature (bāhya-nikāya). This outer world is termed bhājana-loka or "receptacle-world" in that it receives and holds within itself, as though "in a vessel" (bhājana), all the generic and specific families of living beings.

This bhājana-loka (as extrinsic, world-nature) is also posited as the karmic fruition from a collectivity of acts which, although shared by all sentient beings, issue ultimately from the universal élan vital which is adhipati-bala (all-ruling force). In this case, however, the universal, "all-ruling" or "supreme" force exercises the mode of causality which was designated as kāraṇa-hetu, i.e., the "efficient" cause par excellence, the first of the hetus. The external world is created, not through the transmission of the nikāya-sabhāga (biological nature), but through the direct and entitative "projection" which ensues from the universal KARMIC WILL. This world therefore is also a kind of "all-ruling" or "supreme fruition" (adhipati-phala) which results from an outer projection equally effected by the universal karma as "supreme force," as this now exerts such a form of causality which is kāraṇa, i.e., outwardly "efficient" and "creative." Hence the kāraṇa-hetu exerted by the adhipati-bala or "supreme force"--becomes also an adhipati-pratyaya (supreme or "all ruling" condition) for the common fruition by all sentient beings of "supreme" and "all-ruling" effects (adhipati-phala), effects which this time are outer and extrinsical (i.e., the WORLD) to our own shared natures as living beings. Thus the patterns of both forms of universal causation, the one effected through the sabhāga-hetu and the one effected through the kāraṇa-hetu--as exerted by universal ACTION in order to bring about universally shared effects--run parallel to one another. On the one hand, the universal, "all-ruling" FORCE exerts the sabhāga-causality as the "supreme" condition (adhipati-pratyaya) for the fruition of intrinsically shared natures through the "vertical" "down-stream" of life-generation (naiṣyandika-adhipati-phala = "down-flow" of all-ruling fruition). On the other hand, the universal FORCE further exerts the kāraṇa-hetu as the "supreme condition" (adhipati-pratyaya) for the fruition of extrinsical and outerly "projected" effects (bāhya-adhipati-phala or "external and all-ruling fruition"). These latter effects constitute the "horizontal" aspects of our common and external "world-object." The Abhidharmakośa explicitly refers to the "all-ruling" or "supreme KARMA," as different from individual karma, and as "maturing" into the production of a _bhājana-loka_ or "world-receptacle" which is shared by all sentient beings:

> The _dharmas_ which do not directly constitute the sentient beings--such as mountains and rivers, etc.--are, by their nature, common to all. Everybody shares their experience. However the fruit of retribution (_vipāka-phala_) is, by definition, absolutely individual: no one except me can ever savor the fruits of the _karma_ which I alone have performed. Therefore, beyond this individual fruit of retribution, _karma_ (as universal) produces also _supreme, all ruling_ effects (_adhipati-phala_). This _all-ruling_ fruition is shared by all sentient beings in common, on account of the generality of the _karma_ which concurs to its creation.[36]

And in another passage:

> The _kāraṇa-hetu_ is the first of all forms of causality. . . . Its fruit (or effect) is called _adhipaja_ (as generated by the supreme _karma_) or also _ādhipata_ (as belonging to the level of the supreme _karma_). Thus it is thought that the _kāraṇa-hetu_ adopts the form of a _supreme_ or _all-ruling_ (_adhipati_) force. . . . It is regarded as a _sovereign_ cause because it possesses command, and because it is exerted as productive and predominant activity. . . . Thus for example. . . . the collective KARMA of all sentient beings is _supreme_ or _sovereign_ (_adhipati_) in regard to the production of the world-receptacle (_bhājana-loka_).[37]

Here the acknowledgment of a universally shared FORCE which is _ādhipata_ (supreme, sovereign, all-ruling) in that it produces "supreme effects" (_adhipati-phala_)--such as the external manifestation of a common world-object--is obvious. But in verse 62 d the qualification of _ādhipata_ is also directly attributed to the _kāraṇa-hetu_: _adhipatiḥ kāraṇam ucyate_ ("the _kāraṇa_-cause is called _supreme_ or sovereign"). However it is clear otherwise that this qualification--as "supreme causality"--is justified only inasmuch as it is exerted and applied by the adhipati-bala (or "supreme FORCE") in order to produce such a "supreme" and universally shared effect as the "world-receptacle." It is in this sense that the kāraṇa-hetu is, hand in hand with the sabhāga-hetu, also a "supreme" instrumental condition (adhipati-pratyaya) applied towards the fruition of universally shared aspects of existence:

> The adhipati-pratyaya, namely, the class of causal condition called supreme or all-ruling refers (together with the sabhāga-hetu) to such a cause (hetu) which is considered the proximate "reason of being;" thus the kāraṇa-hetu is also a supreme condition (adhipati-pratyaya).[38]

From the above it is clearly implied that both the sabhāga-hetu and the kāraṇa-hetu play the role of "all-ruling" or "supreme conditions" (adhipati-pratyaya) inasmuch as they are exerted and directed by the supreme KARMA (adhipati-bala) in order to bring forth the fruition of supreme and universal effects. Thus the quality of "supreme" or "sovereign," as it applies to these two modes of causality, is adventitious and not intrinsic, and is due to the instrumental directionality or purpose applied to them by the universal FORCE itself. Hence the two hetus become also adhipati-pratyayas in the level of the in-order-to or "final" causality, as this is infused into them by the very source of activity which exercises them in a universal range. Here then the form of an implicit "final" or "scope-causality," as adding to the generative-formal cause (sabhāga-hetu) and to the universal efficient cause (kāraṇa-hetu), comes to the fore.

In sum, the causal elements intervening in the production of universal and "all-ruling" effects can be listed according to the following sequence:

a) A Universal Force or Supreme karma (adhipati-bala) as source of universal action.

b) Two modes of causation as exerted by this universal karma: Sabhāga- and kāraṇa-hetus.

c) The impregnation of universal "seeds" in the karmic carriers of all individual sentient beings implanted by this Universal karma, as this latter exerts these two forms of causation.

d) The "ordination" of the sabhāga- and kāraṇa-hetus as instrumental conditions (adhipati-pratyayas) towards their universal objectives (artha).

e) The actual fruition of universally shared effects as such (adhipati-phala).

Finally, in order to interrelate at a glance all the karmic functions as a whole including both individual karma as it undergoes the process of the vipāka-hetu (maturation or heterogeneous causality), and the universal or supreme KARMA (adhipati-bala) as exerting both the sabhāga- and the kāraṇa-hetus ("common nature" homogeneous causation, and efficient "universe-causation"), we offer the following chart.:

KARMA CAUSATION	INDIVIDUAL KARMA (or cetanā-karma)	exerts	Vipāka-hetu	In order to produce the "heterogeneous" maturation of individual seeds (vipāka-bījas).	To fructify as: Vipāka-phala either as A) bāhya-bhāgya, or external world-allotment, or as B) ādhyātmika-bhāgya, or inner, temperamental allotment.
	UNIVERSAL KARMA (or adhipati-bala)	exerts	sabhāga-hetu as adhipati pratyaya I	In order to produce the universal seeds of "homogeneous" generation nikāya-sabhāga-bījas.	To fructify as: adhipati-niṣyanda-phala, or "supreme," "down-flow" fruition of common biological nature (as generic and specific).
			Karaṇa-hetu as adhipati-pratyaya II	In order to produce the universal seeds of "world-" creation or protection bhājanaloka-bījas).	To fructify as: adhipati-bhājanaloka-phala, or "supreme," "world-receptacle" fruition or "share" of a common external universe.

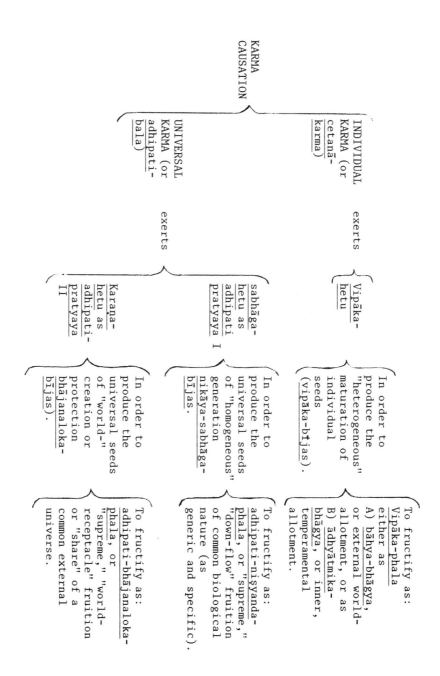

3.- Universal Karma as world-creating *adhipati-bala* (supreme force). Its mystery and entailment.

Unquestionably, the *Sarvāstivāda* doctrine of external world-creation remains obscure and intricate. In the idealistic system propounded by the *Vijñaptimātratā-siddhi*--a commentary to *Vasubandhu's Triṃśikā-kārikā*--the external world is taken only as mental projection produced by "ideation-only" (*vijñaptimātra*). Both the intrinsic share of a biological, generative nature, and the extrinsic share of an external world are due to a universal "permeation" of mental "seeds" (*vijñaptibījas*) as effected by the universal *adhipati-bala* (all-ruling or supreme FORCE). Given its *purely mental* character, the reduction of this world-projection to common or universal mental seeds implanted in the "projecting" mind is more easily explained.

In the realistic context of the *Sarvāstivādins* this explanation of the works of the *kāraṇa-hetu*, as the "supreme condition" for the creation of an external world, is far more difficult and perplexing. That the *sabhāga-hetu provides us with the common seeds of a shared nature (nikāya-sabhāgatā)* which is transmitted through the individual seed-receptacles (*avijñapti* and *citta*) might constitute more of a feasible explanation. *Nikāya-sabhāgatā* is a non-mental force (*citta-viprayukta-saṃskāra*)[39] which can be considered as a universal seed implanted in all the beings sharing the same specific nature, and transmitted--via the parents or generators--to the seed-recipients at the moment of conception. This *nikāya-sabhāgatā* is then a biological force similar to our present notion of genes and chromosomes as containing both the seeds of shared specific nature and the differentiations transmitted individually by inheritance. Thus *nikāya-sabhāga* can be conceived as a universal seed (*sa-ādhāraṇa*) ultimately effected by universal *Karma*. But how the production of an *external* world (*bhājana-loka*) can be reduced to the germination of universal seeds implanted into the *inner* recess of our individual natures is more difficult to see. For the existence of the external world in *Hīnayāna* Buddhism is real and not merely the result of a phantasmagoric projection. And still, given Vasubandhu's manner of speaking, it seems as though the *kāraṇa-hetu* is exercised by the universal life-force (or *élan-vital*), in the form of a supreme condition (*adhipati-pratyaya*), *for the "maturation" of a collectively shared karma*, a maturation which results in a universal, "all-ruling" and *external* fruition. But any maturation of *karma* consists in the germination of "seeds" innerly *implanted* into our intrinsic carriers of karmic seeds (*avijñapti* and *citta* in the case of the *Sarvāstivādins*, *bhavaṅga* or "subliminal life-continuum" in the case of the *Sautrāntikas*). Thus if the *kāraṇa-hetu* (efficient causality), as exercised by the *adhipati-bala* (or supreme force), creates the world by result of a *karmic* maturation and as a *karmic* fruition, this can be done only through the "impregnation" (*bhāvanā*) of universal "seeds" (*bījas* or *vāsanās*). How do these universal but *innerly* shared "seeds" germinate and fructify into an *external* world? Is the world continuously and uninterruptedly emanating from the ever germinating common and universal "seeds" of all the individual sentient beings, *simultaneously* and through the sharing of a common space? Is then the world an external outgrowth from all of us, through generations past and future, all at once and simultaneously? Is then the *bhājana-loka* a commonly emanated--and in this sense "projected"--external world? Or does "universal *karma*" act on its own, independently from the individuals who share its "seeding" effects? If it were so, then the Universal Force would not be acting from "within us," but from "without us," this making such a Force into a transcendent Prime Mover, similar to the Aristotelian God. Nothing would be further from the non-theistic conception of *Hīnayāna* Buddhism. According to the *Kośa*:

> But how is the variety of the world of living beings (*sattva-loka*) and of the "receptacle-world" (*bhājana-loka*)created? It is not by God (*Īśvara*) that it is created intelligently (*buddhi-pūrvaka*). The variety of the world is born from *KARMA* (*karmajaṃ lokavaicitryaṃ*)[40]

Thus the external "creation-projection" of the world remains a mystery. Judging from the contextual manner of speaking of both the canonical and commentarial sources--including Vasubandhu--it seems that there is no way for conceiving the creation of the external world except as a creation "from within us" and not "from without us." Universal karma is also our karma, universally and collectively shared, and cannot be extricated from the warps of our intrinsic karmic mechanism. It seems plausible that the external world-creation, even in the realistic trends of Hīnayāna Buddhism (like in the Sarvāstivāda), has to be conceived as the result of a true maturation and a real fruition of karma. In consequence, no solution is relinquished other than the "projection" idea of a "from within" production of the external world.

If this is the case, a similitude between the notion of world-creation as propounded by the Hindu Sāṃkhyas and the Sarvāstivādins comes to the fore. According to the Sāṃkhya-Yoga, as propounded by Vijñānabhikṣu and Patañjali, the world-object is posterior in the order of evolution to the development of the individual liṅga or "subtle body" of the sentient being. This latter comes to be through the ever changing combinations of the three guṇas or "qualitative" components of the material nature (prakṛti): The guṇa of sattva to bring about the mind (buddhi) and sense-organs, the guṇa of rajas to bring about the organs of motion, and the guṇa of tamas to bring about the constitution of gross matter. The external world (which the Sāṃkhyas consider as "real" and not "māyā-made) is conceived as ontologically (and not merely mentally) evolving from all the individual liṅgas or "subtle bodies" of sentient beings, all at once and simultaneously, throughout all ages and generations. The Sarvāstivāda-conception of the world (bhājana-loka) as the result of a "karmic maturation" and "universal fruition" does not seem to be far from this Sāṃkhya position.[41]

One thing has to be heavily emphasized: Universal karma is a creative action which transcends each individual being as such, but has to be conceived as intrinsically immanent to the whole élan vital that constitutes the whole organic life of the universe.

Although establishing "supreme" acts (*adhipati-karma*) which are beyond the control of the individual being (and which thus escape the doings of the *vipāka-hetu*), the universal or all-controlling FORCE (*adhipati-bala*) is still immanent to the whole realm of the sentient and living beings. It acts, operates and functions *exclusively through it*. What is then the ultimate and intrinsic character of this universal *karma* which we all share? How does it bring to fruition effects which are infinitely removed from the causative range of the individual process of retribution? How is the creation or manifestation of such a vast Universe attributed to it? These are--so far--unanswered questions with regard to the mysterious and all-pervading force which early Buddhism postulates as an intrisic companion to our individual, and thus morally, non-transferable acts of *karma*; for the contribution that universal *karma* offers to our existence extends far beyond the mere fruits of retribution caused by our individual acts. In point of fact, the universal *karma* provides us with the vastness beyond comprehension of a commonly shared stage for such a retribution. The creation of this vast stage has been reserved by most other philosophers (including the *Bhakti-vedāntins* and the later *Sāṃkhyas*) to the work of Infinity, and hence to the doings of the Divine.

At any rate this universal *adhipati*-force of Buddhism is not a novel philosophical happening in the world of Indian thought. The *māyā-vedāntins* of unqualified monism (*aviśiṣṭādvaita*), rooted in the Upanishadic tradition of creation by *māyā*, postulated also a Universal Force that brings about illusory "adjuncts" or limitations (*upādhi*) and a "mirage-like" superimposition (*adhyāropa*) upon the undifferentiated nature of the *nirguṇa-brahman*.[42] This Force has always been acknowledged to be ultimately unknown (*adṛṣṭam*) and unsurpassed (*apūrvam*) in the order of relativity. Here in early Buddhism its pervasiveness and immanent presence throughout the whole process of universal life makes it reminiscent of the Bergsonian *élan vital*. Never transcendent to the whole flux of biological existence, its operations constitute a creation-process *from within*, a creation of a non-living world which appears *as without*, and thus--as said before--as outwardly projected from the *karma*-core of the sentient beings. Theodore Stcherbatsky was fascinated by the Bergsonian redolence of such a universal force of *karma*:

> In the *Abhidharmakośa*, IX, the term *vāsanā* is used identically with *bhāvanā* as a designation of the universal Force which propels life. We have accordingly tried to render it by the Bergsonian *élan vital*, since it seems to possess some of its connotations. . . . It is thus an internal, spiritual force creating the illusion of this external world and might be called the Force of Transcendental Illusion, similar to the *māyā* of the Vedāntins.[43]

However, Stcherbatsky commits--I believe--several mistakes in his effort to determine somehow the otherwise mysterious nature of this universal Force. First of all he takes the terms *vāsanā* and *bhāvanā* to be totally identical and synonymous. Contrary to this assumption, the different connotations attributed by Vasubandhu and his commentators to these two terms are clearly stated in both the *Abhidharmakośa* and in the *Vijñaptimātratā-siddhi*. The latter work expounds the main tenets of Vasubandhu's idealistic theories which were, after all, very much rooted in the original doctrines of his Hīnayānist *Kośa*. *Bhāvanā* is always taken to mean the "active permeation" of seeds as the primary effect ensuing from *karma*, both individual and universal. *Vāsanā*, however, is identical with karmic seeds (*bījas*) themselves and thus reflects rather the passive sense of the accumulated "perfumes," or the passive *saṃskāras* (potential forces) resulting from the act of "perfuming" or "impregnating" which is *bhāvanā*.[44] Although in the *Abhidharmakośa* this term is used also to designate the impregnation of "perfumes" or "seeds" by individual *karma* (like in the case of the term *bhāvanā-mārga*, or "path of the *mind-perfuming-acts* of meditation and contemplation"), in the *Vijñaptimātratasiddhi* the term *bhāvanā* becomes totally universalized as the impregnation of "common" seeds performed by the universal *adhipati*-Force upon the one mental recipient and individual "depository" of karmic potentials. In Buddhist idealism this "one, mental" depository is called the ālaya-vijñāna, or individual "storehouse of consciousness."[45]

Thus bhāvanā becomes the universal act of "impregnation" whereby the adhipati-Force exerts its sabhāga (formal or homogeneous) and kāraṇa (efficient) forms of causation. Vāsanā, however, designates the remaining trail of this universal impregnation as passively pervading "perfumes," ready to re-exhalate at a point in the future. In fact, the Vijñaptimātratāsiddhi prefers the use of the term bījas ("seeds") when referring to the passive result of the causal "fertilization" or impregnation by both sources of karma, the individual and the universal. Thus the seeds ensuing from universal karma are called sa-ādhāraṇa-bījas (common or universal seeds), whereas the ones ensuing from individual karma--as subjected to the vipāka-causality of "heterogeneous" maturation--are referred to as an-ādhāraṇa-bījas or "non-common," individual seeds.[46]

Therefore, Stcherbatsky's error is twofold, first in that he mistakes the term vāsanā for bhāvanā, and second in that he takes the term bhāvanā as the Abhidharmakośa's designation of the adhipati-bala (i.e., the collective Force of Karma). For in the Kośa the term bhāvanā, as we said, refers only to the active "suffusion" of "perfumes"--or active impregnation of "seeds"--as this "suffusion" ensues from any kind of karma, whether it be universal or individual.

Furthermore, Stcherbatsky defines the universal Force of Karma (adhipati-bala) as a "Transcendental Force of Illusion," thus completely assimilating this Force to the māyā of the Vedāntins. This assimilation can be made within the idealist framework of the later Vasubandhu, as transmitted to us by the Vijñaptimātratā-siddhi, but applies in no way to the Hīnayānist doctrines expounded by the Abhidharmakośa along the lines of the Sarvāstivāda and Sautrāntika schools. According to these schools the external World is not an illusion, or phantom-like appearance created by a māyā-force. The bhājana-loka ("world-receptacle") has a reality of its own which is independent from the mind. Although it ensues from the universal "seeds" implanted within us by universal *karma*, and thus comes about as a pro-jection emanating from *within us*, this pro-jection is material and physical, and not a merely mental and phantasmagorical one. The external world, our external bodies alike, is conceived by the *Hīnayāna* philosophers as constituted by real and entitatively existing *dravya-dharmas* of materiality. The objects of the external world are made up of the four *mahābhūtas* (four elements), combining into the material *viṣayas* in order to affect physically and to stimulate our materially constituted sense-organs. The illusion resides therefore *not* in the mistaking of a phantom-world for a real one, but in the false apprehension of it as a permanent and self-abiding substance. For the external world participates of the same marks of *anicca* (impermanence) and *anatta* (no-self-ness) proper to our flowing and fleeing consciousness of it. Hence the Universal Force is only indirectly responsible for the illusion of permanent substantiality that we falsely attribute to both our own existence, and the existence of the external world.

Perhaps Schopenhauer's conception came closest to this Buddhist notion. For the Universal Force can only be conceived as a universal act of WILL (KARMA) which summons and conjures into "momentary" manifestation the "*quantum*-like" aggregates of the *dharmas*. It does project them momentarily upon the absolute screen of *ākāśa* or space. But it really projects them and not just their shadows. Thus the illusion of a permanent and substantial existence--in both its subjective and objective aspects--has to be totally differentiated from the *māyā*-illusion propounded by the *māyā-vedāntins* and--similarly--by the Buddhist idealists.

All the same, and in spite of Stcherbatsky's terminological confusion, this world-creating Force still remains an impenetrable mystery in all instances, whether it be the case of "universal *karma*" as fathomed by the *Hīnayānists*, or it be the "*Māyā*-force" propounded--also in different forms--by the Buddhist *Vijñānavādins* and by the Hindu *māyā-Vedāntins*. Its mystery lies in the fact that this "world-creating" Force is not conceived as ultimately exerted and led by an absolute Power. This is not meant to entail that the conception of an absolute Power as involved in the notion of a transcendent and personal God is free from logical conundrums. It is precisely by the exclusive absolutization or thorough relativization of this "world-creating Force" that the dangerous "rock of Scylla and the currents of Caribdis" emerge over the stormy seas of rationalism.

In the Hīnayānist and early Mahāyānist (Vijñānavāda) framework, the universal karma which is ultimately responsible for world-creation or world-projection is a thoroughly relative Force embedded in the restless flux of existence.[47] The "Absolute" is understood as diametrically opposed to all kinds of action (karma) and sources of action. Only the three asaṃskṛta-dharmas, to be discussed in the third Part, constitute the realm of total Unconditionality. Among them perfect nirvāṇa represents the total stoppage of action. It is from action that all unrest (araṇa) and suffering (duḥkha) arises. Hence, although universally acting and universally manifesting itself, the adhipati-bala or "all-controlling" Force is throughout relative, its activity being a correlate of the individually intransferable and multitudinous acts of individual karma. This correlation to individual karma makes the relativity of the "all-controlling" Force into a circular one, for there is no individul karma without universal KARMA, but, by the same token, there cannot be universal KARMA without individual karma. In consequence, there is no "universe" without "retribution" and there is no "retribution" without a "universe." "Universe" and "retribution" are essentially coexistent (sahabhū) in that the one cannot be without the other, like a North pole cannot be without a South pole and vice versa. And in spite of this--and here the knot of the mystery tightens--universal KARMA is not just the sum total of all the acts of individual karma, for there is always something in the whole as such that is not equal to the sum total of its parts, and thus--somehow--transcends them. Karma's opposition to the absolute QUIET of the Unconditioned makes both its aspects (individual and universal) belong to the sphere of sheer relativity. Thus universal karma is often associated with universal Ignorance (avidyā). The reference to universal karma as to the "Winds of Ignorance," or the "Winds of

Objectivity," are particularly frequent among the works of the *Vijñanavādins*, and in such advanced *Mahāyāna* philosophical *sūtras* as the *Laṅkāvatāra*.[48] These "Winds of Ignorance" are a clear reminder of the Hindu *māyā-force* which brings about the waves of worldly existence upon the ever underlying essence of the *nirguṇa-* (or undifferentiated-*aviśeṣa-*) *Brahman*. Thus also in *Mahāyāna* Buddhist Idealism the "Winds of Ignorance" affect the quiet essence of the universal and supra-spiritual substratum of reality which is designated as *Tathatā* (or Suchness).[49] The "Winds of Ignorance" are the *élan vital* which, in the words of the *Laṅkāvatārasūtra*, produces the waves of objective and worldly manifestation from within the "storehouse of consciousness" (*ālaya-vijñāna*). These "Winds of Ignorance" are synonymous with the universal Force (*adhipati-bala* or *adhipati-bhāvanā*) which impregnates with "universal seeds" our mental receiver and one depository of all karmic "seeds" that is the *ālaya-vijñāna*, for this is the notion which replaces, in early *Mahāyāna* idealism, the dualistic accumulators of passive *karma* of the *Sarvāstivādins* which have been designated as *avijñapti-rūpa* and *citta*. *Nirvāṇa* is nothing but the HALT to the blowing of such world- and existence-generating winds; for this is the literal meaning of the term *nirvāṇa* as the "no-blowing" of karmic winds.

This conception of the Absolute, as totally irrespective to "action" and the very sources of "action," drives the notion of universal *karma* into a logical dead-end. Thus, while a mystery veiled for us the thorough comprehension of the doings of the *vipāka-hetu* (as *heterogeneous*-maturation), another mystery conceals the ultimate essence and origin of "craving" as a source of "suffering." This mysteriousness covers its Wherefrom, its Whereto and its sheer WHY. We were told that the understanding of the reasons why actions--as individual--produce such and such fruits of retribution, was reserved for the Buddhas.[50] Does the total and thorough comprehension of the mystery of universal Action--as "world-generating"--belong also to the domain of the Buddhas? No final answer is provided by the philosophical systems of Buddhist thought as developed from Indian sources. However, the Chinese interpretations of the nature of action will change this picture of mysteriousness. The totalistic schools of Buddhism, as crystalizing in the theoretical schools of T'ien-t'ai and Hua-Yen, and in the practical schools of esoteric, mantric and Ch'an (ZEN) Buddhism, will not acquiesce to the idea that the notion of universal karma is to be left alone, as hiding hopelessly behind the clouds of mystery.

This does not mean that Action will be absolutized in the Judeo-Christian manner. In the view of Buddhism the Universe-creating Action will never be the instrument of Absolute Being, as this still opposes the realm of the Relative. For if the mysterious adhipati-Force of the Sarvāstivādins and Vijñānavādins was nothing more than the Scylla lurking from behind the vast accomplishments of Indian philosophy, the Western notion of God's creatio ad extra might be nothing less than the Carybdis which the real Middle Way wants also to avoid. And there is nothing more Buddhist than the Middle Way (madhyamaka) which has been, from the very outset, at the core of the Suttas-teaching. The philosophers of Buddhism, however, have to grope their way towards Truth by crashing their minds against the rocky blocks of our mental categories, to and fro, back and forth, up towards the summit of "comprehensiveness."

The conceptual separation between the notions of Unity and Plurality, Identity and Difference, Knowledge and Ignorance, Absoluteness and Relativity, turns most systems of philosophy into mental "short blankets," good enough to cover in some cases the head of the issue, in others the tail of it, but never both. Either world-creation is thought of as the action of an Absolute which--or who--draws a whole Relative universe out of the Nothing which It is not, and then we have a problem in comprehending the ultimate purpose of the flaws and pervading ill-effects of its finished product; or the world-creating action is thoroughly relativized and made into the whim of a blind and frustrated WILL TO BE; and in this case we find it impossible to account for the supra-intelligence encrusted within the complex texture of its organic functions. Buddhism will not be contented with the "short blanket," and will try to outgrow the sense of security it gave to its early philosophers. In point of fact, the consideration of "creative action" as WILL already harbors the implicit roots of further philosophical development; these roots are already present in the profound intuitions of the Abhidhamma. Although there is only one Buddhism, this one appears historically as in continuous growth, through the rich spectrum of many self-integrating facets.

From the very outset the purpose of this book has been to delve into the significant accomplishments of Early Buddhist Philosophy. My work The Philosophy of Buddhism: A "Totalistic" Synthesis[51] offers the overall picture of Buddhism, as this "total" picture makes sense of every piece of the jigsawpuzzle that it appears to be. Within the scope of this work, the doctrine that individual action entails "suffering" is to be preserved as utterly Buddhist. This doctrine, together with the doctrines of impermanence and insubstantiality, is ever to be preserved even if deconstructed and synthesized with its opposites through the views of dialectical "complementarity." The "total" surpassing of opposites still will be the goal of self-accomplishing and self-determining Freedom of Being and Freedom in Wisdom.

With this consideration in mind, and an invitation to the further study of the Buddhist Totality, we shall proceed to the discussion of the philosophical conceptions drawn from the third and fourth of the Noble Truths: The Truth of the Cessation of Suffering.

PART III

DUḤKHA-NIRODHA (The Cessation of Suffering) and the Path to Nirvāṇa

Katamañ ca bhikkhave dukkha-nirodhaṃ ariya-saccaṃ? Yo tassā yeva taṇhāya asesa-virāga-nirodho cāgo patinissaggo mutti anālayo . . . . Idaṃ vuccati bhikkhave dukkha-nirodhaṃ ariya-saccaṃ.

Katamañ ca bhikkhave dukkha-nirodha-gāminī-paṭipadā ariya-saccaṃ? Ayam eva Ariyo Aṭṭhaṅgiko Maggo, seyyathīdaṃ sammādiṭṭhi sammā-saṃkappo sammā-vācā sammā-kammanto sammā-ājīvo sammā-vāyāmo sammā-sati sammā-samādhi.

"What, O monks, is the Noble Truth of the Cessation of Ill? The utter fading away and cessation of that very craving, leaving it, giving it up, the being delivered from, the doing away with it . . . . Such is said, O monks, to be the Noble Truth of the Cessation of Suffering."

"What, O monks, is the Path leading to the Cessation of Ill? It is the Noble Eightfold Path of Right View, Right Thought, Right Speech, Right Action, Right Livelihood, Right Exertion, Right Mindfulness and Right Concentration."

Dīgha-nikāya II, 310-313

Chapter 1

The Three Absolute or Non-conditioned Dharmas: Ākāśa (space) and the two nirodhas (cessations). The Buddhist notion of Space (ākāśa) as non-conditioned dharma. Absolute and relative space.

As opposed to the notion of relative or "conditioned" (saṃskṛta) dharmas, the Buddhist notion of absoluteness is far from reflecting the concept of a divine supreme being, the creator or primal cause of the individual existence and its world. As already explained in our treatment of causation, the origination of individual existence and the world that "receives" or "holds" it (bhājana-loka) is due to KARMA understood both as individual and as universal action.

Contrary to possible expectation on the part of the reader, early Buddhist philosophy thinks of Absoluteness in terms of "vacuity" and "negativity." Vacuity is thought of primarily as absolute Space, i.e., the immutable and eternal medium for the manifestation of the relative or saṃskṛta-dharmas. As a "state," the notion of Absoluteness is negatively expressed and represented by two kinds of "cessation" or "extinction" (nirodha). In spite of their semantic negativity the two nirodhas or cessations connote--although indirectly--two ineffable, primordial and ultimate states of Reality. The first of the nirodhas presuposes--according to the Sarvāstivādins--an absolute and primordial state of potentiality from which the noumenal and latent giveness of the dharmas (svabhāva-dharmas) are projected from the future into the momentary manifestation (kṣaṇika-lakṣaṇa-dharma) of the present wherein the dharmas appear in serial and quantum-like interrelations. The second of the nirodhas connotes the ultimate and final state of extinguished individuality as this constitutes the ultimate goal of the ārya or saint, namely the state of nirvāṇa. In spite of the negative overtones of this state as "extinction of individuality," this ultimate state is far from representing a mere nihilation of existence, and is rather a resolution of the latter into a horizon of causelessness and total extrication from the warps of karmic origination.

Thus the Buddhist notion of absoluteness is marked by the triad of the asaṃskṛta-dharmas: ākāśa (or space), the apratisaṃkhyā-nirodha (or cessation without the intervention of wisdom-knowledge) and the pratisaṃkhyā-nirodha (or cessation through wisdom-knowledge). This latter carries out the gradual "disjunction" (visaṃyoga) from the chains of origination that culminates in nirvāṇa. How the second asaṃskrta or first nirodha (extinction without the intervention of knowledge) implies a perpetual state of "dharmic" potentiality will be explained in Chapter 2. How it may support the goals of the second nirodha (cessation through knowledge) and thus indirectly contribute to the realization of nirvāṇa will be explained in the third and final Chapter.

As evidenced by the fact of its inclusion as an "absolute" (saṃskṛta-) dharma on its own right, space (ākāśa) is separated--contrary to Hindu tradition--from the four fundamental elements or mahābhūtas which were established as earth, water, fire, and air (as these represent the forces of Repulsion, Attraction, Heat and Motion). As we saw in Part I, these mahābhūtas constitute the basis for the material constitution of the rūpa-dharmas, i.e., the first of the skandhas.[1] According to the Sāṃkhyas and Vedāntins, the fundamental elements are given--similarly to the presocratics--in the number 5, with the inclusion of space or aether (ākāśa) as the first of them, the rest being air, fire, water, and earth. Given the particular significance and nature of space, the Buddhists take this element aside from the sub-atomic elements of materiality and constitute it into the absolute medium of "dharmic" manifestation. According to Buddhism, in spite of its apparent negativity as vacuity, space (ākāśa) is given the positive attribute of causal effectiveness. In point of fact, ākāśa is considered a kāraṇa-hetu (co-efficient causality) by virtue of its intrinsic "non-hindrance" or "non-impeding" character for the manifestation of the material (rūpāṇi-) dharmas. According to the Abhidharmakośa, "space is everywhere unclosed (or unimpeding) . . ." (tatrākāśam anāvṛtiḥ . . .).[2] This "non-hindrance" (avighna) nature of space is thus considered to offer a positive causal contribution to the momentary actualization of the rūpa-dharmas. Ākāśa proximately co-effects (with KARMA) the fruits of efficient causation and thus is given, together with universal *karma*, the title of *kāraṇa-hetu* of materiality. Thus *ākāśa* becomes a primary root-condition of the elements of materiality.

In this sense, the universal and comprehensive notion of *ākāśa* as absolute space is to be distinguished from the relative aspects of space (or spatial circumscription) as effected on its turn by "empty" material objects such as a jar, a bottle, a box, etc. This relative aspect of "circumscribed" or "delimited" space is given the name of *ākāśa-dhātu* as it depends on the contingent presence of material elements effecting such a delimitation.[3] Hence, whilst *ākāśa* "plain and simple" is--in its primordial infinity--an absolute condition for the origination of material elements, the *ākāśa-dhātu*--as constricted space--is the effect of such material elements themselves. Therefore, *ākāśa-dhātu* shares the relativity of the very elements of materiality which bring it about.

A further significance of *ākāśa* as a "non-conditioned" *dharma* derives from its association with the Path to the ultimate *nirodha* (extinction) or *nirvāṇa*. As will be seen in Chapter 3, space will become the object of "formless" (*ārūpya-*) concentration of the mind in the latter's ascent toward its final purification and deliverance. Thus it will constitute the *ākāśa-bhūmi*, as one of the levels of "formless" consciousness in the higher states of mind-concentration. In this state the *ārya* or saint becomes absorbed into the open and indeterminate (formless, *ārūpya*) nature of infinite space, once he has drained his consciousness from the last remnants of material perception. Hence space is considered also a "con-cause" of the states of mind which realize infinite expansion beyond the "realm of materiality" (*rūpa-dhātu*) as to enter into the "realm of immateriality and formlessness" (*ārūpya-dhātu*). These formless states of consciousness are directed towards the setting of the final condition for the realization of the two wisdom-knowledges (*kṣaya-* and *anutpāda-jñāna*) which precede the total extinction of individual existence. Thus *ākāśa* is intimately connected--as will be seen below--with the two *nirodhas*, i.e., the second and the third of the *asaṃskṛta-dharmas*, namely, the *apratisaṃkyā-* and the *pratisaṃkhyā-nirodha*.

As will be seen in subsequent chapters, the *pratisaṃkhyā-nirodha* (or cessation through the intervention of acts of spiritual knowledge) will directly constitute the total transcendence, overcoming, and final cessation of all the *saṃskṛta-dharmas* as constituents of an individual existence. However, the *asaṃskṛta-dharmas* of space (or *ākāśa*) and the *apratisaṃkhyānirodha* (or cessation which takes place without the intervention of acts of spiritual knowledge) will indirectly contribute to the gradual realization of cessation, but not to the ultimate extinction into *nirvāṇa* which is not possible without the intervention of the *jñānas* or "wisdom-knowledges." The next chapter will be dedicated to further definition, elucidation and contrasting of these two *nirodhas* (cessations).

Chapter 2

Asaṃskṛta-dharmas or "non-conditioned factors" (continued). The two *nirodhas*: *apratisaṃkhyā-nirodha* (cessation without the intervention of wisdom-knowledge) and the *pratisaṃkhyā-nirodha* (cessation through wisdom-knowledge).

The two *nirodhas*--considered as states--constitute the second and third of the "non-conditioned" (*asaṃskṛta-*) *dharmas*. In this chapter we shall define, discuss and contrast the nature of these two "extinctions" or "cessations." In Chapter 3 we shall explain their role within the Path toward ultimate *nirvāṇa*. Let us first concentrate on the nature of the *apratisaṃkhyā-nirodha*, i.e., the state of cessation which follows from acts other than the achievement of spiritual knowledge (*pratisaṃkhyā* = through knowledge).

1. The *apratisaṃkhyā-nirodha*.

Literally this term means the "non-knowledge cessation," or as already stated, the "cessation" which takes place without the intervention of acts of spiritual wisdom-knowledge. The *Abhidharmakośa* classifies this *nirodha* as the third of the *asaṃskṛtas*. Our treatment of it in the second place instead of the third is for didactic reasons. The *kośa* primarily defines it as:

> that suppression . . . . which consists in the absolute obstruction of the origination of (certain) future dharmas . . . . (*utpādātyantavighno'nyo nirodho'pratisaṃkhyayā* . . . . .) It is called *apratisaṃkhyā* because it is attained not by the comprehension of the (noble) truths, but because of the insufficiency of the origination-causes (*pratyayavaikalyāt*).[4]

This *nirodha* has been understood (and misunderstood) in more than one way. One of the early misunderstandings was propounded by the *Mahāsaṃghikas* who mistook it for the universal extinction of the momentary *dharmas*, which as such exist only for the moment (*kṣaṇa*) of their manifestation in the present.[5]

This general extinction to which all the *saṃskṛta-dharmas* are subject constitutes a general law in early Buddhist philosophy. This law is formulated as *kṣaṇikavāda* (momentariness); in its negative connotation of necessary extinction after the moment of "appearance" is called *anityatānirodha* or "extinction which is due to the law of impermanence." The *apratisaṃkhyā-nirodha*, as one of the *asaṃskṛta-dharmas*, has nothing to do with this general law of "dharmic" extinction. The *nirodha* in question refers rather to the "obstruction" (*vighna*) of the very appearance of certain aggregations of *dharmas* belonging to the serial "dharmic" stream of a particular individual existence. Thus, these *dharmas* are prevented from manifesting themselves either by the absence or by the suppression of the causes which otherwise would have brought them into manifestation. This "absence" or "suppression" of the causes of their manifestation either takes place spontaneously or is brought about by certain acts other than wisdom-knowledge.

According to the *Kośa*, this "obstruction" of dharmic manifestations is therefore understood in two different ways:

A) An obstruction (*vighna*) of *dharmas* which disappear *from a marginal or potential present into the past*. This obstruction or impediment of certain *dharmas* from a potential present into the past occurs spontaneously, not only without the intervention of spiritual knowledge (*pratisaṃkhyā*) but also without the intervention of the will. Hence this non-manifestation is totally spontaneous and occurs continuously within the normal range and field of consciousness. Thus the *Kośa* says:

> For example, whilst the organs of sight and of the mind are occupied with a certain visible object, such *dharmas* as sounds, odors, and tactile impressions pass from a potential present into the past . . . . This occurs on account of the lack of the causal conditions for their origination.[6]

When I look at an orange from a distance and go away without eating it, the possible *dharmas* of its fragrance, taste and tactile impressions go from a potential present into the past--the causal conditions for the manifestation of such possible *dharmas* were never made to concur. This holds as well for the manifestation of the visual *rūpas* of a clock whose "tick-tock" sound I hear behind me without turning to look at it. This obstruction (*vighna*) affects, then, sets of *dharmas* which reach the limits of the marginal present without their ever making it into the actual field of awareness. Such a suppression of *dharmas* is the first understanding of the *apratisaṃkhyā-nirodha* in the view of the *Sarvāstivādins*. Its nature from the point of view of moral quality, moral involvement, and karmic retribution is *per se* neutral and inconsequential. Keith, who confined his understanding of the *apratisaṃkhyā-nirodha* to this first notion of "dharmic prevention," stated that this *nirodha* is of "slight importance."[7] A blundering statement from a scholar of no small caliber, for nothing can be further from the truth. Keith's statement does not only disregard the extensive relevance that the second notion of *apratisaṃkhyā-nirodha* will have in regard to the practice of the Path; Keith also neglects the fact that even this apparently irrelevant and neutral understanding of this *nirodha*, as spontaneous "extinction" of marginal *dharmas* from the present to the past, presupposes--at least according to the *Sarvāstivādins*--an extraordinary factor in the explanation of reality as "momentary manifestation." This factor is an abiding "state of potentiality" from which the *dharmas* come into the present and whereto the *dharmas* of the present go into the past. According to the *Sarvāstivādins* the law of karmic retribution which is based on a reaction in the future of acts which are somehow recorded in the past, demands a latent state of potentiality. In this state all conditioned *dharmas* abide potentially as *svabhāva-dharmas* (noumenal *dharmas*) in a status different from their actual phenomenal manifestation in the present (*svalakṣaṇa-dharmas*) which is "momentary."[8] The potential and latent availability of the *dharmas* is ever abiding and perpetual and allows for the assertion that not only the present moment of time exists, but also the future and the past. It is only in this sense that the *Sarvāstivādins could account for the reactibility of the past upon the future. Hence the mere neutral passing from a possible or marginal present moment into the past also presupposes this "state of potentiality" which is positively, albeit indirectly, connoted by the apratisaṃkhyā-nirodha* understood in its primary sense.

This "state of potentiality" is not of slight importance, even if negated by the *Sautrāntikas* who, in their metaphysics of "economy," rejected also the givenness of this *nirodha* as non-conditioned *dharma*.

B) The second understanding of this *nirodha*, far from being insignificant, is, according to the *Kośa*, of the utmost relevance in conjunction with the practice of the Path, and thus also in conjunction with acts of the will. Some exponents of Buddhist thought are given to think of this *nirodha* as an extinction which occurs without an act of knowledge and without the intervention of the will, "just like the fire which extinguishes itself by the lack of fuel." These authors apparently failed to investigate the vast role attributed explicitly and implicitly to this *nirodha* in regard to the "obstruction" of *dharmas* destined to appear *from the future into the present*. This "obstruction" consists in the "prevention" or "shunning" of rebirths in lower levels of existence, such as conceptions in the animal matrices, or births in the hells, or as *pretas* (hungry spirits) etc. The avoidance of these rebirths in lower existences is attributed to the neutralization of unwholesome karmic deposits as effected by the performance of such wholesome acts of *karma* which are still unrelated to the exercise of spiritual knowledge (*pratisaṃkhyā*). Thus, the *apratisaṃkhyā-nirodha*, understood as the "obstruction" of *dharmas* *from the future into the present*, is different from the first understanding of *this nirodha* as a "prevention" of *dharmas* *from the present into the past*. This latter "failure to appear" occurs spontaneously and without the intervention of the will and is somehow comparable to the extinction of fire due to the exhaustion of fuel. However, the extinction of *dharmas* *from the future into the present* as the negative result of acts which are suppressive of evil karmic deposits does not occur without the intervention of the will, even if they certainly occur without the intervention of the "still-to-be-achieved" wisdom-knowledge of the Path (*jñānas*, *parijñās*).

The *Sthaviras* (*Theravādins*) already propounded--prior to the *Sarvāstivādins*--the givenness of the *apratisaṃkhyā-nirodha* as "the future non-origination of ill, namely, of certain punitive existences, by reason of the disappearance of the passions (*anuśayas*), and[9] not directly by reason of spiritual knowledge." Chapters II, VI and VIII of the *Kośa* are pervaded by mentions of the apratisaṃkhyā-nirodha in this second and more significant way. In Chapter VI, 23 b, the Kośa propounds the doctrine of the Sarvāstivādins (as recorded in the Vibhāṣā, 32, 9) according to which by the exercise of the kṣāntis (or "patiences," i.e., the acts of faith and right exertion which are "receptive" of knowledge, but which do not yet constitute the acquisition of the knowledges or jñānas) "one avoids or obstructs evil destinations" (kṣāntilābhy anapāyagah):

> For those who attain the kṣāntis, certain ill destinies are prevented through the entrance in the condition of non-origination of dharmas (anutpattidharmatā) as the apratisaṃkhyā-nirodha of such evil destinies in animal matrices, lower corporeal forms, being born among the two species of eunuchs, or among androgynous beings . . . . The exercise of the kṣāntis (prior to the exercise of the jñānas or parijñās = spiritual knowledge) can even prevent certain good destinies such as being reborn as mahābrahmās or asaṃjñi-sattvas (thus expediting the final realization of nirvāṇa by the proper acts of knowledge) . . . . This abandon (vihāna) by obstruction (vighna) of certain future destinies takes place in relation to the degree of the patience (kṣānti) . . . .[10]

Thus both the Theravādins and the Sarvāstivādins advocate the possibility of progress along the Path as a result of the realization of the apratisaṃkhyā-nirodha by the way of the kṣāntis or "patiences." These kṣāntis prepare the way to the attainment of the jñanas or knowledges, but are prior to the latter. They involve the exercise of wholesome karma. Hence, the implication is that the extensive exercise of wholesome karma which is not intrinsically motivated or pervaded by acts of already acquired wisdom-knowledge have not only the positive effect of a rewarding retribution as a happier future existence, but also--and prevalently--the negative effect of neutralizing the evil accumulations from past unwholesome deeds. Thus the exercise of the kṣāntis produce the "obstruction" (vighna) and "abandonment" (vihāṇi) of certain future ill destinies previously predetermined by such evil deposits. In point of fact the _Theravādins_ refer to the _apratisaṃkhyā-nirodha_ as the avoidance of evil destinies by the destruction of _anuśayas_ (passions) which are primarily understood as the "karma-formed" (_abhisaṃskṛta-_) germs or seeds (_bījas_, _vāsanās_) of future "suffering" retribution. These evil destinies are thought of as compounded by "expectant" _dharmas_ of the future--this is the reason why the _Sarvāstivādins_ maintain that the _dharmas_ of the future exist. If the proper causal conditions concur, then these _dharmas_ will come to manifestation; if the concurrence of the conditions does not take place (spontaneously) or is made not to take place (by the will) then such _dharmas_ of the future will not manifest themselves. In any of these cases, the _apratisaṃkhyā-nirodha_ is being realized as the "absolute non-appearance" of _dharmas_ or "obstruction" of dharmic manifestation by any acts _other than acts of knowledge_."

It must be further emphasized that the _apratisaṃkhyā-nirodha_ can refer to the extinction of pure (_anāsrava-_) _dharmas_ as much as it refers to the extinction of impure (_saāsrava-_) _dharmas_. It is obvious that the practice of the _kṣāntis_ (or "patiences" prior to the acquisition of knowledge) are acts which realize the _apratisaṃkhyā-nirodha_ of impure _dharmas_. It is in this sense that this _nirodha_ is meant to contribute to the advancement in the Path. But the "obstruction" or "cessation" of pure, wholesome _dharmas_ often constitutes the object of the _apratisaṃkhyā-nirodha_ as well. Thus, the mere "non-manifestation" of marginal _dharmas_ of the present on account of the spontaneous lack or absence of "manifestative" conditions affects _dharmas_ that can be either pure, impure, or neutral. In the _Kośa_ explicit reference is made also to the special case when a premature death is caused by extrinsic causes other than the determination by previous _karma_. This happens, for instance, in the case of suicide, or even death produced by accident or by the calculated exposure to life-perils and risks. In all these cases both the wholesome and unwholesome _dharmas_ of the rest of the thus interrupted existence are "obstructed" from coming into manifestation. Death which is produced by such acts represents therefore a further aspect of the _apratisaṃkhyā-nirodha_.[11] Finally, the _Kośa_ also makes mention of specific cases where only the "obstruction" of pure *dharmas* takes place. Such, for instance, is the case where a particular state of *samādhi* (or state of high concentration) in an upper level of consciousness is interrupted by a "relapse" (*parihāṇi*) into a lower level.[12] Here the further manifestation of pure *dharmas* as constitutive of such states of *samādhi* is also being "obstructed" by the relapse into the lower level. It is then also proper to assert that in this case the *apratisaṃkhyā-nirodha* of such a *samādhi* has taken place. The possibility of obstruction of both pure and impure *dharmas* is considered a major difference between the *aprati-* and the *pratisaṃkhyā-nirodha*. For this latter exclusively represents the extinction of impure *dharmas*.

2. The *pratisaṃkhyā-nirodha*.

As already mentioned, this is the state of extinction or cessation (*nirodha*) which takes place through acts of "wisdom-knowledge" (*jñāna*, *parijñā*, *prajñā*). Thus, the *pratisaṃkhyā-nirodha* is the result or "fruition" due to the achievement of the *jñānas* or knowledges of the truths. The objects of these "knowledges" are always the Four Noble Truths in that these must be thoroughly grasped as they apply to the three spheres of existence, namely, the *kāma-*, *rūpa-*, and *ārūpya-dhātus*. Hence the *jñānas* are divided into ten, eight of them obtaining the *pratisaṃkhyā-nirodha* of the *kāma-*, *rūpa-* and early stages of the *ārūpya-dhātus*, and the last two realizing the *pratisaṃkhyā-nirodha* of the last stage of the *ārūpya-dhātu*, thereby immediately securing the entrance into the state of complete *nirvāṇa*. These stages will be enumerated and described in the subsequent chapter on the Path.

It is obvious that this *nirodha*, as the result of the acquisition of the pure *jñānas* or "wisdom-knowledges," can refer only to the extinction or cessation of impure *dharmas*. This essential aspect of the *pratisaṃkhyā-nirodha* has already been emphasized. A further differentiation from the *apratisaṃkhyā-nirodha* is given, so to speak, in the way by which this *nirodha* is obtained as a result of such acts of knowledge. While the *apratisaṃkhyā-nirodha* is achieved by way of "obstruction" (*vighna*), the *pratisaṃkhyā-nirodha* is brought into fruition by way of "disjunction" (*visaṃyoga*). "Obstruction" or *vighna* is mainly understood in terms of the avoidance or prevention of certain future destinies, whether pure or impure. "Disjunction" or visaṃyoga, however, as the event leading to the pratisaṃkhyā-nirodha of a certain level of existence refers not to the prevention of a future status, but to the elimination of a present level of existence, this elimination (or nirodha) "securing" the progress to rebirth in a higher level. The apratisaṃkhyā-nirodha, through the "obstruction" of impure dharmas of the future, impedes the "relapse" (parihāṇi) into lower levels of existence.[13] This is all the apratisaṃkhyā-nirodha can do in terms of advancement and progress towards final emancipation, for avoiding or "obstructing" a relapse into a lower level does not secure per se the ascent into a higher level. In the lower level of the kāma-dhātu, such as hells, world of pretas, animals, etc. any advance toward rebirth in the upper levels of the kāma-dhātu, such as the world of humans, is always made possible by the "obstruction" (vighna) of impure dharmas and not by the "disjunction" (visaṃyoga) from impure dharmas. "Obstruction" merely allows, but does not secure, advancement. The possibility of "relapse" (parihāṇi) is always present. A human who has not yet obtained any of the jñānas has not yet secured either the final "disjunction" (visaṃyoga) from the level of existence in which he is. Through the pratisaṃkhyā-nirodha that follows the acquisition of a particular jñāna, certain total "disjunction" from a particular aspect of existence takes place. The final consecution of the first eight jñānas (as will be further explained in Chapter 3) will have secured the total "abandonment by knowledge" (prahāṇa-parijñā)[14] of the kāma-dhātu or "realm of desire," thus ensuring also rebirth in the purer levels of the rūpa-dhātu. Such an ārya who has secured such a higher state of existence is a "non-returner" (anāgāmin), also called a "non-relapser" (avaivartika, anivartya, or "one who does not slide or fall back"). The pratisaṃkhyā-nirodha as visaṃyoga (disjunction) finally and definitively produces, not only the moral detachment, but also the ontological severing of a particular individual from his actual level of existence and from the possibility of "relapse" into it.

It is also very important to note that the "abandonment" (prahāṇa) which is proper to the realization of the pratisaṃkhyā-nirodha (or "cessation through knowledge") follows a gradual ascent through a number of "disjunctions." Therefore--contrary to the apparent assumption by some authors--the *pratisaṃkhyā-nirodha* is far from being singular and equal to the final realization of complete *nirvāṇa*. Complete *nirvāṇa* is only the crown to a stage-wise realization of a sequence of *pratisaṃkhyā-nirodhas*, and therefore, of a sequence of *visaṃyogas* or "disjunctions." According to the *Abhidharmakośa*:

> Each one of the "disjunctions" taken apart is in itself a cessation through knowledge (*pratisaṃkhyā-nirodho yo visaṃyogaḥ pṛthak pṛthak*) . . . . It is to be understood that there is a single *pratisaṃkhyā-nirodha* of all the impure *dharmas* at once? By no means: each disjunction (*visaṃyoga*) taken in itself and apart from the others is *pratisaṃkhyā-nirodha*. The objects of the "disjunction" are as numerous as the objects of the "junctions" (*saṃyogadravya*). Hence, for each kind of "junction" (or destiny for rebirth) there is also a kind of "disjunction" . . . .[15]

The "abandonment" entailed by the avoidance or "obstruction" of a future state as *apratisaṃkhyā-nirodha* is thus called "*vihāṇi*," whereas the difinitive "abandonment" of a present state through the *visaṃyoga* or "disjunction" proper to the *pratisaṃkhyā-nirodha* is called the *prahāṇaparijñā* or "abandonment produced by the supreme knowledges." Thus, the knowledges or *jñānas* (*parijñās*) are the supreme conditions (*adhipatipratyaya*) for the gradual realization of the *pratisaṃkhyā-nirodha*. Every "disjunction" or stage of the *pratisaṃkhyā-nirodha* leaves behind an eternal blank in reference to the stage that has been thus definitively "abandoned." As the ascent through the series of "disjunctions" progresses, the eternal blank becomes more and more pervasive. In the last of the "disjunctions" the one remaining thread of existence is thus cut off and complete *nirvāṇa* is attained--the eternal blank of individual existence is totally realized as total "cessation" or *nirodha*. This is called the *nirupadhiśeṣa-nirvāṇa* (or *nirvāṇa* "without substratum or karmic adjuncts") which involves the total "non-origination of all passions and all suffering" (*sarvotpannānuśaya-janma-nirodha*).[16] At this point, this complete state of *nirvāṇa* (as the supreme *dharma*) takes the place of all the "abandonments," regardless of whether they were effected through the "obstructions" of the *apratisaṃkhyā-nirodha* or realized by the "disjunctions" of the *pratisaṃkhyā-nirodha*. But it is also stated that every "disjunction" in particular, together with the previous "obstructions" that might have been realized prior to it, carries with itself a true, though partial realization of *nirvāṇa*. Each stage of the Path in the realization of the "disjunctions" produces the fruition of a further and higher aspect of *nirvāṇa* until total and complete *nirvāṇa* is possessed as a result of the final "disjunction." Hence, the *nirvāṇa* which results from the sequence of partial "disjunctions" proper to each *pratisaṃkhyā-nirodha* is called *sopadhiśeṣa-nirvāṇa*, i.e., "*nirvāṇa* with residual adjuncts," or "*nirvāṇa* with residual karmic substratum," or again, "*nirvāṇa* with karmic remnants and attachments."[17] As long as the individual existence carries the seeds of *karma*, including wholesome *karma*, the inevitability of rebirth is not yet overcome. As we shall see, the acts of meditation and states of concentration resulting thereof are in themselves wholesome acts of *karma*. Under the sway of the knowledges the Path of meditation and contemplation (*bhāvanā-mārga*) will have as its fruition the gradual but irreversible neutralization of all karmic residues (or "adjuncts of attachment" = *upadhi*). The fruition of such purer karmic "seeds" as sown by acts of wisdom-knowledge consists therefore in the neutralization of already pre-stored lower "seeds" and in the stoppage (*nirodha*) of their fruition. Hence the direct fruition from the acts of concentration and contemplation is the stoppage of lower--even if good!--fruitions from previously stored karmic seeds not yet neutralized. It is in this sense that the *pratisaṃkhyā-nirodha* with its sequence of *visaṃyogas* or "disjunctions" is always considered--contrary to the *apratisaṃkhyā-nirodha*--to be a true fruition (*phala*) from the wholesome acts of meditation. Any partial realization of *nirvāṇa* is fruition, because the *visaṃyogas* entailed by it are also fruition. The *prahāṇas* or "abandonments" produced by the *visaṃyogas* are fruitions inasmuch as they result directly from the meritorious acquisitions of the *jñānas* or knowledges and the subsequent contemplation and meditation of the truths (*bhāvanā-mārga*). However, *nirvāṇa*, partial or complete, is considered a fruition from "meditative" karma in the sense that only its obtention, and not its creation, is effected by such acts of "abandonment" (prahāṇa) and "disjunction" (visaṃyoga). Nirvāṇa is eternal and absolute, and thus the pratisaṃkhyā-nirodha is only its "obtention" or "attainment," not its "creation" or causal "production." Nirvāṇa, therefore, is mere fruition (visaṃyoga-phala) from pure "meditative" acts, but not the causal effect (sahetuka-phala) of such acts.

Contrary to this conception of the pratisaṃkhyā-nirodha as a fruition sui generis deriving from knowledge (jñāna) the aprati-saṃkhyā-nirodha is never considered to be a proper fruition in any way.[18] The reason for this is that the apratisaṃkhyā-nirodha is merely a negative outcome deriving from the absence of causal conditions and is never intended in the acts by which it is attained. A good act of wholesome karma other than an act of knowledge might provide a rewarding retribution in a happier rebirth in the same plane of existence where such an act was posited. Through this positive retribution other evil retribution which was determined by the previous storage of evil or impure seeds has been averted or impeded. Hence, an apratisaṃkhyā-nirodha results as the negative outcome of some previous causes for evil retributions having been neutralized by new causes of good retribution. Thus, only the good retribution is the fruit (vipāka-phala) of a good or wholesome karmic act, not the negative outcome whereby an evil retribution has been, in this way, averted or "obstructed." Differently from this, every stage of visaṃyoga (disjunction) as "cessation brought about by knowledge" (pratisaṃkhyā-nirodha) is the direct result and intended outcome (although by "obtention" and not by "causation") of purer acts of the will under the sway of wisdom-knowledge. It is in this sense that nirvāṇa can be said to be an ultimate fruition, even if nirvāṇa is "uncaused" because "absolute" and "eternal."

Finally, as an important remark which affects the nature of the two "cessations" it must be emphasized that both the apratisaṃkhyā and the pratisaṃkhyā-nirodhas are "non-conditioned" (asaṃskṛta-, absolute) dharmas in that they are states of cessation, and thus should not be mistaken for the acts which bring us to their "obtention" or "possession." All the individual acts resulting in vihāṇi (abandonment through "obstruction" or vighna) or in prahāṇa (abandonment through "disjunction" or *visamyoga*) are of relative character. The "obstruction" proper to the *apratisaṃkhyā-nirodha* is indirectly realized by sheer acts of wholesome *karma* without the *jñanas* or knowledges. The "disjunction" proper to the *pratisaṃkhyā-nirodha* is directly intended and realized by acts of knowledge *per se*. All these acts bring about the possession of the *nirodhas*, either indirectly (not as a fruition) or directly (as a fruition). The first *nirodha* is possessed (*not created*) through acts of wholesome *karma* (without knowledge) and is the negative outcome of the fruition of such good *karma*: this fruition, as good, displaces--and thus "obstructs"--an evil fruition which otherwise would have taken place without the positing of such good acts. The second *nirodha* is possessed (*not created*) by acts of knowledge whose immediate and direct outcome is the effecting of "disjunction." Such acts of knowledge are also relative and hence *saṃskṛta* (created), whereas the state into whose possession we enter through them is an eternal, uncreated and non-produced (*asaṃskṛta*) *dharma*. By emphasizing this point we should resist the temptation to define the *nirodhas* as "acts of suppression." The *nirodhas* are not "acts" but "states," and it is only as "states" that they can be considered "non-conditioned" (*asaṃskṛta-*) *dharmas*. All acts are acts of *karma*, no matter how pure they might be. Thus, there is no such a thing as acts of "suppression" or "cessation." Cessation (*nirodha*) is a state whose possession can be made possible by such acts, but not effected as the causal product of such acts.

With the explanation and contrasting of the two *nirodhas* we bring to conclusion the second chapter on Cessation. In the following and final chapters we shall delve into the roles played by these two *asaṃskṛta-dharmas* as these are attained throughout the stages of the Path to Cessation, i.e., the last of the Four Noble Truths (*nirodha-mārga-ārya-satya*).

Chapter 3

The Path (*mārga*) to *Nirvāṇa* and the two Cessations (*nirodhas*).

The canonical basis for the interpretation of the Fourth Noble Truth, i.e., the "truth of the Path to the Cessation of Ill," was laid down in the Sermon of Benares as the celebrated *ārya-aṣṭāṅgika-mārga* or, the "Noble Eightfold Path." This "eight-membered" (*aṣṭāṅgika*) formulation of the Path has been cited twice in the present work, first in the Introduction as quoted from the *Saṃyutta-nikāya* and then again at the beginning of Part III as taken from the *Dīgha-nikāya*: "It is the Noble Eightfold Path of Right View, Right Thought, Right Speech, Right Action, Right Livelihood, Right Exertion, Right Mindfulness, and Right Concentration."[19]

The commentarial literature, however, does not view the Eight *aṅgas* as the exclusive formulation of the *mārga*, even if it sees it as the core of the latter. As a matter of fact the two *maggas* (*Vimutti-*, and *Visuddhi-magga*), the two *Vibhāṣās* and the *Kośa* relate to a plurality of *mārgas* as subordinate aspects of the universal Path. There is reference to the *laukika-mārga* or "mundane" Path[20] as the previous and preparatory exercise of wholesome acts by the *Pṛthagjana*-s or the "common people" who are still alien to the *saṃgha* (Buddhist community). The *Pṛthagjana*, and even the heretics themselves, might be induced either by intrinsic or extrinsic factors to the practice of wholesome deeds. These wholesome deeds would associate them with the *laukikāgra-dharmas* or "supreme mundane *dharmas*,"[21] the "purest" *dharmas* to be attained outside the discipline of the *saṃgha* and prior to the proper practice of the Eightfold Path. It is by the adherence to the *saṃgha* and through the practice of the Eight *aṅgas* that the *laukika-* or *prayoga-mārga* (mundane or preparative Path) is abandoned in favor of the entrance into the *lokottara-mārga* (supra-mundane Path).[22] By the entrance into this Path, the *Pṛthagjana* becomes a *srota-āpanna-ārya* (the "ascetic who has entered the stream" of the pure *dharmas*).[23] Such a beginner is also called a *śaikṣa*, a disciple or novice in the *saṃgha*.

The further practice of the eight aṅgas gradually turns the srota-āpanna-ārya into a full-fledged ārya or noble, saintly person. Ārya-hood, however, is far from constituting the final stage of purification. The ārya still is to become an anāgāmin or "one who does not return to the kāma-dhatu," but is reborn in the lower levels of the rūpa-dhātu to begin his ascent through the higher spheres of both the rūpa- and the ārūpya-dhātus.[24] The anāgāmin, however, (who is a "non-relapser" or avaivartika as far as the kāma-dhātu is concerned) has yet to reach the highest state of the arhat (or aśaikṣa) wherefrom ultimate and complete nirvāṇa is finally reached. This state of arhat (or arahant) is later partially assimilated to bodhisattva-hood, a final stage toward perfect buddha-hood which plays a pervasive role in the soteriology of Mahāyana Buddhism.

As corresponding to these diverse stages in the practice of the Path, the "Eight Aṅgas (members, "limbs" of the Path) are bifurcated and further subdivided in a number of specific subordinate mārgas or paths. Thus the practice of the first seven aṅgas will take the śaikṣa or ārya through the so-called darśana-mārga or "Path of seeing," which in its turn subdivides into the ānantarya- and the vimukti-mārgas.[25] The ānantarya-mārga will entail the practice of the "patiences" or kṣāntis, these latter constituting a sequence of eight states of "knowledge-receptivity," states which are prior to the consecution of the proper wisdom-knowledges or jñānas.[26] The term ānantarya given to this aspect of the Path connotes the character of "immediacy" (ānantatva) whereby the kṣāntis are causally followed by the jñānas. Whilst the kṣānti- practices throughout the ānantarya-mārga are preparatory to the attainment of the knowledges (jñānas), these latter constitute the proper acts whereby the different visaṃyogas (disjunctions) are gradually accomplished. Thus both the kṣāntis and the jñānas will be intimately connected with the apratisaṃkhyā- and the pratisamkhyā-nirodhas.[27] The eight kṣāntis which constitute the ānantarya-mārga are not merely repetitive of the "Eight Aṅgas," since, as already said, they themselves are constituted by the practice in different levels of the seven first aṅgas. Thus, the eight kṣāntis are nothing but "states of mind" which are receptive of the knowledge of the Four Noble Truths as these apply on the one hand to the kāma-dhātu, and on the other as they apply further and per modum unius to the rūpa- and ārūpya-dhātus. Hence, the first eight jñānas (of a total of ten) will constitute the formal possesion of eight "wisdom-knowledges" having as objects the Four Noble Truths as they apply to the kāma-dhātu (four dharma-jñānas) and as they further apply to the rūpa- and ārūpya-dhātus (four anvaya-jñānas).[28] Thus, there will be a perfect correspondance between the eight "kṣāntis" and the eight first "jñānas" in that each of the jñānas will be the causal effect of each one of the kṣāntis; each of the jñānas will be of a similar nature to its preceding kṣānti, this latter being therefore considered as sabhāga-hetu (formal, "resemblance" cause) of its subsequent jñāna (which will be correspondingly considered as niṣyanda-phala or the "down-the-stream-effect" of its precedent kṣānti).[29]

Kṣānti, therefore, constitutes a preparatory state of mind which is pre-cognitive in that it is still pervaded by "doubt" (sa-vicikitsā), but which is volitively intentional in regard to the actual vision or "seeing" (darśana) of any of the Four Noble Truths. In this respect they are appropriately designated as "knowledge-receptivities." The jñānas, however, represent the casting out of the doubt (nir-vicikitsā) and the total ascertainment of Truth in any of its four-fold form as it gradually applies to the kāma-dhātu on the one hand, and to the rūpa- and ārūpya-dhātus on the other. The stage-wise consecution of each one of the jñānas, from the first to the seventh, constitutes the vimukti-mārga (Path of emancipation from passion), each one of these following the practice of each one of the kṣāntis, from the first to the seventh kṣānti. When the seventh jñāna has been obtained by the practice of the seventh kṣānti, then the practice of the eighth kṣānti signals the final stage of the darśana-mārga (Path of seeing) and hence also the end of the two serial components of the darśana-mārga, namely the ānantarya-mārga (constituted by eight kṣāntis) and the vimukti-mārga (constituted by seven jñānas). When as a result of the eighth kṣānti the eighth jñāna is achieved, then the practice of the last (eighth) aṅga of the eightfold Path, namely the aṅga of "right concentration," is started. This practice of "right concentration" or meditation constitutes the bhāvanā-mārga (Path of contemplation) which is subsequent to the completion of the darśana-mārga.[30] The bhāvanā-mārga (Path of contemplation) takes the ārya through the stages of the anāgāmin or "non-returner to the kāma-dhatu." The stages of the anāgāmin in his ascent through the levels of the rūpa- and ārūpya-dhātus (rūpa- and ārūpya-bhūmis) up to the third ārūpya-level constitutes the anāgamya-mārga[31] which contains the initial phases of the bhāvanā-mārga (Path of contemplation). All these stages of the anāgamya-mārga are attained under the sway of the eighth jñāna which is defined as "the vision of the Truth of the Path as it applies to the rūpa- and ārūpya-dhātus" (marge'nvaya-jñāna).[32] When the anāgāmin reaches the fourth level of the ārūpya-dhātu he enters the final stage of the aśaikṣa or arahant in which the two last jñānas (ninth and tenth) are achieved, namely the kṣaya-jñāna and the anutpāda-jñāna, (i.e., the "knowledge" which destroys all remaining upadhis or adjuncts of karmic residues, and the "knowledge" whereby one knows that there is no further rebirth for him).[33] After these two knowledges are achieved the arhat's tenuous thread of existence is broken off through the final and total visaṃyoga (disjunction), and thus complete nirvāṇa is accomplished.

In order to visualize the diverse aspects of the mārga (the Path) as already mentioned, and to lay down the clearest possible basis for further commentary of the complex character of its stages, I include some systematic charts. The first chart will offer a preliminary view of the Eightfold Path as this bifurcates into the darśana-mārga and the bhāvanā-marga, the former in its turn subdividing into the ānantarya- and vimukti-mārgas and the latter into the anāgamya- and aśaikṣa-mārgas respectively:

CHART OF THE PATH (MĀRGA)

LAUKIKA-MĀRGA (Mundane Path)
(Path of the Pṛthagjana or "common person" in association with the laukikāgra-dharmas, or "supreme mundane dharmas)

↓

LOKOTTARA-MĀRGA (Supramundane Path) or ĀRYA-AṢṬĀNGIKA-MĀRGA (Noble Eightfold Path):

1.- Right View (Samyagdṛṣṭi)
2.- Right thought (Samyaksaṃkalpa)
3.- Right speech (Samyagvāc)
4.- Right Action (Samyakkarmānta)
5.- Right livlihood (Samyagājīva)
6.- Right exertion (Samyagvyāyāma)
7.- Right mindfulness (Samyaksmṛti)

(1–7) → DARŚANA-MĀRGA (Path of "seeing") Path of the srotāpanna-ārya or -śaikṣa (the "ascetic" who has entered the stream of pure dharmas). Characterized by: saṃtīraṇa ("judgment") and parimārgaṇa ("search")

→ I. ĀNANTARYA-MĀRGA (Path of "immediate accession to the "wisdom-knowledges" through eight kṣāntis ("patiences" or "knowledge-receptivities") Characterized by: sa-vicikitsā ("with doubt")

↓

II. VIMUKTI-MĀRGA (Path of "liberation" through seven jñānas ("wisdom-knowledges") Characterized by: nir-vicikitsā ("without doubt")

↓

8.- Right concentration (Samyaksamādhi) — BHĀVANĀ-MĀRGA (Path of "contemplation") Characterized by: asaṃtīraṇa ("without judgment") aparimārgaṇa ("without search")

→ III. ANĀGAMYA-MĀRGA (Path of the anāgāmin or "non-returner to the kāma-dhātu"). Consisting in the exercise of one jñāna (the eighth), five rūpa-concentrations, and three ārūpya-contemplations.

↓

IV. AŚAIKṢA-MĀRGA (Path of the Arhat, the saint in the threshold of enlightenment). Consisting in the fourth ārūpya-contemplation and in the attainment of two final jñānas. These last jñānas constitute total enlightenment (saṃbodhi).

↓

NIRVĀṆA

As visible in the preceding chart, the practice of the seven first *aṅgas* of the Eightfold Path constitutes the Path of the *srota-āpanna-ārya* or *śaikṣa* as the *darśana-mārga* or "Path of seeing." The purpose and goal of this path is to obtain thorough realization of the Four Noble Truths. "Right view" and "right mindfulness" constitute the cognitive efforts toward this vision of the Truths. "Right thought," "right speech" and "right action" constitute the wholesome (*kuśala-*) acts of *mental*, *verbal* and *bodily karma*. "Right livelihood" and "right exertion" encompass all the meritorious efforts and bring them to their crown. The "right mindfulness" is the continuing application of the mind to the recollection (*smṛti*) of the Truths, our keeping them in mind, and our becoming "recipient" to them; thereby the *kṣāntis* as the state of mind "with doubt" (*savicikitsā*) called "knowledge-receptivity" sets itself as the *conditio sine qua non* for the rejection of doubt (*nirvicikitsā*)[34] and the establishment of the *jñānas* as "certain knowledge."

Furthermore the *darśana-mārga* (Path of seeing) involves the practice of the "patiences" or *kṣāntis* (as predispositions to knowledge) and the exercise of the *jñānas* in the two respective Paths of the *ānantarya-mārga* and *vimukti-mārga*. The *ānantarya-mārga* contains eight *kṣāntis* whereas the *vimukti-mārga* involves only seven of the ten *jñānas*. In all these cases the pre-vision (*kṣānti*) and the vision of the Truths (*jñānas*) are both accompanied by *vikalpa* (discursive thought with "judgment"), and are characterized by the "spirit of search." For these reasons the *darśana-mārga* is designated as *saṃtīraṇa* ("with judgment" and "I-conditioned") and as *parimārgaṇa* ("with search").[35]

The *bhāvanā-mārga*, however, represents the long path to be covered by the acts of meditation and contemplation as prescribed by the last *aṅga* of the Eightfold Path ("right concentration"). The *bhāvanā-mārga* begins with the attainment of the eighth *jñāna* and guides the *ārya* and *anāgāmin* through the levels of nine *dhyāna-bhūmis* (levels of meditation) corresponding to the five levels of existence in the *rūpa-dhātu* and the four psycho-cosmic levels of the *ārūpya-dhātu*. The *bhāvanā-mārga*, in contrast with the *darśana-mārga*, covers the "vision" of the truth not with *saṃtīraṇa* and *parimārgaṇa* (through discursive thought and volitive search) but through totally balanced, "settled," direct contemplation and thorough cognitive possession (*asaṃtīraṇa* and *aparimārgaṇa* = without judgment and without search).[36] Through the possession of the eighth *jñāna*--which gives him direct and immediate knowledge of the Path as this applies to the *rūpa-* and *ārūpya-dhātus*--the earthly *ārya* becomes an *anāgāmin* by an irreversible self-grounding upon the levels of the *rūpa-dhātu*. His ultimate goal in the ascent through the *rūpa-* and *ārūpya-bhūmis* ("form-" and "formless" levels of existence) is the attainment of the last two *jñānas*, the *kṣaya-jñāna* and *anutpāda-jñāna*, which, as mentioned above, puts him on the threshold of complete *nirvāṇa*.[37] In order to exhibit the proper parallels and correspondances between the eight *kṣāntis* and the ten *jñānas* as the proximate goals of each one of the mentioned aspects of the Path, the following chart will be of assistance:

Correspondances between the Eight Kṣāntis ("patiences" or "knowledge-receptivities") and the Ten Jñānas (wisdoms or knowledges)

ur dharma-āntis (1-4)

or "pre-cognitive acceptances" and "knowledge-receptivities" or the Four Noble Truths:

1. Suffering (duḥkha)
2. Origination (samudaya)
3. Cessation (nirodha)
4. Path (mārga)

as they apply to the kāma-dhātu

producing Four dharma-jñānas (1-4)

or "thorough knowledges" of The Four Noble Truths:

1. Suffering
2. Origination
3. Cessation
4. Path

as they apply to the kāma-dhātu

↓

ur anvaya-āntis (5-8)

or "knowledge-receptivities" of the Four Noble Truths:

5. Suffering
6. Origination
7. Cessation
8. Path

as they apply to rūpa- and ārūpya-dhātus

producing Four anvaya-jñānas (5-8)

or "thorough knowledges" of the four Noble Truths:

5. Suffering
6. Origination
7. Cessation
8. Path

as they apply to rūpa-and ārūpya-dhātus

↓

Two supreme jñānas (9-10) (abhijñās):

9. kṣaya-jñāna
↓
10. anutpāda-jñāna

→ samyaktva (absolute goal) as last visaṃyoga (disjunction from ārūpya-dhātu) = complete nirvāṇa

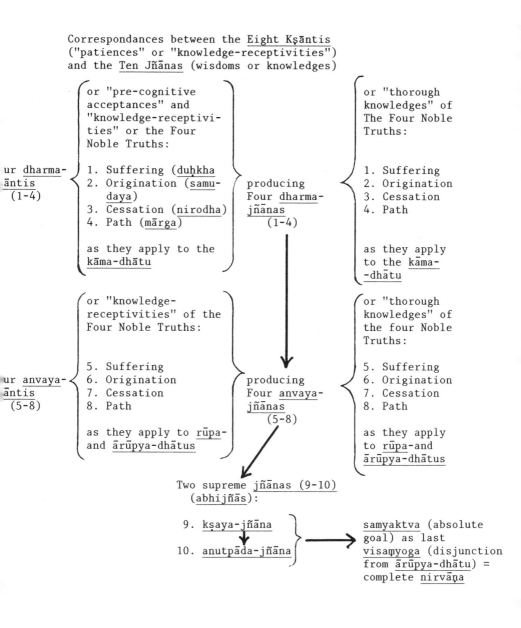

It should be noted that the first three anvaya-jñānas (i.e., from the fifth to the seventh jñānas inclusively), as directed toward the thorough understanding of the three Truths of Suffering, Origination and Cessation in the rūpa- and ārūpya-dhātus are "knowledges with certainty" (nirvicikitsā) about the extremely subtle nature of still present "suffering" (duḥkha) in such purer spheres of higher existence (rūpa- and ārūpya-dhātus), about the latter's continuing subjection to the laws of karmic retribution, and about the futher possibility of cessation (nirodha) and "disjunction" (visaṃyoga) from such levels. This knowledge, however, does not yet transcend the kāma-dhātu and hence does not entail direct intuition and possession of such higher states. Only the eighth jñāna (or fourth anvaya-jñāna)--which has as its object the "seeing" of the Path to Cessation as this has to take place in the higher levels of existence in the rūpa- and ārūpya-dhātus--sets the ārya directly upon the very Path which consists in direct contemplation of such higher levels. This is the logical consequence of the fact that the Path "as it applies to the rūpa- and ārūpya-dhātus" is the "path of contemplation" (bhāvanā-mārga) and thus "its vision" (darśana) is reduplicatively the Vision "of the Path of direct Vision." The three previous anvaya-jñānas were considered as indirect (though certain) "visions" (darśana) of the rūpa- and ārūpya-dhātus attained only through the mediate process of discursive thought, and thus they involved only a cognitive certainty by unshakable inference and not by direct contact. However, the eighth jñāna, its vision being a "vision of the Path as it applies to the rūpa- and ārūpya-dhātus," involves already the direct "Path of contemplation" (bhāvanā-mārga) of such levels and hence their direct cognitive possession.

In view of all this, the darśana-mārga (Path of seeing) establishes itself as a path involving a total of "fifteen stages" which consecutively go from each kṣānti to its corresponding jñāna, and which proceed alternately from the ānantarya-mārga to the vimukti-mārga. When the XV stage--which corresponds to the 8th kṣānti--is attained, then the ārya becomes a contemplative, this achievement signaling his entrance in the bhāvanā-mārga, or Path of Contemplation.[38] His success in this Path as a beginner will secure his visaṃyoga (definitive disjunction) from the kāma-dhātu and will ensure his rebirth in the first psycho-cosmic level of the *rūpa-dhātu*. Thus he has become an *avaivartika-anāgāmin* (a "non-relapsing non-returner").

The next chart will visualize the total relationships of the fifteen stages of the *darśana-mārga* (eight *kṣāntis* plus seven *jñānas*) and their connection with the last three *jñānas* of the *bhāvanā-mārga*, as these latter secure the *ārya*'s ascent to the realization of the *nirupadhiśeṣa-nirvāṇa* or complete "*nirvāṇa* without karmic residues." This chart will also show the roles to be played by the various *apratisaṃkhyā-nirodhas* (extinctions without the intervention of knowledge) and the gradual *pratisaṃkhyā-nirodhas* (or extinctions through acts of wisdom-knowledge). As already stated, these two *nirodhas* designate--within this context--either the negative outcome from wholesome acts posited under the influence of the *kṣāntis*, or the fruition of the acts of knowledge that the *jñānas* are in themselves. I suggest that the reader closely examine the following chart prior to proceeding with the text.

Chart of the DARŚANA-MĀRGA (Path of Seeing) and the BHĀVANĀ-MĀRGA (Path of Contemplation) with EIGHT KṢĀNTIS, TEN JÑĀNAS, TWO NIRODHAS (aprati-, pratisaṃkhyā-) and NIRVĀṆA.

D A R Ś A N A - M Ā R G A (Fifteen stages) Path of the Ārya (saṃtīraṇa, parimārgaṇa = "with judgment" or "I-conditioned" and "with search").

- APRATISAṂKHYĀ-NIRODHA of certain lower levels of KĀMADHĀTU (birth in hells, as pretas, or as eunuchs, androginous, pṛthagjanas, etc.)
- APRATISAṂKHYĀ-NIRODHA of some good destinies in RŪPA-DHĀTU (mahābrahmās and asaṃjñi-sattvas)

ĀNANTARYA-MĀRGA with EIGHT KṢĀNTIS		VIMUKTI-MĀRGA with SEVEN JÑĀNAS
I. 1st kṣānti (duḥkhe-dharma-kṣ.)	→	II. 1st jñāna (duḥkhe-dharma-jñ.)
III. 2nd kṣānti (samudaye-dharma-kṣ.)	→	IV. 2nd jñāna (samudaye-dharma-jñ.)
V. 3rd kṣānti (nirodhe dharma-kṣ.)	→	VI. 3rd jñāna (nirodhe-dharma-jñ.)
VII. 4th kṣānti (mārge-dharma-kṣ.)	→	VIII. 4th jñāna (mārge-dharma-jñ.)
IX. 5th kṣānti (duḥkhe' (nvaya-kṣ.)	→	X. 5th jñāna (duḥkhe'nvaya-jñ.)
XI. 6th kṣānti (samudaye'nvaya-kṣ.)	→	XII. 6th jñāna (samudaye' nvaya-jñ.)
XIII. 7th kṣānti (nirodhe nvaya-kṣ.)	→	XIV. 7th jñāna (nirodhe'nvaya-jñ.)
XV. 8th kṣānti (mārge' nvaya-kṣ.)	═	END OF DARŚANA-MĀRGA

Goal: PRATISAṂKHYĀ NIRODHA of superior levels of KĀMA-DHĀTU

BEGINNING OF BHĀVANĀ-MĀRGA

B H Ā V A N Ā - M Ā R G A (Nine stages) (asaṃtīraṇa, aparimārgaṇa = "without judgment" and "without search")

(See detailed chart on pp. 171-175)

- ANĀGAMYA-MĀRGA Path of the anāgāmin (non-returner)
  - 8th jñāna (mārge'nvaya-jñāna)
    - I to V stages (pp. 171 - 173) (Five rūpa-concentrations and Five rūpa-bhūmi-lokas) — Goal: PRATISAṂKHYĀ-NIRODHA of Five levels of RŪPA-DHĀTU
    - VI to VIII stages (pp. 173 - 174) (Three ārūpya-contemplations and three ārūpya-bhūmi-lokas) — Goal: PRATISAṂKHYĀ-NIRODHA of Three first levels of ĀRŪPYA-DHĀTU
- AŚAIKṢA-MĀRGA Path of the Arhat
  - 9th jñāna (kṣaya-jñāna)
  - 10th jñāna (anutpāda-jñāna)
    - IX stage (Fourth ārūpya-contemplation) Goal: PRATISAṂKHYĀ-NIRODHA of last (4th) level of ĀRŪPYA-DHĀTU (or B H A V Ā G R A)
    - → SAṂBODHI enlightenment)

SOPADHIŚEṢA-(NIRVĀṆA (Nirvāṇa with residues) Successive prahāṇas (abandonments) of doubts (vicikitsā) and passions (anuśayas). Partial vimokṣas (liberations) and visaṃyogas (disjunctions)

NIRUPADHIŚEṢA-NIRVĀṆA (Nirvāṇa without residues) Total visaṃyoga (disjunction)

It must be noted that in spite of the tight continuity in which each *kṣānti* is linked with its corresponding *jñāna*, this is a sequence which follows up the content of the acts of knowledge to be pursued but does not necessarily and strictly constitute a temporal order. The fact that each *kṣānti* effects without intermediary (*ānantarya*) its corresponding *jñāna* does not preclude the possibility of the *kṣāntis* being practiced--temporally speaking--after one another, or several *kṣāntis* being practiced at the same time, temporally prior to the attainment of their matching *jñānas*. The "immediacy" (*ānantatva*) whereby each *kṣānti* is followed by its corresponding *jñāna* is a causal immediacy, not a temporal one. That means that each *kṣānti* will eventually produce its subsequent *jñāna* "without causal intermediary," regardless of whether other *kṣāntis* are also being practiced during the same period of time.

As a result of this it becomes apparent that the *kṣāntis* can by themselves--as acts of wholesome *karma*--achieve the extinction of impure *dharmas*, in this case being of course still "extinctions without the intervention of wisdom-knowledge." This--as frequently said--constitutes a particular kind of *apratisaṃkhyā-nirodha*. The exercise of the *kṣāntis* hence is able to produce the "obtention" or "possession" of the *apratisaṃkhya-nirodha* (cessation "without knowldege") of rebirths in levels of existence of the *kāma-dhātu* which are inferior to the level of the humans. It is in this way that the "Path of Seeing" (*darśana-mārga*) begins by "obstructing" the maturation of previously accumulated impure "seeds." Thus, the *kṣāntis* produce the avoidance of rebirth in hells, or in the animal levels, or in the level of the *pretas* (or beings subjected to the feelings of thirst and hunger, a lesser state of evil retribution above the hells and closer to the level of humans). For that matter the *kṣāntis* can go as far as "impeding" rebirth as a *pṛthagjana* (a human who still is an outsider to the Path) or even as an *uttarakuru* (the hightest karmic destination within the level of humans, as an inhabitant of *Uttarakuru* or the "Northern Continent").[39] An individual can reach this level of the *uttarakurus* just through the *kṣāntis* and without the proper acquisition of the *jñānas*. Thus, this level can be considered as prior to the *anāgamya*-level, i.e., the level of the "non-returners to the *kāma-dhatu*." In fact, the kṣāntis can bring about the state of apratisaṃkhyā-nirodha (extinction without the jñānas) of all the levels of the srota-āpanna (the one who "has entered the stream" of the Path or āryas) up to the level of the sakṛd-āgāmin, i.e., the "one who still has to return once" to the level of the humans,[40] which is said to be the highest level of the kāma-dhātu.

Furthermore, according to the Kośa, the kṣāntis might--under certain circumstances--bring about the apratisaṃkhyā-nirodha of some levels of the rūpa- and ārūpya-dhātus. The accumulation of meritorious "seeds" through the practice of the kṣāntis might be intense enough to produce the "skipping" of certain good destinations beyond the kāma-dhātu, such as the level of the brahma-devas who occupy the first region of the rūpa-dhātu, i.e., the Brahma-loka. Thus, thanks to his previous exertion (pradhāna) in the exercise of the kṣāntis, an individual who has attained the first seven jñānas and thus is to become an anāgāmin (non-returner to the kāma-dhātu) might--by virtue of such kṣānti-merits--caper his rebirth in the Brahma-loka and be reborn in the subsequent higher level of the parīttābha-s (or "radiant beings"). The Kośa goes so far as to mention the possibility of avoiding being reborn as an asaṃjñisattva in the higher levels of the rūpa-dhātu (world of form).[41] The asaṃjñisattvas are individuals who have been absorbed into a cataleptic state after reaching the highest states of "pure form" (rūpa-dhātu) through the effort of meditation and concentration. Such beings--when dying in such a state of unconsciousness (asaṃjñisamāpatti) are reborn--according to early Buddhist mythology--in a high region of the rūpa-dhātu where they still remain withdrawn into unconsciousness. As the Brahma-loka or region of the brahma-devas constitutes the inferior region at the base of the rūpa-dhātu (world of pure form), the asaṃjñisattva-bhūmiloka (or Bṛhatphala-loka)[42] belongs to the highest sphere of the same dhātu, just below the Akaniṣṭha-loka (sphere of "equanimous" beings).[43] Both stages, even if due to pure dharmas and wholesome karma, can delay faster progress within the Path. They may produce such delay for totally disparate reasons: the Brahma-loka because of the still high degree of attachment due to the exuberant use of the organs of sight and hearing, and to the mental activities of the "imaginative process" (vitarka) and "sustained thought" (vicāra)[44] as well as the presence of emotion of less than balanced elation and exultant joy (*saumanasya*, *saṃpraharṣa*). However, the *asaṃjñisattva* state (of unconsciousness) delays the final attainment of the last two *jñānas* (*kṣaya-* and *anutpāda-jñāna*) precisely because of the lack of the still necessary though highly purified state of consciousness needed to realize them. In point of fact, the *asaṃjñisattva* is supposed to "relapse" into the higher spheres of the *kāma-dhātu*.[45] Hence, the *ārya* who is advancing through the psycho-cosmic stages of the *bhāvanā-mārga* (path of contemplation) might get detained--at least temporarily--in the first level, or even "thrown back" from the penultimate level of the *rūpa-dhātu*: the first because of an excessive and still egotistic state of individual happiness, the last because of the *ārya's* relapse back into the *kāma-dhātu*. The proper *apratisaṃkhyā-nirodha*--in this case as "extinction" of pure *dharmas*--might therefore expedite the ascent through the *bhāvanā-mārga* on the basis of previous accumulations of meritorious "seeds" in the practice of the *kṣāntis*, by impeding rebirth even in these *rūpa-dhātu* stages which can cause a delay in the progress.

The *Kośa* also advocates the further possibility of other particular *apratisaṃkhyā-nirodhas* (or extinctions "without knowledge") taking place in the ascent across the *rūpa-dhātu*. Thus, the organs of sexuality are already absent in the *Brahma-loka*,[46] whereas the organs of taste and smell are also relinquished in the second and third stages of the *rūpa-dhātu* which in its cosmic level is termed *Parīttābha-* and *Apramāṇābha-lokas* (realms of "limited" and "unlimited radiance") as the *Ābhāsvara-loka* (realm of "translucent beings"). In the fourth cosmic level of the *rūpa-dhātu* or *Subhakṛtsna-loka* (realm of the "pure mind fixation") the touch organ is also relinquished,[47] and finally in the supreme level of the *rūpa-dhātu* or *Akaniṣṭha-loka* (realm of the equally young)[48] the organ of sight, even if not yet abandoned, is not exercised. In this level the sight-organ is exercised only inasmuch as the individual in the *Akaniṣṭha-loka* is still able to re-live its former experiences in the inferior levels of the *rūpa-dhātu*.[49] At any rate the gradual loss and "abandonment" of these sexual and sensorial organs in the progress upward towards the *ārūpya-dhātu* are not due to acquisition of new knowledge. This is due to the fact that all these stages--as already explained--are attained under the sway of the eighth (8th) *jñāna* (mārge'nvaya-jñāna)[50] and entails only the contemplation of truths already acquired at the beginning of the bhāvanā-mārga as an anāgāmin or non-returner. Hence, the Kośa considers the abandonment of the sex and sense organs as apratisaṃkhyā-nirodhas. Such abandonments are therefore to be designated as vihāṇis (i.e., "riddances" produced by the kṣāntis) and not as prahāṇas ("riddances" produced by the jñānas). It is then to be understood that the exercise of the eight kṣāntis in the ānantarya-trail of the darśana-mārga already accumulates the merits which necessarily will attain the "extinction" and "riddance" of such lower bodily organs throughout the progress along the bhāvanā-mārga (or Path of Contemplation). The great extent and wideranging importance of the role played by the apratisaṃkhyā-nirodha in the progress along the Path to nirvāṇa can be gathered from all the above said. This carries a clear verdict by the Vibhāṣās and the Kośa against the shallow statement that "the apratisaṃkhyā-nirodha is of relatively slight importance."[51]

As for the role of the pratisaṃkhyā-nirodha (extinction through knowledge) it clearly shows from the above chart: the seven jñānas (knowledges) as acquired in the vimukti-mārga (second aspect of the darśana-mārga) produce the prahāṇa (abandonment), the vimokṣa (liberation), and the subsequent visaṃyoga (disjunction) from the superior levels of the kāma-dhātu, thus enabling the ārya to become an anāgāmin, i.e., a non-returning inhabitant of the rūpa-dhātu. The further exercise of the eighth (8th) jñāna as underlying the practice of the bhāvanā-mārga (Path of Contemplation) allows the anāgāmin to complete the "riddance" (or prahāṇa) of each one of the five levels of the rūpa-dhātu and of each one of the first three levels of the ārūpya-dhātu. When the anāgāmin reaches the ninth (9th) and tenth (10th) jñānas he becomes an aśaikṣa or arhat and, if reborn, he exists for a while in the highest level of the ārūpya-dhātu, namely, the Bhavāgra-bhūmi,[52] wherefrom--after the further realization of the two last jñānas--he obtains the final pratisaṃkhyā-nirodha of the last level of the ārūpya-dhātu (Bhavāgra) thus accomplishing total or "traceless" nirvāṇa.

The vihāṇis or "riddances" obtained by the different apratisaṃkhyā-nirodhas together with the subsequent prahāṇas or "riddances" produced through the gradual attainment of the *pratisaṃkhyā-nirodhas*, from level I to level XV of the *darśana-mārga*, and from level I to level VIII of the *anāgamya-mārga* (first part of the *bhāvanā-mārga*), bring about the "possession" of the *sopadhiśeṣa-nirvāṇa* or "*nirvāṇa* with residues." The final *prahāṇa* or *visaṃyoga* of the *Bhavāgra*-level (*arhat*-level) which is the result of the final *pratisaṃkhyā-nirodha* coincides with the possession of the *nirupadhiśeṣa-nirvāṇa* or "*nirvāṇa* without residues." With this last *pratisaṃkhyā-nirodha*, the final goal of the Path has been accomplished and the extinction of suffering and origination has taken place for the *ārya* who has exerted himself through such arduous stages.

As a completion of this chapter, a schematic description of each one of the nine stages of the *bhāvanā-mārga* and of the nine psycho-cosmic levels of existence which correspond to these stages of meditation and contemplation is in order.

Bhāvanā-mārga
(the Path of Contemplation)

As we already have said, the eighth (8th) *jñāna* signals the entrance in the Path of Meditation and Contemplation. With the eighth (8th) *jñāna* the way of judgment (*saṃtīraṇa*) and investigative search (*parimārgaṇāśaya*) which is proper to the *darśana-mārga* is superseded by stages of pure and "settled" contemplation.

It has been repeatedly suggested that there is--according to early Buddhist tradition--a correspondance between psychological states of contemplation reached by the mind of an individual who might still reside in the *kāma-dhātu*, and the cosmic levels of rebirth into which any individual might be reborn after he has achieved mastery in any of those stages of mental discipline within the *bhāvanā-mārga*. Therefore, the *bhāvanā-mārga*, which designates as a whole the total Path of Meditation and Contemplation, encompasses both a total of nine stages of phenomenological progress within the recess of the individual mind, and nine cosmic levels of existence into which anyone practicing the *bhāvanā-mārga* might be reborn in his progression toward *nirvāṇa*. Thus, the progression toward the final *visaṃyoga* (disjunction) can be realized both psychologically and cosmically. An *ārya* endowed with great capability of right exertion (*samyagvyāyāma*, *pradhāna*) might be able to climb up the ladder of the *rūpa* and *ārūpya-dhātus* in a purely mental way, thus accomplishing the *pratisaṃkhyā-nirodha* either of several or even of all the stages and levels of the two superior *dhātus* (world of "form," and "formless" world).

The implication seems to be that the ascent through the cosmic levels is not absolutely necessary and inevitable. However, in most of the cases an individual practicing the *bhāvanā-mārga* will master certain degrees of concentration or contemplation in this life (in the highest level of the *kāma-dhātu* as a human). If he dies at the point of such mastery, he will be reborn as an *anāgāmin* (non-returner) in the level corresponding to such a stage of merely mental mastery and attainment. Thus, the possibility of rebirth from the *kāma-dhātu* into any of the higher levels of the *rūpa*- and *ārūpya-dhātus* as an *anāgāmin* is perfectly admissible. The degree of mastery and application of the eighth (8th) *jñāna*, under whose sway he meditates and contemplates, will determine in which of the cosmic levels he will be reborn. Hence, there is no impossibility in the event of an *ārya* acquiring such a mastery of the last and final mental states of "formlessness" that he would not be reborn in any of the cosmic levels at all, not even those of the *ārūpya-dhātu* (formless world). It is then feasible--according to Buddhist tradition--to obtain final *visaṃyoga* (disjunction) from all the *dhātus* through mere ascent accross the mental states of the *rūpa*- and *ārūpya* stages of concentration and contemplation. Later on we shall give a concordant and parallel definition of each one of the mental states as compared to each one of its matching and corresponding cosmic levels.

The mental stages of the *rūpa-dhātu* are attained by five *rūpa-aikāgryas* of "form-concentrations" corresponding to five possible levels of cosmic rebirth or *rūpa-lokas* ("form-locations"). The mental stages or trances (*samādhis*) of the *ārūpya-dhātu* are in their turn attained through four *ārūpya-dhyānas* or "formless contemplations," each one of them corresponding to four *ārūpya-bhūmis* or "formless levels of existence" as possible cosmic plains of "reward-birth" for the thusly advanced _ārya_ or _anāgāmin_.

The entrance in the _rūpa-aikāgryas_ (form-concentrations) demands a preliminary effort on the part of the _śaikṣa_ (or disciple) which is called the _kṛtsna_- (Pali: _kasiṇa_-) practices. _Kṛtsna_ (_kasiṇa_) means "totality" or "completeness," and is the designation given to the totality of mental absorption (_samādhi_) sought by the _śaikṣa_ in his effort to develop the capability of concentration. For that purpose he uses the well known _maṇḍalas_ or circles made of different materials and exhibiting - most of the time-- a particular color. Other figures such as triangles, squares, rhombuses, etc., are also acceptable. A wide variety of _kṛtsna_- (_kasiṇa_-) _maṇḍalas_ is suggested by the commentarial literature, especially the two _Maggas_ (_Visuddhi_- and _Vimuttimagga_).[53] One of the most popular _kasiṇa-maṇḍalas_ used for this preparative purpose (as conducive to the proper attainment of the _rūpa-aikāgryas_ or _rūpa-samādhis_, i.e., stages of "form-concentration") is the so-called earth-_kasiṇa_. In this case the beginner makes a circle out of clay on the ground, in the quiet place where he intends to meditate. Such is the way--as an example--suggested by the _Vimuttimagga_:

> If a yogin desires to make a maṇḍala on the ground, let him at first select a calm place in the monastery, or a cave, or a place under a tree, or a deserted, covered place unlit by the sun, or a place on an unused road. In all such places, let him keep a distance of one fathom, sweep the place clean and make it smooth. In such places let him, with clay of the colour of dawn, prepare the ground in order to cause the arising of the sign. Taking a moderate quantity in a vessel, let him carefully mix it with water and remove grass, roots and dirt from it. With the edge of a cloth let him remove any dirt that may be on the swept place. Let him screen the sitting place and exclude the light, and make a couch of meditation. Let him make a circle according to rule, neither too near nor too far. Let the circle be flat and full and without markings. After that let watery

> clay unmixed with any other colour or unmixed with special colour be applied. When it is dry it should be edged with another colour. It may be of the size of a round rice-sifter, a metal gong and may be circular, rectangular, triangular[54] or square. Thus it should be understood.

The maṇḍalas can be also made of colored circles to hang on the wall. The beginner is supposed to gaze at such maṇḍalas for a period of time that increases in length according to progress in the exercise. The color-maṇḍalas or color-kasiṇas are always of one particular color, such as the red-kasiṇa, the yellow-kasiṇa or the white-kasiṇa, etc. After the disciple obtains greater skill in concentrating his sight upon the clear image of the earth- or color-kasiṇa, he will be able to stand for hours in his quiet, gazing-position. After a long period of gazing he will close his eyes, with an "after-image" replacing in darkness the real or external vision of the kasiṇa-maṇḍala or kasiṇa-triangle, etc. This "after-image" will be retained after he has closed his eyes for a length of time which will be proportional to the time he spent in actually gazing at the external maṇḍala. The longer the actual gazing, the longer this "after-image" will remain in his closed-eyes-vision. Consequently, he will increase the time of the gazing in order to intensify further and to prolong the presence of the "after-image." Proportionally to the gazing and closed-eye-concentration on the "after-image" he will also increase the size of the kasiṇa-figure, thus also expanding the size of the "after-image." In the effort towards expansion within his concentrative state, the disciple will lose track of the color and material aspect of the kasiṇa, whereby the object of concentration will idealize itself and become more abstract and purer. The object of concentration still will be, nevertheless, a circle or any other suitable "form" as previously chosen. The figure of the "after-image" will thus correspond to the geometrical figure of the selected kasiṇa.

The first material or sensorial "after-image" that is subsequent to the prolonged gazing of the kasiṇa is called[55] (in Pali) uggaha-nimitta or "grasped original sign." The second quasi-dematerialized form of the "after-image" is called patibhāga-nimitta or "counterpart-sign."[56] After this "second reflex" image or "counterpart image" has been obtained, the Buddhist yogi might begin to experience great elation and an intense sense of joy, followed later on by a quiet and happy state of blissful calmness. These are signs that he is entering in the proper states of rūpa-concentration or aikāgrya-stages. As the disciple applies himself to the production of the patibhāga-nimitta (abstract form of concentration) he still is conditioned by two particular acts of the mind, namely the functions called vitarka and vicāra. Both functions of vitarka and vicāra are phenomenologically more primordial and basic than the function of vikalpa or "discursive thought" which is still proper to the darsána-mārga, and which--as said--is conditioned by saṃtīraṇa (scrutiny, judgment) and parimārgaṇa (search, investigation). In the initial stages of rūpa-concentration, the function of vikalpa in both of its forms, namely, saṃtīraṇa and parimārgaṇa, is gone. The function of vitarka and vicāra, however, are still present in such inital stages of the rūpa-meditation. Both vitarka and vicāra seem to imply the function designated by Kant as the synthesis of apprehension proximately based on the "schemata" of the imagination.[57] Through vitarka the disciple is still actively involved in the effort of "applying" his attention to the imaginative presence of the purified "after-image" (either as a circle, or as a triangle, square, etc.). Thus vitarka has been translated often as "applied thought," whereas vicāra is a finer state of the mind as this settles in the sustained contemplation of the "pure form" or dematerialized after-image. Hence vicāra is mostly translated as "sustained thought." Vitarka requires an effort of attention towards the "after-image" so as not to drop it from the "mental" sight. Vicāra, however, quietly and effortlessly settles in the mental possession of the "purified after-image" (patibhāga-nimitta). It seems as though the vitarka function involves an applied move of the will (cetanā-viśeṣa, cetanāvṛtti), whereas vicāra does not.[58] When vicāra or "sustained thought" (mental vision) of the purified after-image is attained, the strong emotion of overjoy and elation (prīti-saumanasya)[59] overpowers the practitioner until a more balanced state of calm bliss (sukha, śānta) brings this overjoy to subsidence. At the end, the mental vision of the after-sign is only accompanied by upekṣā (Pali: upekkhā, upekkā) or perfect and serene "equanimity."

In view of this explanation there are five mental factors intervening in the process of the rūpa-aikāgryas or "pure form-concentrations." They can be listed in the following way:

I	II	III	IV	V
VITARKA	VICĀRA	PRĪTI	SUKHA	UPEKṢĀ
Applied thought	Sustained thought	Exultant joy	Calm bliss	Perfect equanimity

The progress upwards through the levels and stages of the rūpa-dhātu will then consist in the prahāṇa (riddance or abandonment) of each one of the first four factors successively until only a pure state of upekṣā (equanimity) remains in the vision of the "purified after-image." By dropping in succession each one of components in the sequence established above, a total of five stages is obtained:

1st stage: vitarka-vicāra-prīti-sukha-aikāgrya
2nd stage: vicāra-prīti-sukha-aikāgrya
3rd stage: prīti-sukha-aikāgrya
4th stage: sukha-aikāgrya
5th stage: upekṣā-aikāgrya[60]

When the disciple commands the state of pure upekṣā (serenity, equanimity) at the peak of "pure-form concentration" (rūpa-aikāgrya) then he is able to go into this state directly without the further intervention of the vitarka-vicāra process and skipping the emotions of exultation (prīti) and even blissful calmness (sukha, śānta). At this point either of the two following events might occur: either the Buddhist yogi loses track of the "pure-form" (purified "after-image") and thereby enters into a cataleptic state of total unconsciousness (asaṃjñi-samāpatti),[61] or his awareness increases in intensity, with an accompanying sense of expansion ad infinitum of the pure geometrical "form" which still remains the object of his concentration. If the second happens, then the "form" will eventually diffuse totally into the experience of an awareness of unlimited space (Skt. ākāśānantyāyatana or Pali: ākāsānañcāyatana). The achievement of this samādhi (state of concentration or absorption) signals the abandonment of the realm of "pure form" (rūpa-

<u>dhātu</u>) and constitutes the mental entrance into the realm of "formlessness" (<u>ārūpya-dhātu</u>).[62] As the <u>yogi</u> continues his process of "formless" and expansive awareness, his <u>samādhi</u> (or state of concentration) loses its "spatial" character; i.e., the sense of objective three-dimensionality vanishes and a state follows where only the <u>yogi</u>'s awareness in its unlimited indetermination remains. Thus the second stage of "formless" contemplation is reached as the state of "infinite consciousness" (<u>vijñānānantyāyatana</u>, Pali: <u>viññānānañcāyatana</u>). A further step will consist in the <u>prahāṇa</u> (abandonment) of the sense of infinite consciousness as a positive mental energy experiencing itself in its unrestricted and unimpeded expansion <u>ad infinitum</u>, and in its place the experience of the negative vacuity or total absence of "content" entailed by the blank indetermination of this very expansion is established. This stage represents the top of the scale of the <u>anāgāmin</u>, or the end-terminal in the <u>anāgamya-mārga</u>, i.e., the end to the first phase of the <u>bhāvanā-mārga</u> (Path of Contemplation). After this state of "experience of infinite nothingness" begins to subside, the Buddhist <u>yogi</u> might be able to bring about a particular mental state characterized by the tenuity of the abiding awareness, but still pervaded by the purest intention of the will (<u>cetanā</u>). This state is said to constitute the very platform for the realizaton of the last two <u>jñānas</u>, the two "knowledges" which occur in immediate succession and which transform the yogi into an <u>aśaikṣa</u> or <u>arhat</u>. These two <u>jñānas</u> were already mentioned above as:

a) <u>kṣaya-jñāna</u> (knowledge of destruction) = the knowledge whereby the <u>arhat</u> knows that all <u>upadhis</u> (adjuncts or residues of <u>karma</u>) have been destroyed and exhausted.

b) <u>anutpāda-jñāna</u> (knowledge of no further origination) = the knowledge whereby the <u>arhat</u> knows that he is no longer to be reborn in any level of individual existence.[63]

The acquisition of these two "knowledges" within the state of what we could call "tenuous awareness in the purest will-intentionality" constitutes the last and shortest track of the Path as a whole, and of the bhāvanā-mārga in particular. This last trail of the Path is called--as indicated in the above charts--the aśaikṣa-mārga. This particular state of tenuous consciousness, within which this last milestone of the Path is reached, is termed nevasaṃjñānāsaṃjñā-āyatana (Pali: nevasaññā-nāsaññā-āyatana), i.e. the "state of neither perception nor non-perception."[64] Many authors refer to this state as a semi-cataleptic state taking place in the very limit of consciousness. That it is a tenuous stage of awareness is rather obvious. The fact, however, that the two final and most important jñānas have to take place within this state does not favor the interpretation that this stage represents a mental state of torpor or slumber. In point of fact the indication that this final samādhi consists in "neither perception nor non-perception" might refer to the "ineffability" and "sublimity" of this state, rather than to its alleged "twilight" nature or semi-sleepness. Its tenuous character, then, might be understood in terms of its objective or noematic content, and not in terms of its subjective or noetic degree of activity. It represents the very last and hence extremely thin thread of individual existence, where the intentionality of the will is directed to the slim nature of the karmic residue still remaining in the citta or "cumulative" mind of the yogi. It is only in reference to the tenuity of the object of the will's intentionality that this state of awareness might be considered as extremely tenuous and feeble. This, however, does not preclude the possibility of this experience constituting a mighty and powerful state from the noetic point of view, i.e., from the point of view of the mental energy put out by the exertion of the mind. It is only on account of the noetic (from the point of view of the subjective function) extraordinary intensity--if not on account of the noematic or content-wise tenuity of objectivity--that this state is said to end up--by exhaustion--in a cataleptic state similar to the one mentioned above as taking place at the top of the rūpa-aikāgrya (form-concentration) scale.[65] This state of total unconsciousness follows only if the yogi fails to bring about the two last knowledges or jñānas; for when these occur the arhat has become a full-fledged Buddha and his entrance into total nirvāṇa is imminent. The state of total unconsciousness--similarly to the case of the last *rūpa*-concentration--is due rather to the failure to take the further step in the realization of the last of the *ārūpya*-stages. Whilst the state of unconsciousness following the *upekṣā-aikāgrya* (last *rūpa*-concentration) "with equanimity") was called *asaṃjñisamāpatti* (non-perception attainment), the state of unconsciousness following the "tenuous awareness" of the last *ārūpya*-stage is termed *sarvasaṃjñāvedayita-nirodha* or "extinction of all perception and sensation."

All the stages described above are considered as mental states phenomenologically presenting to the mind the different levels of both the *rūpa*- and *ārūpya-dhātus*. As it has been often suggested, these mental states are matched by corresponding levels of cosmic existence. Any *anāgāmin* ("non-returner" to the *kāma-dhātu*) who, at the point of his death, has mastered a certain degree of such mental stages is thought to be reborn in the corresponding cosmic level of either the *rūpa*- or the *ārūpya-dhātus*. These *dhātus*, when considered as cosmic spheres of existence, are called *lokas* or also *bhūmis* (locations, "earths," cosmic plains). It is to be emphasized that the *anāgāmin* who has been reborn in any of these cosmic plains is a "non-returner" only in reference to the *kāma-loka*, but not in reference to the stages of the *rūpa*- or *ārūpya-lokas*. His "non-returning" to the level of the humans will not preclude the possibility of "relapse" (*vinivartanīya* = backsliding) from one level of the superior *rūpa*- and *ārūpya-bhūmis* into the inferior ones. The *anāgāmin* or "non-returner to the *kāma-dhātu*" has overcome the *kāma-dhātu* by the obtention of the first seven *jñānas*. However, his ascension through the *rūpa* and *ārūpya* spheres is due only to his contemplation of the truths as presented to him by the eighth (8th) *jñāna*. No new *jñānas* are developed throughout this ascension until he reaches the last stage of the *ārūpya-dhātu*. Therefore the *pratisaṃkhyā-nirodha* or definitive abandonment (*prahāṇa*) of each one of the *rūpa*- and *ārūpya-bhūmis* has to be attained through the sustained contemplation of the nature of the spheres (*bhūmi-lokas*) themselves as basic states of consciousness. Thus the relaxing or weakening of the intensity in the contemplation of the very nature of such *bhūmi-lokas* might bring about the relapse into an inferior *bhūmi*, without this entailing that one has lost track of the very knowledge given to him by the eighth (8th) jñāna, which is the "knowledge of the Path as it applies to the rūpa- and ārūpya-dhātus" (mārge'nvaya-jñāna).[66] The Path "as it applies to the rūpa- and ārūpya-dhātus" is the Path of Contemplation as subjective activity, regardless of the object of contemplation. The subjective activity of contemplation in the bhāvanā-mārga remains the same throughout stages I to VIII. Only the object of contemplation changes hand in hand with the different natures of the bhūmis from I to VIII (five rūpa- and three ārūpya-bhūmis). As long as the last two jñānas are not acquired, the "relapse" from the last ārūpya-bhūmi (stage IX) to the lower bhūmis is also possible. Thus the advance through stages I to VIII of the anāgamya-mārga is to be secured by holding fast to the objects of contemplation, as these change from sphere to sphere. The final step from the last IX bhūmi to nirvāṇa can only be secured by the obtention of the last two jñānas whereby the final visaṃyoga (disjunction) from all remaining threads of individual existence takes place.

It must be taken into account that the ascent through the mental stages and/or the cosmic spheres of the rūpa-dhātu has as proximate goal the elimination of the material upadhis (karmic "adjuncts" or residual "seeds") accumulated in the form of avijñapti-rūpa. As the avijñapti-rūpa (karmic accumulations from "verbal" and "corporeal" karma) is being diminished and "thinned away," the bodies of rebirth through the rūpa-spheres become more and more subtle. In the upekṣā- (equanimity) state of mind proper to stage V, the avijñapti-rūpa is exhausted, the embodiment of the mind by the rūpa-skandha is abandoned, and one is reborn in the immaterial (arūpa) realms of the ārūpya-dhātu.[67] Thus the proximate scope of the ārūpya-stages from VI to IX (ārūpyāvacara-bhūmis) is the elimination of the mental karmic residues (manokarma-bījas) accumulated in the citta or cumulative aspect of the mind (manas) as constituted by the vijñāna-skandha. The following pages will offer--as promised--a concordant summary of the mental stages (aikāgryas, dhyānas, samādhis) with their corresponding and matching cosmic spheres (bhūmi-lokas):

B H Ā V A N Ā - M Ā R G A
(Path of Meditation and Contemplation)

A) anāgamya-mārga or Path of the Non-returner. Progression under the sway of the eighth jñāna (mārge'nvaya-jñāna):

R Ū P Ā V A C A R A - B H Ū M I S
(Stages of subtle materiality and of "pure form")

Proximate goal: elimination of material upadhis (verbal and bodily karmic residues accumulated as avijñapti-rūpa

Rūpa-aikāgryas (form-concentrations) and rūpa-dhyānas (form-contemplations)	Bhūmi-lokas of Rūpa-dhātu (cosmic plains or cosmic spheres of rebirth)
Mental states of pure form	Worlds of pure form (beings with subtle embodiments or rūpāvacaradevas). Although endowed with subtle bodies, the beings of these spheres are still compounded by all five skandhas.
I. VITARKA-VICĀRA-PRĪTI-SUKHA-AIKĀGRYA: concentration with applied-thought, sustained-thought, exultant joy and calm bliss (the meditator progresses from one element into another throughout the fourfold sequence).	I. BRAHMA-LOKA Sphere of brahmins: retribution of beings endowed with the contemplative functions described in the first aikāgrya. Contains three subspheres or domains: 1. Brahma-pāriṣadya or "assembly of Brahmins." 2. Brahma-purohita-devas or "attendants of Mahābrahma 3. Domain of the Mahābrahmā or "supreme" Brahmin.

II.	*VICĀRA-PRĪTI-SUKHA-AIKĀGRYA*: concentration with sustained-thought, exultant joy and calm bliss (progression through the threefold sequence).	II.	*PARĪTTĀBHA-& APRAMĀṆĀBHA-LOKAS* Spheres of "limited radiance" beings (*parīttābha*) and "infinite radiance" beings *apramāṇābha*): Retribution of beings endowed with the mental functions described in the second *aikāgrya*.
III.	*PRĪTI-SUKHA-AIKĀGRYA*: concentration which begins with exultant joy and ends in calm bliss (progression through a twofold sequence).	III.	*ĀBHĀSVARA-LOKA* Sphere of "translucent" or "transparant" beings (*ābhāsvara*): Retribution of beings endowed with the mental functions proper to the third *aikāgrya*.
IV.	*SUKHA-AIKĀGRYA*: concentration upon a pure form accompanied of calm bliss	IV.	*ŚUBHAKṚTSNA-LOKA* Sphere of beings of "pure mind fixation" (*śubhakṛtsna*): Retribution of beings endowed with the mental state of calm bliss in the contemplation of pure forms.
V.	*UPEKṢĀ-AIKĀGRYA* concentration upon a pure form accompanied by the sense of perfect equanimity. Failure to hold fast to the *upekṣā*- (equanimity) state or to induce the mental stages of "infinite space" (first stage of the *ārūpya-dhātu*) brings about the *asaṃjñi-samāpatti* or "unconscious concentration."	V.	Two main levels of rebirth: 1. *BṚHATPHALA-LOKA* Sphere of rebirth for the *asaṃjñisattvas* or "unconscious beings." They are born conscious but their consciousness is soon suspended until their death, at which point they recover it briefly. They relapse into the higher levels of the *kāma-dhātu*. Their mental state corresponds to the attainment of the *asaṃjñi-samāpatti* ("un conscious concentration") They are the only sentient beings who--being "relapsers" into the *kāma-dhātu*--enter the *rūpa-bhūmi-lokas* without having become *anāgāmins* (non-returners).

2. AKANIṢṬHA-LOKA
Sphere of the śuddhāvāsa-kāyikadevas or "pure abode bodily gods" who stay "equally young" (akaniṣṭha). It is the highest heaven in the rūpa-dhātu and the last level of the embodied (kāyika) beings. The Akaniṣṭha level constitutes the retribution for individuals who persevere until their death in the state of upekṣā-samādhi. There is no aging process in this realm.

Ā R Ū P Y Ā V A C A R A - B H Ū M I S
(Stages of immateriality and "formlessness")

Proximate goal: elimination of mental upadhis (mental karmic residues) accumulated in citta (cumulative mind).

ĀRŪPYA-DHYĀNAS (contemplations) and ārūpya-samāpattis.	-BHŪMI-LOKAS (cosmic plains) of ārūpya-dhātu.
Mental states of "non-form"	"Form-less" plains of existence or "immaterial worlds." (Beings in these plains are compounded only by the mental saṃskāra-skandha and vijñāna-skandha as arūpāvacara-devas).
I. ĀKĀŚĀNANTYĀYATANA: Stage of infinity of space. Attainment of the ākāśānantyasamāpatti or concentration having as object the "infinity of space."	I. ĀKĀŚĀNANTYĀYATANA-LOKA Sphere of the beings retributed for their attainment of the ākāśānantya-samāpatti
II. VIJÑĀNĀNANTYĀYATANA: Stage of infinity of consciousness. Attainment of the vijñānānantya-samāpatti or concentration having as object the "infinity of consciousness."	II. VIJÑĀNĀNANTYĀYATANA-LOKA Sphere of beings retributed for their attaintment of the vijñānānantya-samāpatti

III. ĀKIṂCANYĀYATANA:
Stage of infinity of nothingness. Attainment of the ākiṃcanya-samāpatti or concentration having as object the "infinity of nothingness "

III. ĀKIṂCANYĀYATANA-LOKA
Sphere of beings retributed for their attaintment of the ākiṃcanya-samāpatti

B) Aśaikṣa-mārga or Path of the Arhat. Progression to the ninth and tenth jñānas (kṣaya- and anutpāda-jñāna) as these constitute bodhi (enlightenment):

IV. NAIVASAṂJÑĀNĀSAṂJÑĀ-ĀYATANA:
Stage of neither perception nor non-perception. Mental stage characterized by an extremely tenuous object of awareness and by pure cetanā or pure act of will in reference to the attainment of the last two jñānas. The tenuous objectivity of this state of thin awareness does not preclude the givenness of great subjective (noetic) energy (vīrya) in the exercise of pure cetanā (will to know). Failure to obtain the two last jñānas induces the total state of unconsciousness termed as:

IV. BHAVĀGRA-LOKA
Highest and last sphere of individual existence in the ārūpya-dhātu. Retributive rebirth level for the āryas who have attained mastery of the nevasaṃjñānāsaṃjñā-āyatana state of consciousness. Beings in this level are just intent through pure cetanā on the attainment of the last two jñānas.

Sarvasaṃjñāvedayita-nirodha: "halting to all perception and sensation." This state of unconsciousness--contrary to the asaṃjñi-samāpatti in the last level of the rūpa-dhātu--has no corresponding bhūmi or cosmic plain of rebirth.

After attaining the last two jñānas, the arhat reaches the:

C) End of the *mārga* (Path):

Ninth *jñāna*:	*kṣaya-jñāna*	(the *arhat* knows that the goal of the Path has been accomplished and that all karmic residues--both material and mental--of individual existence have been ex-exhausted)
Tenth *jñāna*:	*anutpāda-jñāna*	(the *arhat* knows that he is no longer to be reborn)
BODHI (enlightenment)	SAMYAKTVA (absolute perfection)	NIRUPADHIŚEṢANIRVĀṆA (*nirvāṇa* without residues)

****

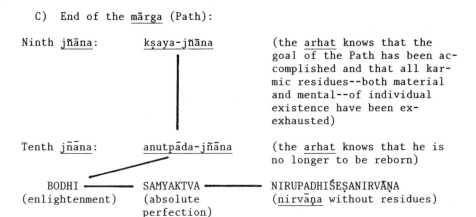

Conclusion

In the _Mahā-parinibbāna-sutta_ (_Dīgha-nīkaya_, XVI) the following account of the passing away of Gautama Buddha is given:

> The Blessed One addressed the brethren and said: Behold, now, brethren, I exhort you: Decay is inherent in all elements of existence! Work out your emancipation with diligence!
>
> These were the last words of the Tathagata. Then the Blessed One entered into the first stage of the (_rūpa_-) meditation. And rising out of the first (_rūpa_-) stage he passed into the second. And rising out of the second (_rūpa_-) stage he passed into the third. And rising out of the third (_rūpa_-) stage he passed into the fourth. And rising out of the fourth (_rūpa_-) stage (of total equanimity) he entered into the (_ārūpya_-) stage in which the infinity of space is alone present. And passing out of the mere awareness of the infinity of consciousness he entered into the (_ārūpya_-) state in which the infinity of consciousness is alone present. And passing out of the mere awarenes of the infinity of consciousness he entered into the (_ārūpya_-) state in which nothing at all is present. And passing out of the awareness of nothing at all he entered into the (_ārūpya_-) state of neither perception nor non-perception. And passing out of the state of neither perception nor non-perception he fell into the state in which there is total lack of perception and sensation.
>
> Then the venerable Ānanda said to the venerable Anurudha: O Lord Anurudha, the Blessed One has attained _parinibbāna_ (perfect _nirvāṇa_)!
>
> No, brother Ānanda, the Blessed One has not yet attained _parinabbāna_. The Blessed One has only entered the state in which

> there is total lack of perception and sensation.
>
> Then the Blessed One, passing out of the state in which there is total lack of perception and sensation, entered back into the state of neither perception nor non-perception. And receding from the state of neither perception nor non-perception he entered back into the state of awareness of nothing. And receding from the state of awareness of nothing he entered back into the state of awareness of infinity of consciousness. And receding from the state of awareness of infinity of consciousness he entered back into the state of awareness of infinity of space. And receding from the mere awareness of infinity of space he entered back into the fourth (_rūpa_-) state (of equanimity). And receding from the fourth he entered back into the third (_rūpa_-) stage. And receding from the third he entered back into the second (_rūpa_-) stage. And receding from the second he entered back into the first (_rūpa_-) stage. And advancing from the first he entered again into the second (_rūpa_-) stage. And advancing from the second he entered again into the third (_rūpa_-) stage. And advancing from the third stage he entered again into the fourth (_rūpa_-) stage (of equanimity). And passing out from the fourth stage (of equanimity) he immediately (expired and) attained _parinibbāna_.
> (_Mahā-parinibbāna-sutta, VI, 10-13._

This passage represents perhaps one of the earliest canonical references to the _rūpa_- and _ārūpya_-stages of the _bhāvanā-mārga_ (Path of Contemplation) as expounded by the non-canonical, commentarial sources. However, in the light of the same commentarial literature, the above passage strikes one as highly enigmatic. The riddle affects two important issues of the passage. First is the particular order in which the Buddha is said to have gone through all the _rūpa_- and _ārūpya_-stages as the final preparation for his death as subsequent attainment of _parinibbāna_ (complete _nirvāṇa_). Why did not the Buddha enter _nirvāṇa_ right after the highest stage of the _ārūpya_-levels in which the two last and final _jñānas_ are achieved? What was the meaning of his rising through all nine stages from the two first _rūpa-aikāgrya_-s of _vitarka_ and _vicāra_ ("applied" and "sustained" thought) to the highest "formless" state, and then back step by step to the very bottom, to climb again gradually the _rūpa_-scale up to the _upekṣā_- (equanimity) top-stage to the _rūpa-dhyānas_? Why did this "equanimity" stage become the door of his entry into complete _nirvāṇa_--instead of the fourth _ārūpya_-stage which is the proper stage of the _arhat_?

This passage poses obvious problems to the commentarial structure of the _bhāvanā-mārga_ (Path of Contemplation). Our attempt to offer a solution to this perplexing account will open the way to a second, no less perplexing question: What is _nirvāṇa_ in the mind of the early Buddhist philosophers? Conceding its inherent ineffability, can _nirvāṇa_ be understood as a _positive_ state and not as a mere nihilation of existence? In other words, does the _Hīnayāna_ metaphysics, as propounded by the _Abhidharma_ literature, allow for a _positive_ interpretation of the state of _nirvāṇa_?

As for the first issue in regard to the sequence followed by the Buddha prior to his attainment of _nirvāṇa_: It is obvious that the _Mahā-parinibbāna-sutta_ does not imply that the Buddha entered the stages of the _bhāvanā-mārga_ for the first time during the moments which immediately preceded his demise. The records maintain that Śākyamuni had exercised himself in such practices prior to his realization under the _bodhi_-tree. His final realization took place--according to tradition--in Gayā ca. 528 BC, i.e., when he was just thiry-five years of age. He died ca. 483 BC at the age of eighty. It is to be assumed that at the time of his enlightenment the Buddha had already attained all the _kṣāntis_ and _jñānas_ which are essential parts of the Path. Thus he did not have to attain the last two _jñānas_ (_kṣaya_- and _anutpāda-jñāna_)--which according to the _Maggas_ and the _Kośa_ are constitutive of enlightenment--at the point of his death. If the last two _jñānas_ are constitutive of enlightenment, then these two _jñānas_ were acquired already under the _bodhi_-tree at Gayā. This provides the basis for the _Mahāyāna_ emphasis on the fact that enlightenment is not necessarily followed by the complete extinction of individuality which is equated with nirupadhiśeṣa-nirvāṇa or "nirvāṇa without residues." If this is the case, were all the upadhis (karmic residues) "exhausted" by Śākyamuni under the bodhi-tree? If yes, then why and how did he keep living as an individual for another forty-five years of worldly existence? If not all of the upadhis were then abandoned in Bodhi-Gayā, which ones were then consumed in Kuśinagara (where he supposedly expired)?

Our previous treatment of the bhāvanā-mārga--as involving the five rūpa-dhyānas and four ārūpya-samādhis--might afford some possible answers to the above questions. It was said that the rūpa-bhūmis were stages of both meditative and psycho-cosmic advancement towards the "disjunction" (visaṃyoga) from the gross material plains of existence, ascending through levels of decreasing coarseness and increasing subtlety. The rūpa-stages have as their proximate goal the visaṃyoga from the factors of materiality (rūpa-skandha). To attain this goal all the upadhis constituted by physical (both verbal and bodily) karma have to be extinguished. Thus the exhaustion of the material upadhis (vacī- and kāyika-karma-bījas)stored as avijñapti-rūpa is the proximate scope of the rūpa-bhūmis.

The ārūpya-stages, however, are directed toward the "exhaustion" of all the mental upadhis (mano-karma-bījas) stored in the vijñāna-dharma as the mind (manas) in its "cumulative" role (citta). Hence it can be said that Śākyamuni did really "exhaust" all the material and mental upadhis when he attained bodhi (enlightenment) at the age of thirty-five, inasmuch as such upadhis were impediments to the purest exercise of mercy and compassion which he chose to perform during the forty-five years of his further existence. It therefore seems thinkable that a continuing accumulation of wholesome material upadhis (as "unsoiled" avijñapti-rūpa) during those forty-five years was well in place. This would have been due to the fact that the Buddha exerted himself both "verbally" and "bodily" for the sake of the enlightenment of others in the foundation of the saṃgha (community). Did this accumulation of pure, unsoiled, material upadhis (as wholesome avijñapti-rūpa) involve a parallel accumulation of mental karmic "seeds" in his citta? It would be congruous to assert that after his enlightenment the Buddha's mind remained undivided and single-intentioned. One could say that his thought, in a perfact way, held fast to the last two *jñānas*, as these were continuously "exhausting" all mental *upadhis* (mental *bījas*, *vāsanās*), these being released by his active mind (*manas*) as he was intentionally involved in the "verbal" and "corporeal" exertion of compassion (*karuṇā*). However, his material *upadhis* (as "unsoiled" *avijñapti*) were absolutely essential to the continuation of his corporeal presence in the level of the *kāma-dhātu* "for the sake of others." Thus his exertion in "verbal" and "corporeal" *karma* of the purest kind was the only basis of his continued existence for forty-five years after his enlightenment. The inertia of the material *upadhis* had to continue past the extinction of his mental *upadhis*. Hence, when his final moment arrived, Śākyamuni re-enacted and undertook his final trip along the *bhāvanā-mārga* (Path of Contemplation) as an immediate preparation for his total *nirvāṇa*. When he reached the highest *ārūpya*-state he found no mental *upadhis* to "get rid of" in his long purified *citta*. Returning all the way down the scale, he started anew from the first *rūpa-bhūmi*, detaining himself in each one of the *rūpa*-stages in order to attain the final *prahāṇa* (abandonment) from all the material *upadhis* of his "verbal" and "corporeal" exertion. In the sublime state of "total equanimity" (*upekṣā-aikāgrya* = fourth *rūpa-bhūmi*) all his material karmic *upadhis* were extinguished like the fire extinguishes itself from lack of fuel. As the last traces of his *avijñapti-rūpa* disappeared both his corporeal demise and his total *visaṃyoga* (disjunction) took place. In this manner Śākyamuni paved the way for the pervasive *Mahāyāna* notion of the *bodhisattva*, i.e., the "enlightened, although still Buddha-to-be sentient being," who for the sake of others renounces final *nirvāṇa* until he has secured the emancipation of others.

But a further perplexing question about the very nature of this complete *nirvāṇa* still haunts the student of early Buddhism. The issue is not about the ineffability of the state of *nirvāṇa*, but about the congruence of its positive nature,[1] affirmed by the scriptures and by the commentaries. That *nirvāṇa* (from the root *vā* = blow, kindle; thus *nir-vāṇa* = "no-blowing") is itself a negative term is obvious. But *nirvāṇa* cannot be thought of as mere nihilation. If the nihilation "plain and simple" of the individual being were the intrinsic nature of nirvāṇa, then the state of sarva-saṃjñā-vedayita-nirodha (extinction of all perception and sensation) would entail its total mental realization. But both the canonical and commentarial literature deny a cosmic correspondence (bhūmi-loka) to this state of mental catalepsis, hence proving that nirvāṇa cannot be equated with a state of absolute "non-perception." The fact that the last two jñānas (as constituting enlightenment) take place in a state of "neither perception nor non-perception" (nevasaṃjñānāsaṃjñā) brings this paradoxical and also undefinable state closer to the conception of a nirvāṇa which is the samyaktva (ultimate "Perfection") and "summum bonum."

How is nirvāṇa then possible as a positive state which is "possessed?" In view of existence as made up of saṃskṛta- (conditioned), momentary, self-extinguishing dharmas, what is relinquished by the individual that becomes de-individualized into the possession of nirvāṇa? In other words, what is the individual ground for this "possession" of the supra-individual? Or what is it that "bridges" what is radically impermanent and "momentary" with what is absolutely permanent and eternal? If all the elements that compound the individual--namely the five skandhas--have to be nihilated and extinguished in order to attain nirvāṇa, then what is it that attains nirvāṇa? How is nirvāṇa a "possession" at all?

Within the Sarvāstivāda's context the possibility of answering these questions might reside in the givenness of an abiding state of potentiality wherein a latent level of "past" and "future" dharmas exists. But as flowing sets of the dharmas are "actualized" for one moment from the state of latent potentiality, to be subsequently extinguished from the present and thus returned to such a latent state, do any of the "potential" dharmas (svabhāva-dharmas) have the virtuality for eternal actualization? Is the vijñāna-dharma (as the mental dharma carrying "knowledge") the basis for such eternal actualization? Does, then, the "momentary" flash of the purest act of vijñāna--as this carries the final acts of wisdom-knowledge--become eternally present to itself by "entering" into such a state of perpetual actualization? In summary: Are the rūpa-dharmas in their interactions with the vijñāna-dharma (as functional vedanā, saṃjñā and saṃskāras) the proximate causes of impermanent individualization, but also the ultimate negative condition for the eternal actualization of *vi-jñāna* as sheer, self-transparent infinite *jñāna*? Would *nirvāṇa* then be the *supreme Dharma* in that It constitutes the eternal act of Freedom which produces this resolution of *vi-jñāna* (as dis-criminative consciousness) into pure *jñāna* or eternal *prajñā* (pure knowledge)?

The preceding questions aim only toward the possibility of bridging the gap which--in the *Sarvāstivāda* context--opens up between the state of the *svabhāva-dharmas* (as latent or potential *dharmas*) and the state of *nirvāṇa*, when this is not to be identified with *nihilum purum*. The mysteriousness of the universal Force of *karma* which propels the life of the universe as such widens the gap. Within the context of the *Sautrāntikas* the notion of *nirvāṇa* becomes even more remote in that they deny the state of latent potentiality attributed by the *Sarvāstivādins* to the *dharmas* of the past and future. The *Sautrāntikas*, however, adhering to a purer kind of phenomenalism, paved the way--together with the *Mahāsaṃghikas*--for the advent of *Mahāyāna* idealism.

Buddhist idealism--even if by some sort of return to the Upanishadic conceptions--reduced the gap between the source of individualized and worldly reality (state of potentiality), the source of Universal action, and the ultimate state of absolute *nirvāṇa*. *Nirvāṇa* becomes then a "return to the source with bliss-bestowing hands."[2] The doctrine of *citta-mātra* (mind-only) underlines all the rich developments of Buddhist thought throughout the *Mahāyāna* schools. In early Buddhist idealism as initiated by the brothers Asaṅga and Vasubandhu the twofold storage of the karmic *upadhis*, i.e., the *avijñapti-rūpa* and the *citta*, are reduced to and merged into only one mental "depository" of karmic seeds called the *ālaya-vijñāna* (storehouse of consciousness). In this term all the notions of potentiality are comprised. The *ālaya-vijñāna* thus becomes the central conception in *Mahāyāna* psychology and metaphysics. For Asaṅga and Vasubandhu the *ālaya* is the individual--and thus plural--bottom-ground for the projection of a purely phenomenal world which is "dreamed-out" from the groundless depths of *citta-mātra* (mind-only). This universal source of "mental" reality is also designated as *Tathatā* or "Thusness."[3] *Tathatā* (Thusness or Suchness), as a designation for the universal and all-pervasive *citta-mātra* (mind only), appeals on the one hand to the unfathomable nature of the original ground of reality, which can be "pointed out" only as SUCH (or THUS), that is, as given in the ultimate cognitive experience. On the other hand, however, the term Tathatā (THUS-ness) takes cognizance of a Hīnayāna appelation of the Buddha as tathāgata or as the "THUS-come" and/or "THUS-gone." This "Thusness" of the Buddha is always eternal and all-encompassing, regardless of the co-relativity of all determined actions and functions of reality which THUS come and go. Tathatā is then by the same token, not only the primordial ground of worldly reality, but--as "mind-only"--it is also the ultimate goal of the karmically individualized mind which appears as the chain of karmic seeds that is the ālaya-vijñāna. The ālaya-vijñāna is not conceived as a permanent subconscious ground of the self; this would run counter to the anātman doctrine which is essential to Buddhism. The individual ālaya is originally conceived as an ever streaming torrent of mental actions and reactions,[4] embedded in the universal citta-mātra that is Thusness. Thus the notion of nirvāṇa as a positive state of infinite and eternal Freedom grounds itself as the "reintegration" of individual mind (pravṛtti-citta) into its original and infinite source as Tathatā.

In the more universalistic idealism propounded by the celebrated Laṅkāvatāra-sūtra the ālaya-vijñāna becomes universalized as the all-embracing depository of the "common seeds" (sa-ādhāraṇa-bījas) which result in the "fruition" of a common and shared Universe. In the view of the Laṅkāvatāra text the ālaya-vijñāna represents the passive aspect of the universal citta-mātra (mind-only) as Tathatā. Hence the individual citta still remains--like in the Sarvāstivādins--the limited depository of individual (an-ādhāraṇa) karmic seeds as planted by individual action (vipāka-karma).[5] The universalization of the ālaya-vijñāna as the passive aspect of Tathatā makes this absolute ground of reality into the recipient of the universal creative ACTION that imparts the "seeds" for the origination of the World-Receptacle (bhājana-loka). This creative ACTION is called the "universal permeation" or "impregnation" of Tathatā (Chinese: chen-ju hsün-hsi).[6] As this universal Creative Action sets itself into motion the World-Receptacle (as object-in-its-totality) and a plurality of individualized minds (subjects) are "conceived" in the "womb" (garbha) of

Tathatā--worldly reality is thus born. Tathatā (or citta-mātra), as the "womb" (garbha) of this universal conception, is then given an appelation which originally meant the "womb of tathāgata-hood" or "womb of Buddhahood," namely the tathāgata-garbha. Primordially meaning the individual potentiality to conceive Buddhahood through the awakening of enlightenment, the notion of tathāgata-garbha came also to designate the eternal and universal potentiality of Tathatā (Thusness) to produce and bear within itself all the aspects of Reality, including the aspects of both "knowledge" and "non-knowledge." In this universalistic and supra-cosmic meaning the tathāgata-garbha--according to the Laṅkāvatāra and later progressive Buddhism--was nothing else than the ālaya-vijñāna inasmuch as this contains within itself the principle of its own activation into "cosmic manifestation."[7]

Through such basic developments of later Buddhist idealism the four notions of tathatā, ālaya-vijñāna, tathāgata-garbha and nirvāṇa become aspects of One and the Same primordial and ultimate reality. The Citta-s and/or manas as individual minds (limited and plural seats of subjectivity and discrimination) are exhibited as "the waves of limitation stirred by the winds of Action upon the ocean of Tathatā as ālaya-garbha" (store of karmic "seeds" and womb of conception). The individual consciousness--in its twofold aspect of citta (cumulative mind) and kliṣṭa-manas (afflicted; active mind)--is the multiple carrier of both "ignorance" (with its concomitant "suffering"), and the potentiality to purification and enlightenment whereby Tathatā comes back to itself and knows itself eternally.

Based upon such texts as the Laṅkāvatāra-sūtra, the Lotus-sūtra, the Avataṃsaka-sūtras and the Chinese work Ta-ch'eng ch'i-hsin-lun ("Awakening of Faith in Mahāyāna"), the foundation of dialectical Buddhism is laid down and its march toward the "totalistic" doctrines of the T'ien-t'ai and Hua-yen schools is set forth. Through this progression "enlightenment" is approached as a state of mental integration which supersedes the mere negative content of the last two jñānas of the bhāvanā-mārga. Thus enlightenment becomes, not only the knowledge of the "destruction of karmic attachments" (kṣaya-jñāna) and the knowledge of "no further rebirth" (anutpāda-jñāna), but also the cognitive realization of total reality as the *One in Many and the Many in One* (*li-shih wu-ai*) or--in a more perfect formulation--the vision of "each thing in all things, all things in each thing" (*shih-shih wu-ai*). *Nirvāṇa* is thus the subsequent total Freedom from "limitation and non-limitation" that ensues from the re-integration into the Infinite Totality that *Tathatā* itself is, as It comprises the totality of the one Substance (t'i), its Function as eternal self-activation (*yung*) and its Manifestations (*hsiang*).[8] Thus the totality of the Manifestations embraces all aspects of the plural and individual minds as these experience the objective world from the state of original, potential "knowledge" (*pen-chüeh*), through the narrow straights of suffering in the realms of "non-knowledge" (*pu-chüeh*), back to the state of "explicit knowledge" (*shih-chüeh*)[9] and the "lands" of Buddhahood (*Buddha-kṣetra*).

At the summit of totalistic Buddhism *nirvāṇa* does not only represent the surpassing of individual limitation, ignorance and sorrow. It also includes the possession of an unrestricted Freedom which, in the words of the *Laṅkāvatāra*, moves through the infinite realms "beyond limitation and non-limitation," "beyond form and non-form" and "beyond individuality and non-individuality." Perhaps the early Buddhists found a similar expression to apply to the state which constitutes the threshold of *nirvāṇa* when they described it as a state which is "beyond perception and non-perception" (*nevasaṃjñānāsaṃjñā-āyatana*), where ultimately a supreme and otherwise inexpressible "identity-in-the-difference" is attained. In this "identity-in-the-difference," the tiny flower in the midst of a meadow contains within itself the whole of *Tathatā* in its undivided unity and--by the same token--the whole of the Universe in its plurality. It is this "identity-in-the-difference," as the experience which is "beyond limitation and non-limitation," that led a *Ch'an* (*Zen*) Master called Yün-men to exclaim:

> "This staff of mine has transformed itself into a dragon and has swallowed up the whole universe! Oh, where are the rivers and mountains and the great earth![10]

NOTES
to
EARLY BUDDHIST PHILOSOPHY

Notes to Introduction

1. *Abhidharmakośa* (henceforth abbreviated as *Abh.k.*), I, 2 a.
2. *Abh.k.*, I, 2 b.
3. *Abh.k.*, ibid.

Notes to Part I

1. On *kṣaṇikavāda* (momentariness) and the real existence of past and future *dharmas* see *Abh.k.*, II, 46 a-b.
2. *Abh.k.*, I, 7 c-d.
3. *Abh.k.*, I, 8 c.
4. *Abh.k.*, I, 7 c-d. See also II, 45 c.
5. *Abh.k.*, I 7 c-d.
6. *Lalitavistara*, 420. 4-5 (Edition by Lefmann, Halle, 1902).
7. *Dhammasaṅghaṇi*, 124 (584) :*tattha katamaṃ sabbaṃ rūpaṃ? cattāro ca mahābhūtā catunnañ ca mahābhūtānaṃ upādāya rūpaṃ--idaṃ vuccati sabbaṃ rūpaṃ*. See also *Vimuttimagga*, XI, 1.
8. *Abh.k.*, I, 12 a-b.
9. *Abh.k.*, I, 12 c-d. See also *Vimuttimagga*, XI, 1 and *Visuddhimagga*, 351-2.
10. *Abh.k.*, I, 36. See also *Dhammasaṅghaṇi*, 616 and 628.
11. *Abh.k.*, I, 13; I, 20 a-b; I, 29 a-b, b-c; I, 42.

12. *Abh.k.*, I, 9 c-d.
13. *Abh.k.*, I, 43 c-d.
14. *Abh.k.*, I, 35 d; I, 43 c-d. Or also *saṃghātastha*, *saṃcita*, I, 13.
15. *Abh.k.*, I, 36.
16. *Abh.k.*, I, 44 a-b.
17. *Vimuttimagga*, XI, 1 (taken from the *Abhidhammāvatāra*, 66). *Abh.k.*, ibid.
18. *Vimuttimagga*, ibid.
19. *Vimuttimagga*, ibid.
20. *Abh.k.*, I, 44 a-b.
21. *Vimuttimagga*, XI, 1.
22. *Abh.k.*, I, 10 a.
23. *Abh.k.*, I, 10 b. See *Dhammasaṅghaṇi*, 621.
24. *Abh.k.*, I, 10 b-c.
25. *Abh.k.*, I, 10 c. *Dhammasaṅghaṇi*, 625.
26. *Prakaraṇa*, 13,b 1.
27. *Abh.k.*, I, 10 d.
28. *Abh.k.*, ibid.
29. *Abh.k.*, ibid.; *Vibhāṣā*, 127, 1; *Dhammasaṅghaṇi*, 648. See also *Abh.k.*, I, 35 a-c.
30. *Abh.k.*, IV, 2 a. *Vijñapti* is that "which makes known" (*vijñapayati*) the volitive intentionality of a thought, either through a gesticulation of the body, hands, face, etc. (*śarīraceṣṭā*, *viṣpanda*) or through the verbal expression of sound. On *vijñapti* as bodily gesticulation see *Dhammasaṅghaṇi*, 636; and *Aṭṭhasālinī*, 323. On *vāgvijñapti* (verbal intimation) see *Abh.k.*, IV, 3 d. See also *Visuddhimagga*, XIV, 61.
31. On the "karmic" quality of the *vijñaptis* (external manifestation of the will) as morally right (*kuśala*), wrong (*akuśala*) and neutral (*avyākṛta* = morally "undefined") see *Abh.k.*, IV, 7 a and ff. See also *Visuddhimagga*, XIV, 61 ff., 79; XVII, 61.
32. *Abh.k.*, IV, 7 a ff.; 16 a-b ff. and passim. On the necessary correspondance and corelativity between *vijñapti* and *avijñapti* (an *avijñapti* for each *vijñapti*) see *Abh.k.*, IV, 16 c-d ff.; 67 a ff. On the passive, cumulative character of *avijñapti* see *Abh.k.*, IV, 16 a-b: "the *avijñapti* is *karma* because it is both the effect and the cause of *karma*." As "effect" of *karma* it is

passively accumulated; as the cause of *karma* it "re-acts."

33. On the possible connection between *hṛdayavastu* (heart-basis) and *avijñapti* (as the former being the "store" of the latter) see *Visuddhimagga*, XIV, 60-61; 78.
34. *Abh.k.*, I, 11.
35. This seems to be Saṃghabhadra's interpretation in his *Samaya-pradīpikā*. Thinking that Vasubandhu's notion of *avijñapti* was somewhat incomplete, he substituted the above mentioned *kārikā* (verse) of the *Abh.k.* for the following: *vyākṛtāpratighaṃ rūpaṃ sā hy avijñaptir iṣyate*. See *Vyākhyā*, 31.16 and 34.5.
36. Both *vedanā* (sensations) proximately and *saṃjñā* (perception) ultimately originate from the *triple contact* (*trisparśa*) among *viṣaya*, *prasāda* and *vijñāna*. See *Abh.k.*, II, 24 and 44 d: Contact (*sparśa*) is said to be "the encounter of the triad of consciousness (*vijñāna*), sense-organ (*prasādendriya*) and material object (*viṣayālambana*); by virtue of this contact there is sensation (*vedanā*) and perception (*saṃjñā*)."
37. *Abh.k.*, I, 14 c; II, 7, 8, 24; III, 32. See also *Saṃyutta-nikāya*, III, 96; *Dhammasaṅghaṇi*, 3.
38. The mental, noetic function of *vijñāna*, whereby the raw sensations presented by *vedanā* are integrated into the full *noematic* "presence" of an object (*saṃjñā*) is henceforth designated as *saṃgrahaṇa* (com-prehension) and *ud-grahaṇa* (apprehension). See forthcoming part of the text.
39. *Abh.k.*, I, 14 c-d.
40. *Abh.k.*, II, 24. See also II, 34 b-d.
41. See above, note 36.
42. *Visuddhimagga*, XVII, 44-47.
43. *Visuddhimagga*, ibid. See also other post-canonical works such as the *Kāśyapa-parivarta*, 79 (2); *Divyāvadāna*, 78 (5), 78 (25), 467 (1); *Mahāvastu*, I, 26 (7).
44. *Visuddhimagga*, ibid. See also *Abh.k.*, I, 15 a-b.
45. *Abh.k.*, II, 66-72; IV, 8 b, 127 a-b; V, 18 c-d, 19.
46. *Abh.k.*, II, 38 c, 53 b, 57 a-b, 71 b, 72; IV, 8 a-c, 94 c-d, 127 c-d.

47. See above, pg. 41 f.(on saṃjñā).
48. See above, ibid.
49. Abh.k., I, 9 c-d.
50. See David Hume, A Treatise of Human Nature, Part IV, Sec VI.
51. Vijñāptimātratā-siddhi, I, passim; II, 28, b, 29 a-b; VII, 8 a. The grāhaka-grāhya correlation is also designated as vikalpa--yad vikalpyate or "illusory perceiving--that which is falsely perceived." Vikalpa carries the māyā (or illusory) character proper to the idealist notion of perceiving, discriminating or imagining.
52. Abh.k., I, 16 a. The Vyākhyā (II, 24) defines upalabdhi as vastumātra-grahaṇa or "simple apprehension of the thing," thus refering to vijñāna as the function of pure apprehending regardless of the particular character of the apprehended itself. The characteristics and material determinations of the apprehended object appear in association with vedanā and saṃjñā: ."..vedanādayas tu caitasikā viśeṣagrahaṇarūpāḥ (Vyākhyā, ibid.).
53. Abh.k., ibid.
54. Abh.k., II, 34 a-b.
55. On "triple contact" (trisparśa) see above pg. 38 f. and note 36. According to the Abh.k. the eighteen dhātus are listed as to offer a proper material "support" to the purely mental activities of vijñāna as manas (ṣaṣthāśrayaprasiddyartham dhātavo' ṣṭādaśa smṛtāḥ, Abh.k., 17 c-d.
56. Abh.k., I, 17 a-b.
57. Textual reference to primary sources in regard to the three rūpalokas and their bhūmis (or stages) will be made later in the third part of this work.

Notes to Part II

1. See *Abh.k.*, II, 48 c-d and IX, 12 b, 13 a.
2. *Abh.k.*, II, from 48 c-d to 65 d.
3. *Abh.k.*, II, 50 a.
4. *Abh.k.*, II, 50 c-d, 51.
5. *Abh.k.*, II, 47 b-c; 57 a-b.
6. *Abh.k.*, II, 53 c-d.
7. *Abh.k.*, I, 37.
8. *Abh.k.*, II, 61 d.
9. *Abh.k.*, II, 62 d.
10. *Abh.k.*, IV, 1 b.
11. See above, pgs. 35-38 and Note I, 32.
12. *Abh.k.*, II, 34 a-b: *citraṃ śubhāśubhair dhātubhir iti cittam* or in Paramārtha's interpretation: *citaṃ śubhāśubhair dhātubhis tān va cinotīti cittam*. The Tibetan version carries: " because the *citta* is loaded (*bsags-pas*) with good and bad elements." This "cumulative" aspect is also emphasized by the *Aṭṭhasāliṇī*: *ālambanaṃ cintetīti cittam* (293).
13. According to the *Aṅguttara-nikāya* (VI, 63), there are--from the temporal point of view--three kinds of *karma*-maturations: a) maturation during this lifetime (*diṭṭha-dhamma-vedanīya-kamma*); b) mattration in the next birth (*upapajja-vedanīya-kamma*; c) maturation in successive births (*aparā-pariyavedanīya-kamma*).
14. See *Visuddhimagga*, XIV, 132, 135; XVII, 61, 292f.; XXI, 37, 38, 80; XXII, 5, 79, 113ff.
15. *Abh.k.*, II, 30 a-b.
16. *Abh.k.*, II, 36 c-d.
17. *Abh.k.*, IV, 123, c-d. Or in the words of the *Bhāṣya* (gloss to the *Kośa*'s verses): *cittaṃ vāsayati guṇais tanmayīkaraṇāt saṃtateḥ puṣpais tilavāsanāvat*. See also *Vijñaptimātratā-siddhi*, II, 15 b.
18. On the *ālayavijñāna* (storehouse of consciousness) and its "perfumation" (*bhāvanā*) see *Vijñapti-mātratā-siddhi*, from II, 12 a-b to IV, 12 a.
19. *Abh.k.*, II, 36 c-d. In point of fact, *saṃtatipar-iṇāmaviśesa* (transformation or "metamorphosis within the series") is a *Sautrāntika* expression

applicable to the "heterogeneous" causality of the vipāka-hetu.

20. Avijñapti refers to the Sarvāstivāda doctrine, whereas bhavaṅgasrotas or saṃtāna expresses the vipāka-theory of the Sautrāntikas. Avijñapti is only material accumulation (differentiated from citta as carrier of mental accumulations) whereas bhavaṅgasrotas is the subconscious "perfuming" of the whole stream of existence, both mental and material.
21. See above pg. 87 and note II, 19.
22. On the pratītya-samutpāda (interdependent coorigination) doctrine see Abh.k., III, 20-38 b, and Visuddhimagga, VII, 8- 16;XVIII passim.
23. Majjhimanikāya I, 256; Saṃyuttanikāya, II, 1. See also Vimuttimagga, XI, 1.
24. Abh.k., III, 28, a-b. Vibhāṣā, 33, 11.
25. Abh.k., I, 29 b-c. There are three kinds of pratighāta (resistance, clash, collision): a) āvaraṇapratighāta, the "obstacle" (āvaraṇa) offered by any external body to occupy the same space with other body, or impenetrability." b) viṣayapratighāta, the collision of the sensorial organ with its corresponding external viṣayas or matters. c) ālambanapratighāta, the final "objection" of the total external object (through vedanā and saṃjñā) to the mental faculty or manas, whereby the subject-object opposition is established.
26. See above, pgs.41-42, and notes I, 38 and 40.
27. See above, pgs.87-91, and note II, 19.
28. Abh.k., IX, 15 a-b.
29. See above, pgs. 73-74.
30. Abh.k., II, 57 c.
31. Abh.k., I, 40 c and 41a: "There is an entity (dravya) called nikāya-sabhāga (or sabhāgatā); it is a (citta-viprayukta-) dharma in virtue of which all the living beings as well as all the entities that fall within the class of sentient beings (sattva-saṃkhyatā) are similar to one another (samāna, sadṛśa). See also Vibhāṣā, 27 (4).
32. Abh.k., I, 41 a.
33. Abh.k., II, 57 a-b.
34. See above, pgs. 77-78.

35. Abh.k., II, 57 a-b. In point of fact, the Kośa attributes to the sabhāga-hetu (homogenous causation) the role of adhipati-pratyaya (sovereign, all-ruling condition) already in the micro-cosmic foundation of similitude among the dharmas: "As said by the Mahāśāstra, the great elements (mahābhūtāni) which are about to pass (within the serial flux) constitute the hetu (proximate cause) and the adhipati (the "rulers" or "regulators") of the great elements which are about to come. By adhipati one has to understand the adhipati-pratyaya (the "supreme" condition that presets the form of each element as specifically identical to the preceding one) and as hetu one has to understand the sabhāga-hetu (i.e., the mode of causality by which a dharma begets a subsequent dharma of the same form.)." (Abh.k., II, 52 a).
36. Abh.k., II, 57 b.
37. Abh.k., II 56 b.
38. Abh.k., II, 62, b.
39. See above, note II, 31.
40. Abh.k., IV, 1 a.
41. On primary sources in regard to the Sāṃkhya-yoga system see: Gerald J. Larson, Classical Sāṃkhya, Motilal Banarsidass, New Delhi, 1969. Radhakrishnan, Moore, A Sourcebook in Indian Philosophy, Princeton University Press, 1957. James H. Woods, The Yoga-system of Patañjali (translation), Harvard University Press, 1914 (reprint by Motilal Banarsidass, New Delhi, 1966).
42. Nirguṇa-brahman or "non-qualified," "attributeless" or "impersonal" brahman which extends ad infinitum above the saguṇa-brahman or Brahmā (with personal attributes).
43. Theodore Stcherbatsky, Buddhist Logic, reprint by Dover Publications, N.Y. 1962, Vol. II, pg. 368. See also Th. Stcherbatsky, The Central Conception of Buddhism, reprint by Motilal Banarsidass, New Delhi, 1974, pg. 19f.
44. See Abh.k., IV, 123, c-d, and Vijñaptimātratā-siddhi, II, 15 b: "Bīja (seed) is another name given to vāsanā (perfume as seminal impregnation). Vāsanā (the perfume) remains indeed (in the ālaya-vijñāna = "storehouse of consciousness") by reason

of *bhāvanā* (or the perfumation), similarly to the scent of the sesamum-grains (*tilagandha*) which remains in them by reason of the flowers which perfume them." See also above, pg. 85 and note II, 17.

45. *Vijñaptimātratā-siddhi*, II, 14 b - 18 a. See also above, note II, 18.
46. *Vijñaptimātratā-siddhi*, II, 29 b.
47. This relativity of the world-creating Force is very remindful of the notion of Life in Wilhelm Dilthey's *Lebensphilosophie*.
48. *Laṅkāvatāra-sūtra*, II, 46.
49. See *Vijñaptimātratā-siddhi*, II, 19 a-b; VIII, 30 a-b; 32 b; IX, 2 b; 12 a-b and passim.
50. See above, pgs. 105-106.
51. Forthcoming. In the process of publication by MARTINUS NIJHOFF BV, The Hague.

Notes to Part III

1. See above, pgs. 25 ff.
2. Abh.k., I, 5 d. Glosse: "Space has as its nature not to impede (āvṛṇoti) matter (rūpa) which, effectively, 'takes place' freely within space; furthermore (space) is not impeded (āvriyate) by matter, since the former is never dislodged by the latter." The Sautrāntikas deny the reality of space as an absolute dharma: "The Vaibhāṣikas (or Sarvāstivādins) assume in the Abhidharmaśāstra that ākāśa is a reality of its own (vastu), not realizing that the scriptures confine themselves to giving a name to an unreality, to a pure nihil (avastusato'kiṃcanasya)..." (Catuḥ^śatikā, 202, Ed. Assoc. of Bengal, 1914, III, pg. 483). See also Abh.k., II 55 c-d, and Kathāvatthu, VI, 6-7.
3. Abh.k., I, 28 a-b. "The cavity or void of the door, of the window, etc., is the external space-element (bāhya-ākāśadhātu); the cavity of the mouth, nose, etc., is the internal space-element (ādhyātmika-ākāśadhātu)."
4. Abh.k., I, 6 c-d. See also Vibhāṣā, 32 (5).
5. Abh.k., II, 55 d.
6. Abh.k., I, 6 c-d.
7. A. Berriedale Keith, Buddhist Philosophy in India and Ceylon, Chowkhamba Sanskrit Series, Vārāṇaśī, Fourth ed. 1963, pg. 160.
8. Abh.k., V, 27 b-c.
9. Abh.k., II, 55 d.
10. Abh.k., VI, 23 b.
11. Abh.k., ibid.: "For example, after a (premature) death before its time (antarāmaraṇa) interrupts the individual existence there is apratisaṃkhyānirodha of the dharmas which would have been generated if such an existence had been continued."
12. Abh.k., VIII, 26, c-d. On parihāṇi (relapse) see Abh.k., VI, 22 c.
13. Let us keep in mind that as the apratisaṃkhyānirodha of impure dharmas impedes a relapse (parihāṇi) into lower levels, by the same token an

apratisaṃkhyānirodha of pure dharmas may produce such a relapse; see above, pgs.139 f.and note 12.

14. Abh.k., II, 55 d; V, 63 c-d to VI, 1 a-b. Vibhāṣā, 79 (1).
15. Abh.k., I, 6 a-b.
16. Abh.k., II, 55 d; II, 4; VI, 37 a-c; 65 b.
17. Abh.k., II, 55 d; VI, 37 a-c.
18. Abh.k., II, 55 c; II, 57 d; VI, 46. The pratisaṃkhyānirodha does not have a direct cause (as it is only obtained and not produced); it is, however, a cause (kāraṇa-hetu) of visaṃyoga (disjunction) and is in itself a fruition (vipākaphala) from the meritorious acts of the Path. See Abh.k., II, 50 a; 55 c and 57 d. See also Prakaraṇa, 33 b (16): na phaladharmāḥ katame? ākāśam apratisaṃkhyānirodhaḥ (Which dharmas are never a fruition? The space and the apratisaṃkhyānirodha).
19. See above, pg. 2 and 129. Abh.k., VI, 54d.
20. Abh.k., VI, 1 c-d; 49 a-c; 53 c-d. Visuddhimagga, XIV, 9, 202; XVIII, 8f.; XXII, 39, 46, 124, 128, and passim.
21. Abh.k., VI, 25, c-d; 26 a; see also II, 40 b-c. Vibhāṣā, 3 (6).
22. Abh.k., VI, 1 c-d;; 48 c-d. Visuddhimagga, XIV, 8f., 88, 105, 127, 158, 182, 202; XXII, 36, 122, 124, 128, and passim.
23. Abh.k., II, 16 c-d; IV, 54; V, 9; 43 b-c; VI, 29 c-d; 34 a-b; 58 b. Visuddhimagga, XXII, 18; XXIII, 7, 18, 55.
24. On the anāgāmin ("one who is destined to return no more to the kāma-dhātu") and anāgamya-mārga ("path of the anāgāmin") see Abh.k., VI, from 36 d to 45 a. Visuddhimagga, XII, 2f., 21, 28f., 45; XXIII, 7, 18, 25, 28, 56f.
25. Abh.k., VI, 1 a-b and ff.; VII, passim.
26. Abh.k., VI, 25 c-d and ff; 28 a-b and ff.; VII, passim.
27. On kṣāntis as effecting the apratisaṃkhyānirodha of certain inferior levels of existence, see Abh.k., VI, 23 b, and above pg. 138. On jñānas as effecting the pratisaṃkhyānirodha of passions as "liberations" (vimokṣas) thereof, see II, 55 d.

28. Abh.k., VI, 26 a-b, b-c; VII, 3 b-c, c-d.
29. Abh.k., VI, 26 a; II, 52 d.
30. The total of the eight kṣāntis and their subsequent eight jñānas constitutes the sixteen stages of the abhisamaya or "truth-comprehension." The darśana-mārga (path of intellectual "truth-seeing") stops, however, in the fifteenth stage, i.e., the eighth kṣānti. The eighth jñāna, which is subsequent to the eighth kṣānti, lays down the basis for the bhāvanā-mārga (or path of "truth-contemplation"). See Abh.k., VI, 27 b-d and 28 c-d: "At the stage XVI there is nothing to intellectually understand that has not been already understood. This moment, in which one contemplates the truth such as it has been (intellectually) seen (yathādṛṣṭabhāvanāt), is an essential part of the bhāvanā-mārga (path of contemplation)..."
31. See above, note III, 24.
32. See Abh.k., VI, 28 c-d, VII, 3 c-d; 20 a-c; 22 b. See above note II, 28.
33. Abh.k., VI, 67 a-b: The kṣaya- and anutpāda-jñānas, in point of fact, constitute final enlightenment: kṣayānutpādayor jñānaṃ bodhiḥ. See also VI, 50 and VII, 1, 4 b, 7. According to the Vibhāṣā, 96 (8): The kṣaya- and the anutpāda-jñānas receive the name of bodhi (enlightenment) because they entail the complete understanding of the four (noble) truths..."
34. Or also vicikitsā (doubt) and niścita (certainty): see Abh.k., VII, 1 a.
35. Abh.k., VII, 1 a (saṃtīraṇātmakatvāt, parimārgaṇāśayaḥ).
36. Abh.k., VII, 1 b (asaṃtīraṇa-aparimārgaṇāśayatvāt).
37. See above, pg. 149 and note 33.
38. See above, pg. 149 and note 30.
39. Abh.k., VI, 23 b (see above page 138). Uttarakuru (northern continent) or the superior continent on this earth. According to early Buddhists, the earth contains four dvīpas or continents: the Jambudvīpa in the South of the central Mount Meru, the Pūrvavideha in the East, the Godaniya in the West, and the Uttarakuru in the North. See

Abh.k., III, 53 b - 55 d. Listed also in Lalitavistara, 19 (15 f.); 149 (19f.). See also Divyāvadāna, 214 (25) and Mahāvastu, III, 378 (2).

40. Abh.k., VI, from 31 a-b to 36 d. The proper sequence of the disciple or śaikṣa is that of the srota-āpanna (the "one who has entered the stream" of the Path), the sakṛd-anāgāmin (the "one who is to return only once to the kāma-dhātu"), the anāgāmin (the "one who is not to return to the kāma-dhātu"). The last state is that of the Arahant (arhat) or aśaikṣa who has obtained the last two jñānas or bodhi (enlightenment).

41. See above, pg. 138, and note 10.

42. Bṛhatphala or Pali Vehapphalā (-loka or -devas); see Abh.k., II, 41 d; Lalitavistara 150 (9); 396 (16); Mahāvastu, II, 314 (8); 319 (6); 349 (1); 360 (21); Divyāvadāna, 68 (16); 138 (23); 367 (13).

43. The Akaniṣṭha-loka, the supreme realm of the rūpa-dhātu or "world of form." Akaniṣṭha means literally a place "without a youngest," namely the place of the "equally young" or "of the never aging."

44. Vitarka and vicāra designate two aspects in the function of the synthesis of apprehension (saṃgrahaṇa) which will be explained later in the text.

45. Abh.k., II, 41 d. See also Abh.k., II, 42 d: "The pṛthagjanas (ordinary people as outsiders to the Path) commonly mistake this state of unconsciousness (asaṃjñika) with the true deliverance..." A similar state of unconsciousness takes place at the very top of the ārūpya (formless) stages (nirodhasamāpatti or sarvasaṃjñāvedayitanirodha), prior to the obtention of the two last jñānas.

46. Abh.k., II, 12. In the interpretation of the Kośa, all beings in the rūpa-dhātu (world of form) are males in spite of lacking the corresponding male sexual organ. Their masculinity reflects in the form of the body and the sound of their voice. See also II, 2 c-d.

47. See complete list of devas and lokas in the rūpa-dhātu in Abh.k., III, 2 b-d; 5 a - 6 a; 75; 77 and passim.

48. See above, note III, 43.
49. Abh.k., I, 38 c-d; VIII, 13 a-c.
50. See above, pg. 149 and note 32.
51. See above, pg. 136 .
52. Abh.k., I, 22 b-d; II, 43 c; 44 d; III, 6 b; 6 c-d; 8 b. The Bhavāgra is the cosmic level of the Arhat, corresponding to the highest state of contemplative mind which is defined as nevasaṃjñānāsaṃjñā-āyatana, i.e., the "level wherein there is neither perception nor non-perception." This is a very subtle state in which only a very thin activity of awareness remains, but which is characterized by the intensity of the pure will (cetanā) towards the acquisition of the last two jñānas as these constitute final bodhi (enlightenment). See Abh.k., I, 22 b-d: "The fourth level of the ārūpya-dhātu (formless realm), at the very summit of individual existence (bhavāgra) is characterized by (pure) volition (cetanā), the saṃskāra par excellence..." More will be explained about this extremely subtle state of the mind which is exclusively proper to the arhat or aśaikṣa.
53. A brief listing of these methods of sensorial concentration (kṛtsnas, Pali, kasiṇas) is given by Abh.k., VIII, 36 a. The canonical literature mentions them in Aṅguttara-nikāya, V, 46, 60; Majjhima-nikāya, I, 423; II, 14; Dīgha-nikāya, III, 268. The Visuddhimagga explains them in great detail in chapters IV and V. So also does the Vimuttimagga in chapter VIII, 1-3.
54. Vimuttimagga, VIII, 1. See also the Visuddhimagga on the making of the "earth-kasiṇa" in IV, 24-26.
55. Visuddhimagga, IV, 27-29; Vimuttimagga, VIII, 1 (grasping sign).
56. Visuddhimagga, IV, 31-34; Vimuttimagga, ibid.
57. See above, pg. 158 and note 44.
58. See definitions of vitarka-vicāra in Abh.k., I, 32 c-d; II, 33 a-b: vitarkavicāraudāryasūkṣmate ("Vitarka and vicāra are gross and subtle aspects of the process of thought"). According to this text, vitarka seems to designate a searching motion of the mind "examining" and trying to make sense of a manifold of sensorial data, a function

designated by Husserl as vorverbildliche Anschauung (prefigurative viewing), whereas vicāra appears as the primal evidence resulting from this "searching intentionality of the mind." In Husserlian terminology, this primal evidence is designated as vorpraedikatives Urteil" (pre-predicative judgment). Heidegger refers also to these functions as Vorsicht (fore-seeing) and Vorgriff (fore-conception). See Edmund Husserl, Cartesian Meditations, I, 4; III, 25. See also Martin Heidegger, Sein und Zeit, IV, 32 (pg. 191). In the words of the Kośa: Vitarkya vicārya vācaṃ bhāṣate nāvitarkya nāvicārya ("it is after having examined and having judged that one talks, not without having examined and having judged." See also Saṃyutta-nikāya, IV, 293: pubbe kho...vitakketvā vicaretvā pacchā vācaṃ bhindati.

59. Or also prīti-saṃpraharṣa (Abh.k., II, 8 a). See also Abh.k., VIII, 2 a-b; 11 c-d; 12.
60. See explanation of these aikāgryas or rūpadhyānas (Pali, rūpa-jhānas) in Visuddhimagga, IV, 79-202; Vimuttimagga, VII, 1-2. In these texts the second and third jhānas (Skt. dhyānas) are reckoned per modum unius as only one stage; hence the listing of four instead of five rūpa-stages. See Visuddhimagga, "The Fivefold Reckoning of Jhāna," IV, 198-202. See also Abh.k., VIII, from 7 to 13 d.
61. See above, pg. 158 .
62. The four stages of the ārūpya- (formless, immaterial) contemplation are explained in Abh.k., VIII, from 2 c to 4 c-d. See also detailed description in Vimuttimagga, VIII, Sec. 2. The Visuddhimagga lists them briefly quite a number of times, like, for instance, in I, 140; III, 105f.; IX, 119, 122; XV, 25f.; XXIII, passim; detailed account is given in chaper X.
63. See above, pg. 149 and note 33
64. See above, pg. 160 and note 52.
65. See above, pgs. 158 f. and notes 42, 45, where the asamjñika or asaṃjñisamāpatti is described as the mental state of unconsciousness proper to the beings born in the Bṛhatphala cosmic level of the rūpa-dhātu, just underneath the Akaniṣṭha realm which corresponds to the fifth rūpa-aikāgrya of

total equanimity (upekṣā).

66. See above, pg. 149 and notes 30, 32.

67. On the gradual riddance of the elements of materiality (rūpa-skandha) see Abh.k., III, from 5 a to 6 b; VIII, 3 c.

Notes to Conclusion

1. On the positivity of nirvāṇa see Visuddhimagga, "Discussion on nibbāna," XVI, 67-74.
2. From the "Ten Oxherding Pictures" by Kuo-an Shih-yuan, a Zen master of the Sung dynasty belonging to the Lin-chi school, pictures IX and X.
3. On the notions of ālaya-vijñāna and tathatā, see above, pgs. 122f. and notes (Part II) 45 and 49.
4. The ālaya-vijñāna "evolves like the violent torrent of a flood..." (tac ca vartate srotasoghavat)...it perpetually originates and perishes at every instant...it is at the same time cause and effect...(Vijñaptimātratā-siddhi, III, 7 b - 8 a).
5. See Laṅkāvatāra-sūtra, Chapter II, 100-106.
6. Hsün-hsi (permeation, impregnation, suffusion) is the usual version of the Skt. bhāvanā used by the VI century Chinese translator of Skt. texts, Hsüan-tsang, and by the author of the celebrated Ta-ch'eng ch'i-hsin-lun (Treatise of the Awakening of Faith in Mahāyāna). Vāsanā (perfumes, traces, permeation in the passive, receptive sense) translates commonly as hsi-ch'i (habit energy).
7. Laṅkāvatāra-sūtra, Chapter VI (Sec. LXXXII).
8. Ta-ch'eng ch'i-hsin-lun, Taishō Daizōkyō, 32:1666. 575-576.
9. Ibid., 32:1666.576b.
10. Quoted from Kubose-Ogura, Zen Kōans, Chicago, 1973, pg. 35.

EARLY BUDDHIST PHILOSOPHY

GLOSSARY - INDEX OF SANSKRIT TERMS

(LISTING OF TERMS FOLLOWS THE ENGLISH ALPHABET ORDER)

EARLY BUDDHIST PHILOSOPHY
SANSKRIT-ENGLISH GLOSSARY AND INDEX
(in the English alphabet order)

ābhāsvara-loka
Cosmic plain of the "translucent" beings, the third psycho-cosmic region of the Real of Form (*rūpa-dhātu*).
pp. 159, 172

Abhidharma
The ultimate "Dharma" or "Teaching;" also connoting the treatises dealing with the "inferred," "non-empirical" nature of the factors of existence (*dharma-s*). Often translated as "metaphysics".
pp. 6-8, 13, 26, 138

abhinna
Not specifically differentiated, as said of generic qualities.
pp. 110

abhisamaya
Truth comprehension
pp. 196

abhisaṃkaraṇa-saṃskāras (or *abhisaṃskaraṇa-*)
Volitive forces which are "*karma*-forming."
pp. 43, 45-6, 48

abhisaṃskṛta-saṃskāras
Volitive forces or propensities which are "*karma*-formed."
pp. 43, 45, 48, 58

acaitasika-saṃskāras
Forces which are non-mental, sublimimal, purely biological.
pp. 45, 48, 63

acchatva
Translucidity, transparency.
pp. 24

adhipati
Sovereign, all-ruling, supreme, as said of universal karma (adhipati-karma, adhipati-bala) and its effects (adhipati-phala).
pp. 77-8, 110-19, 121-23, 125-27, 192

adhvan, adhvanaḥ
Road, roads (of time), i.e., future, present and past.
pp. 15, 17, 19, 101-02

ādhyātmika
Inner, subjective.
pp. 24-6, 57

ādhyātmika-bhāgya
Inner (temperamental) karmic allotment, as determined by previous deeds.
pp. 99, 117

ādhyātmika-phala
Inner karma-fruition (as temperamental disposition, proclivities, etc.)
pp. 88

adṛṣṭa
Non-seen, invisible, sometimes used in the sense of "transcendental."
pp. 110, 121

aikāgrya
State of concentration upon objects of the Realm of Form (rūpa-aikāgrya-s)
pp. 165-66, 170-72, 199

ākāśa
Space, one of the three asaṃskṛta- (non-conditioned) factors (dharma-s)
pp. 18, 124, 130-33, 194

ākāśa-dhātu
The element of space as limited or circumscribed by a container, room, etc.
pp. 132

ākāśānantyāyatana
Stage of mental experience of infinite space as a form-less (*ārūpya*) state of concentration (*samādhi*, *samāpatti*).
pp. 166, 173

Akaniṣṭha (-loka)
The cosmic sphere where there is "no youngest;" or plain of the "equally young." Fifth and uppermost sphere of the Real of Form (*rūpa-dhātu*).
pp. 158-59, 173, 197, 199

ākiṃcanyāyatana (or *ākiñcanya-*)
Mental state in which "infinite nothingness" is experienced as a form-less (*ārūpya*) state of concentration.
pp. 174

ālambana
Objective "support" as said of the mental objects of abstract or ideal cognition.
pp. 41, 75

ālambanapratighāta
The object's "opposition" (resistance) to the subject.
pp. 191

ālaya-vijñāna
Storehouse of consciousness, depository of all karmic seeds of existence according to Buddhist idealism.
pp. 87, 123, 126, 182-4, 192, 201

amalaprajñā
Non-tinged, immaculate knowledge.
pp. 8

anādhāraṇa-bījas
"Non-common" (i.e., individual) karmic seeds, as posited by individual action.
pp. 111

anāgāmin
The "non-returner" to the Realm of Desire (kāma-dhātu)
pp. 141, 147, 149-52, 156, 158, 160, 162-63, 167, 169, 195, 197

anāgamya-mārga
The path of the "non returner" to the kāma-dhātu.
pp. 149-150, 156, 161, 167, 170-71, 195

ānantarya-mārga
The path of "immediate succession" between the practice of the kṣānti-s (patiences) and the acquisition of the jñānas (wisdom-knowledges).
pp. 147-151, 154, 156

ānantatva
Immediacy (like between the cause and its effect).
pp. 147, 157

anantya
Endlessness, infinity.
pp. 58

anāsrava-dharma-s
Pure, non-soiled factors of existence.
pp. 17-18, 44, 58

anātman (Pali: anatta)
No-self, no (existence of) soul.
pp. 11, 96, 183

aṅga-s
"Limbs" or "members" as said of the stages of the Path.
pp. 146-47, 151

anidarśana
Not directly perceptible, invisible.
pp. 26, 38

anitya (Pali: anicca)
Impermanence, destructibility of factors due to the doctrine of "momentariness" (kṣaṇikavāda).
pp. 11, 96

anityatā
(Force of) destruction.
pp. 46, 48, 77

anityatānirodha
Succesive extinction of dharma-factors of existence due to the law of impermanence (anitya) and theory of momentariness (kṣaṇikavāda).
pp. 135

anivartya
An ārya (saintly person) who does not "fall back" (or "relapse") into lower spheres of rebirth.
pp. 141

anivṛta
"Non-obfuscating," "non-obscuring," not offering hindrance to the performance of good deeds.
pp. 84

anivṛta-avyākṛta
"Non hindering (but morally) undefined, as said of certain karmically alloted proclivities.
pp. 47-48

antarāmaraṇa
Premature death.
pp. 194

anuśaya-s
Evil propensities or passions.
pp. 44-48, 56, 84-85, 88-89, 97, 102

anutpāda-jñāna
Knowledge of "non (future) origination," the last of ten "wisdom-knowledges" (jñānas).
pp. 132, 149, 152-53, 156, 159, 167, 174-75, 178, 185, 196

anvaya-jñāna-s
"Wisdom-knowledges" of Four Noble Truths as these apply to rūpa (form) and ārūpya-(formless) dhātus (psycho-cosmic spheres).
pp. 153-156

anvaya-kṣānti-s
"Pre-cognitive receptivities" (literally, patiences) of the Four Noble Truths as these apply to the *rūpa* and *ārūpya-dhātus*. They precede and are causes of the *anvaya-jñāna-s* (see above).
pp. 153, 156

āp
Water-element
pp. 23, 52

apramāṇābha-loka
Region of the "unlimited radiance" beings in the second cosmic plain of the Realm of Form (*rūpa-dhātu*).
pp. 159, 172

aprāpti
Force (*saṃskāra*) of "non-acquisition" or metabolic "rejection".
pp. 43, 48

aparimārgaṇa
"Without search" or "without investigation," said of the stages of the *bhāvanā-mārga* (Path of Contemplation).
pp. 150-52, 156

apratigha
"Non-resistance," penetrability.
pp. 24, 50

apratisaṃkhyā-nirodha
Extinction of *dharma*-factors of existence, mostly in reference to the avoidance of some future karmic destinations, an extinction which takes place "without the intervention of the wisdom-knowledges" (*jñāna-s*).
pp. 18, 131, 134-45, 155, 157-61

apūrvam
"Non-surpassed," ultimate.
pp. 110, 121

arahant, arhat
The advanced disciple who has reached the last stage of the Path, prior to achieving perfect enlightenment, Buddhahood and complete nirvāṇa.
pp. 18, 147, 149, 160-61, 167, 169, 174-75, 178, 197-98

araṇa
Unperturbed, untroubled (by passions, etc.).
pp. 17, 58, 125

araṇa-prajñā
"Passion-free" wisdom.
pp. 56

artha
Objective, purpose, scope.
pp. 116

ārūpya-dhātu
Realm of Formlessness (see dhātu-s).
pp. 132, 140, 147-49, 151-54, 158-60, 162, 167, 169-70, 173-74, 198

ārūpya-loka-s
Plains or cosmic spheres of the Realm of Formlessness.
pp. 64, 132, 169, 173

arūpāvacara-bhūmi-s
Stages and levels within the Formless spheres.
pp. 170, 173

arūpāvacara-devas
The (superior) beings belonging to the Formless spheres.
pp. 173

ārya
The saintly or noble person who follows the Noble Path.
pp. 18, 130, 132, 141, 147, 149, 151-52, 154-55, 159-63

ārya-aṣṭāṅgika-mārga
The "Eightfold Noble Path."
pp. 146, 150

<u>aśaikṣa</u>
The no-beginner, i.e., the <u>arhat</u>
pp. 147, 149, 160, 167, 197-98

<u>aśaikṣa-mārga</u>
The path of the <u>arhat</u> or of the "no-longer-a-novice," the last track of the Path closest to Buddhahood.
pp. 149-150, 156, 168, 174

<u>asamāna</u>, <u>asabhāga</u>
Unlikeness, heterogeneity.
pp. 107

<u>asaṃjñika</u>, <u>asaṃjñi-sattva-s</u>
Said of the sentient beings in the higher levels of the Path who enter into a state of unconsciousness.
pp. 156-159, 172, 197, 199

<u>asaṃjñisamāpatti</u>
State of unconscious concentration or cataleptic state as proper to the <u>asaṃjñika-s</u>.
pp. 158, 166, 169, 172, 174

<u>asaṃskṛta-dharma-s</u>
Non-conditioned, eternal factors.
pp. 18-19, 56, 132-134, 145

<u>asaṃtīraṇa</u>
"Without judgment." A characteristic of the Path of Contemplation (<u>bhāvanā-mārga</u>).
pp. 150-152, 156

<u>āśraya</u>
Support, basis of reliance.
pp. 9, 53, 57

<u>aśubha</u>
Impure, soiled.
pp. 46

<u>aśubha-bīja-s</u>
Impure, soiled (karmic) seeds.
pp. 46, 85

asukha
Unpleasant, disagreeable.
pp. 29, 39

atīndriya
Supersensitivity.
pp. 24

aupapattika-bīja-s
Pure karmic "seeds" originating from deeds which are performed under the sway of wholesome propensities.
pp. 85

avaivartika
See anivartya
pp. 141, 147

āvaraṇa
Hindrance, obstacle.
pp. 84, 191

āvaraṇa-pratighāta
Bodily resistance, impenetrability.
pp. 84

avidyā
Non-knowledge, ignorance.
pp. 75, 95, 97, 125

avighna
Offering no-hindrance or no-obstacle.
pp. 131

avijñapti-rūpa
"Non-manifest," (non intimated) material element, as said of the karmic, subliminal residue from verbal and corporeal karma.
pp. 34, 36-7, 44, 56, 62-63, 82, 97-8, 109, 126, 170-71, 179-80, 182

avyākṛta
Morally undefined or neutral.
pp. 46-7, 84, 187

bāhya
External, objective.
pp. 24-5, 57, 112

bāhya-adhipati-phala
External, objective, "sovereign" fruition originating form Universal *karma*, i.e., the world-receptacle (*bhājana-loka*).
pp. 113

bāhya-bhāgya
External (worldly) karmic "allotment."
pp. 89, 99, 102, 117

bhājana-loka
The "world-receptacle," or external world-universe.
pp. 112-14, 117-20, 123, 130, 183

bhautika- (or upādāya-) rūpa
Derivative *dharma-s* of materiality (as deriving from the four great elements).
pp. 24-5, 33

bhava-cakra
The "wheel of existence," said of the twelve-linked chain of dependent co-origination (*pratītya-samutpāda*).
pp. 93, 96-7

Bhavāgra
Cosmic plain of the Arhat, the summit of the Realm of Formlessness.
pp. 160-61, 174, 198

bhāvanā
The active "permeation" or "impregnation" of seeds or perfumes, as enacted by *karma*.
pp. 85, 105, 110, 119, 122-23, 190, 193, 201

bhāvanā-mārga
The Path of Contemplation, as enacting the "impregnation" (bhāvanā) of the mind (citta) with the purest seeds or perfumes (vāsanāḥ).
pp. 85, 122, 143-44, 148-151, 154-56, 159-62, 167-171, 177-80, 184, 196

bhavaṅga-srotas
Subliminal stream of conscious existence as "impregnated" by karmic perfumes.
pp. 86-87, 191

bhava-saṃtāna
Serial (dharma-) flux of existence.
pp. 65, 79

bhinna
Specifically determined (as the species vs. the genus).
pp. 110

bhinna-sāmānya
Specific sameness.
pp. 111

bhūmi
Mental stage as it corresponds to cosmic plains of existence.
pp. 58, 170, 174, 189

bhūta
Primordial element of materiality (see mahābhūta-s).
pp. 23

bīja-s
The "seeds" of karma, as sown by human action for future germination of fruition.
pp. 89-92

bīja-saṃtati-pariṇāma-viśeṣa
Serial transformation or "metamorphosis" of the karmic seeds into their "heterogeneous" fruitions.
pp. 87-92, 104

bodhisattva
A Buddha-to-be, literally meaning "enlightened being", though not yet in possession of perfect nirvāṇa.
pp. 147, 180

brahma-deva-s
Beings of the Brahma-loka, first cosmic plain of the Realm of Form.
pp. 158, 171

Brahma-pāriṣadya
Assembly of the Brahmins in the Brahma-loka.
pp. 171

Brahma-purohita-deva-s
Attendants of Mahā-brahmā, the one who presides over the Brahma-loka.
pp. 171

Bṛhatphala
"Great Fruition" realm, a cosmic plain below the Akaniṣṭha heaven. It houses the asaṃjñika-sattva-s ("unconscious beings").
pp. 158, 172, 197, 199

buddha
The "enlightened one," or the "one who has reached the ultimate goal."
pp. 1, 4-7, 93, 105, 126, 147, 169

buddha-kṣetra
Buddha-lands, realms of Buddhahood.
pp. 185

caitasika-saṃskāra-s
Mental forces and conscious volitive functions.
pp. 43-48, 62-65, 73

cakṣur-indriya
Sight-faculty or visual organ.
pp. 25, 74, 77

cakṣur-vijñāna
Sight-awareness
pp. 77

catvāryāryasatyāni
The Four Noble Truths.
pp. 1

cetanā
The act of the conscious, free will (the formal constituent of individual *karma*).
pp. 43-5, 48-9, 58, 62-63, 68, 73-5, 80-1, 84, 108, 117, 167, 174, 198

cetanāviśeṣa
The changing, applied moves of the conscious will.
pp. 165

cetanāvṛtii
See *cetanāviśeṣa*.
pp. 165

cetayitvā-karaṇam
Human action as posited by the will (active *karma* as producing karmic deposits or "seeds").
pp. 80, 89-92

citta
The mind (*manas*) as "cumulative" of memories and of mental karmic seeds.
pp. 44, 48, 53, 82-3, 85-6, 97-9, 109, 118-19, 126, 168, 170, 173, 179-80, 182-84, 190-91

citta-mātra
"Mind-only" (a tenet of Buddhist Mahāyāna idealism).
pp. 182-84

darśana-marga
The Path of Seeing, intellectual vision or understanding of the Four Noble Truths as still previous to the Path of direct Contemplation (*bhāvana-mārga*).
pp. 147-157, 160-61, 165, 196

devakṣetra
The lands of the Gods or "superior beings" in the realms of Pure Form and Formlessness.
pp. 57

devaloka
Divine (superior) plains or cosmic levels of existence.
pp. 57

dhāraṇī
Supporter, said mainly of the earth (as support of life).
pp. 8

dharma
Duty, rule, teaching, law, characteristic, property.
pp. 73-7, 86, 97-8, 108, 114, 124, 130-31, 137, 143, 145, 181, 186, 191, 194

dharmāḥ (dharma-s)
Ultimate "factors" or constituents of existence.
pp. 8-9, 13, 15-6, 55-6

dhātu-s
"Elements" or also realms, spheres, whether mental or cosmic.
pp. 22, 54-58, 148

dhyāna
Meditation, exercise in concentration.
pp. 199

dhyāna-bhūmi-s
Stages or levels of meditation.
pp. 151

dravatva
State of liquidity, fluidity, wettness.
pp. 23

dravya
Substance, entitative factor.
(see also dravyaka-dharma).
pp. 17, 29, 49, 52, 64

dravyaka-dharma-s
"Entitative" (as distinguished from "functional") factors of existence.
pp. 49, 64

duḥkha
Suffering, first of the Four Noble Truths.
pp. 11-2, 17-8, 96, 125, 153-54

duḥkha-nirodha
Extinction of suffering, third of the Four Noble Truths.
pp. 129

duḥkha-samudaya
Origination of suffering, second of the Four Noble Truths.
pp. 65-66

dveṣa
Hatred.
pp. 45

dvīpa-s
The continents of earth as they deploy themselves in the four points of the compass around the mithical mount Meru.
pp. 196

garbha
Matrix, womb.
pp. 184

grāhaka-grāhya
The "grasping" (knowing) - "grasped" (known) correlation (subjective function - objective content) similar to Edmund Husserl's noesis-noema.
pp. 51, 189

ghrāṇa-indriya
Smell faculty or olfactory organ.
pp. 25

gotra-dhātu-s
Family-related elements of conscious experience, given in the number of three interrelated sixtuplets (eighteen dhātu-s).
pp. 53-54, 65, 75

hetu-pratyaya
"Root" (principal, proximate) causal conditions and concomitant (subordinate, remote) causal conditions.
pp. 67, 70

hetu-s (hetavaḥ)
"Root" causal conditions, as referred to six principal, proximate forms of causation.
pp. 97

hīnayāna
The "Small Vehicle" of Buddhism.
pp. 3, 7, 35, 52, 87, 93, 104, 118-120, 183

hṛdaya-vastu
The "heart-basis", material organ which seats the mind (manas, citta).
pp. 37-38, 188

indriya-s
Sources of "energy" or "power," i.e., faculties or organs of mental (manendriya), sensorial (prasādendriya), or of other bodily functions (kāyendriya).
pp. 24-26, 39, 58, 75-77, 98

īr-ṇakarman
Material quality of "motion" as proper of the air-element (vāyu), one of the four primary, great elements (mahābhūtāni).
pp. 23

īrṣyā
Jealousy
pp. 45

Iśvara
Proper name given --in Hinduism-- to the personal manifestation of God (sa-guṇa Brahman).
pp. 119

Jambudvīpa
The continent at the South of the mount Meru.
pp. 196

jarā
Decay, deterioration, aging.
pp. 10, 46, 48, 101

jarā-maraṇa
"Old age and death," last link in the twelvefold chain of codependent origination (pratītya-samutpāda).
pp. 94-95, 101

jāti
(Force of) causal generation.
pp. 46, 48, 77, 92-95, 100

jihvā-indriya (jihvendriya)
Taste organ.
pp. 25

jīvita-saṃskāra
"Vital energy," a force determining the span of life in an individual.
pp. 45

jñāna-s
"Wisdom-knowledges," listed as ten in number, eight deriving from eight kṣānti-s and the last two attained through the Path of contemplation (bhāvanā-mārga).
pp. 49-52, 59, 62, 74, 133, 137-40, 145-47, 150-57, 160-62, 168-71, 178-81, 196-97

kāma-dhātu
Realm or sphere of desire, lowest of three psychocosmic spheres (see also rūpa- and ārūpya- dhātu-s).
pp. 56-7, 64, 141, 147-50, 153-54, 157-62, 169, 172, 180, 195-96

kāraṇa-hetu
The efficient, generative and "non-hindrance" cause (first of six principal causes or ṣaḍhetavaḥ).
pp. 72-3, 76-8, 106-07, 113-16, 118-19, 131-32, 195

karma
Human action as carrying its own future retribution.
pp. 4, 15, 36-7, 43-4, 46-8, 56, 58, 67-71, 75-6, 78-82, 84, 86-8, 90-91, 93-4, 96-7, 100-05, 107, 109-17, 119-27, 132, 137-39, 143-45, 157-58, 167, 170, 179-80, 182, 187-88, 190

karmabhava
Karmic existence or "becoming," tenth link in the twelvefold chain of codependent origination (pratītya-samutpāda).
pp. 68, 95, 100

karmaphala
The fruition of karma (reactive karma) as retribution.
pp. 44, 46

karuṇā
Mercy
pp. 12, 180

kāya-indriya (kāyendriya)
The tactile faculty or touch organ.
pp. 25

kāyika-vijñapti
Corporeal or bodily intimation (external manifestation) of the inner will.
pp. 35-6, 82

kāyika-karma
Corporeal action as morally qualified and distinguished from verbal (vācika-) and mental (mano-) karma.
pp. 36, 69-70, 80-1

khakkhaṭatva
State of solidity proper to the earth-element, the first of four primary or great elements (mahābhūtāni).
pp. 22

khāra
Repulsion, repelling force, the characteristic of the earth element (pṛthivī).
pp. 22

kleśācchādita
Veiled by defilement (see also nivṛta).
pp. 84

kleśa-s
Defilements, afflictions, evil passions (see also anuśaya-s).
pp. 56, 89

kliṣṭa-manas
The "afflicted"-mind or Ego-, thought- and will-center, according to Buddhist idealism.
pp. 184

kṛtsna (Pali: kasiṇa)
"Totality," "completeness," referring to the state of total absorption reached through the practice of concentration upon maṇḍalas and other devices.
pp. 163-66, 198

kṛtyika-dharma-s
"Functional" factors of existence as distinguished from "entitative" factors (dravyaka-dharma-s).
pp. 49, 64

kṣaṇa
The "moment" of existence or manifestation of any conditioned factors of existence (saṃskṛta-dharma-s).
pp. 134

kṣaṇika-saṃsarga
"Momentary co-emission" of dharma-s.
pp. 18, 74

kṣaṇika-vāda
The theory of "momentary" manifestation of the dharma-factors of existence.
pp. 108

<u>kṣānti-s</u>
"Patiences" or pre-cognitive states of dedication to the acquisition of the <u>jñāna-s</u> or "wisdom-knowledges" of the Four Noble Truths (see also <u>ānantarya-mārga</u>).
pp. 138-139, 147-160, 196

<u>kṣaya-jñāna</u>
"Knowledge of destruction," the ninth of ten "wisdom-knowledges" whereby the <u>arhat</u> knows that all his karmic residues (<u>upadhi-s</u>) have been destroyed.
pp. 149, 152-53, 156, 167, 174-75, 184

<u>kuśala-karma</u>
Wholesome, good <u>karma</u> producing rewarding retribution.
pp. 43, 48, 80

<u>laghusamudīraṇatva</u>
"Mobility" on account of lightness, the characteristic of the air-element (<u>vāyu</u>), fourth of the Great Elements.
pp. 23

<u>laghutva</u>
Lightness, weightlessness.
pp. 23-24

<u>lakṣaṇa</u>
Character, mark, attribute, phenomenal manifestation.
pp. 21-22

<u>laukika-mārga</u>
"Mundane Path," the one practiced by the <u>Pṛthagjana</u> (common person) as a preparation to enter the "supramundane Path" (<u>lokottaramārga</u>).
pp. 146, 150

<u>laukikāgra-dharma-s</u>
"Supreme mundane <u>dharmas</u>," or pure <u>dharmas</u> (factors) which prepare the "outsider" (<u>pṛthagjana</u>) to the Path to enter the latter.
pp. 150

loka-dhātu-s
Cosmic spheres as corresponding to the three mental levels of the "desire" (kāma-), "form" (rūpa) and "formless" (ārūpya) realms.
pp. 53, 64-65

mahābhūta-s
The "Great Elements," said of four primary factors materiality (rūpa-s): air, fire, water and earth, as representing the characters of motion, heat, liquidity and solidity.
pp. 28, 32-33, 37, 72-76, 124, 131, 186, 192

mahāsaṃghika-s
Followers of a pre-idealistic school of Buddhist thought.
pp. 86, 134, 182

Mahāyāna
The Great Vehicle of Buddhism.
pp. 3, 6, 12, 35, 71, 87, 93, 126, 147, 178, 180, 182, 184, 201

māna
Pride.
pp. 45

manas
Active aspect of the mind as distinguished from the passive or cumulative aspect (citta).
pp. 35, 37-38, 40-44, 49-59, 65, 75, 77, 82-83, 86, 98, 170, 179-80, 184, 189, 191

manasa-ālambana
Mental (abstract) objects of thought.
pp. 77

manasikāra
Mental attention.
pp. 45

maṇḍala
A "circle," used mostly as the means of concentration called kṛtsna-s (or Pali, kasiṇa-s), preliminary practices conducive to the mental states of the Realm of Form (rūpa-dhātu).
pp. 93, 163-64

manodhātu
The "mind" element (see manas).
pp. 55

mano-karma
Mental or intentional moral action, as distinguished from "bodily" (kāyika-) and "verbal" (vācika-) karma.
pp. 55, 69, 81-82

manovijñāna
"Mental" awareness as superior to the five kinds of "sensorial" awareness. In Buddhist idealism, however, this term designates the center of perception and apprehension, second of seven faculties deriving from the ālaya-vijñāna (storehouse of consciousness).
pp. 65

maraṇa
Death
pp. 92

mātsarya
Envy
pp. 45

mati
Thought, notion, understanding.
pp. 50, 59-63, 73-74

māyā
Force of illusion, creative force of Brahman, according to Hinduism. Deceit.
pp. 45, 104, 120-24, 189

moha
Stupidity
pp. 45

<u>naiṣyandika-srotas</u>
The "homogeneous" stream of generic and specific sameness in living beings.
pp. 74, 77, 109

<u>nāmabīja-s</u>
Mental (karmic) "seeds."
pp. 86

<u>nāsāpuṭī</u>
The nose.
pp. 27

<u>nevasaṃjñānāsaṃjñā-āyatana</u>
Mental level of "neither perception nor non-perception, "the highest level of the <u>ārūpyadhātu</u>, corresponding to the <u>Bhavāgra</u> cosmic plain.
pp. 168, 174, 185

<u>nidāna-s</u>
"Links," "members," as applied to the twelve links of the chain of interdependent co-origination (<u>pratītya samutpāda</u>).
pp. 94-102, 107

<u>nikāya-sabhāga</u>
"Community of nature," the force which transmits sameness from generator to generated.
pp. 45-56, 109-110, 113, 118, 191

<u>nimitta</u>
"Mark," "sign," said often of objective determinations (<u>pariccheda</u>).
pp. 42

<u>nimittodgrahaṇa</u>
Mental apprehension of objective, specific determinations (see <u>udgrahaṇa</u>).
pp. 41-42

<u>nirodha</u>
Cessation, state of extinction.
pp. 4, 18-19, 56, 130-32, 134-37, 139-43, 153-54

<u>nirodha-samāpatti</u>
Mental state of total arrest of conscious activities (see <u>asaṃjñi-samāpatti</u>).
pp. 197

nirupadhiśeṣanirvāṇa
nirvāṇa with no karmic residues or adjuncts, i.e., complete nirvāṇa.
pp. 143, 155, 161, 175, 179

nirvāṇa
State of extinction or emancipation from individual bondage, whether it be incomplete (partial) or it be complete (total).
pp. 7-9, 18, 56, 58, 101, 125-26, 130-34, 138, 140, 142-44, 147, 149, 152-53, 155, 160-62, 169-70, 175-85, 201

nirvicikitsā
"Without a doubt," certain.
pp. 151, 154

niṣyanda-phala
"Down-the-stream" fruition, as it follows from the universal sabhāga-hetu or "shared," "homogeneous" causation of specific and generic sameness in living beings.
pp. 74, 109, 112, 148

nivṛta
"Obfuscating," impeding, hindering, as said of the evil passions (anuśaya).
pp. 47, 84

nivṛta-avyākṛta
Morally undefined (neutral) but "obfuscating" and "hindering" as said of karmically alloted passions.
pp. 47-48

nivṛtābhisaṃskṛta-saṃskāra-s
Karmically "formed" obfuscating and hindering forces (kleśa, anuśaya).
pp. 58

pañcaskandhāḥ
The Five Assortments or Division of existence-factors (dharmāḥ). (See skandha-s).
pp. 19

<u>pañcendriyāṇi</u>
The Five Sense-organs (see <u>indriya-s</u>).
pp. 24, 54

<u>paramāṇu-saṃghāta</u>
Conglomerations of subtle atoms of <u>rūpaprasāda</u> (essential contituent of the sense-organs).
pp. 26

<u>parinirvāṇa</u> (Pali: <u>parinibbāna</u>)
Perfect, supreme <u>nirvāṇa</u>.
pp. 19, 176, 177

<u>pariccheda</u>
The mental discrimination or discernment of objective characteristics or determinations (see <u>nimitta</u>).
pp. 42, 50

<u>parihāṇi</u>
"Relapse" into an inferior level of existence.
pp. 140-41, 194

<u>parijñā</u>
Wisdom-knowledge of the highest realms of existence.
pp. 137-38, 140, 142

<u>parikalpita</u>
Imagination, said mostly of the illusory character of the external objects in Buddhist idealism.
pp. 16

<u>parimārgaṇa</u>
Search, investigation, as proper to the <u>darśana-mārga</u> or "Path of seeing".
pp. 150-51, 165

<u>pariṇāma</u>
Process of transformation.
pp. 96

<u>parīttābha-s</u>
Beings of "limited radiance," reborn and living in the second region of the Realm of Form (<u>rūpa-dhātu</u>).
pp. 158, 172

<u>pradhāna</u>
"Exertion," "effort," as applied to the following of the Path.
pp. 158, 162

<u>prahāṇa</u>
"Abandonment" of levels of existence as "alloted" by the karmic process.
pp. 142, 144-45, 160-61, 166-67, 169, 180

<u>prajñā</u>
Supreme "wisdom," as proper to the enlightened person. Predominantly used in the <u>Mahāyāna</u> schools.
pp. 8, 41, 57, 140, 182

<u>pramāda</u>
Negligence, carelessness.
pp. 45

<u>prāpti</u>
The force (<u>saṃskāra</u>) of "acquisition," specially in reference to vegetative processes.
pp. 45, 48

<u>prasāda</u>
See <u>prasāda-rūpa</u>
pp. 23-24, 27-28, 33, 39, 42, 53, 188

<u>prasāda-rūpa</u>
Sutle matter which is constitutive of the sense-organs and which is "non-resistant" (<u>apratigha</u>) and "translucent" (<u>accha</u>) to the subjective awareness (<u>vijñāna</u>).
pp. 54, 59-60, 74, 98

<u>pratighāta</u>
"Collision," "obstruction," "resistance," mostly said of the external object as it "collides" against the subjective faculties or organs.
pp. 23-24

<u>pratisaṃkhyā-nirodha</u>
One of the three "unconditioned" (<u>asaṃskṛta-dharmas</u>) as the absolute extinction of <u>one by one</u> of the karmic levels of existence as obtained by the acquisition of the wisdom-knowledges (<u>jñānas</u>).
pp. 19, 131-32, 134-45, 147, 155, 160-62, 169

<u>pratītya-samutpāda</u>
"Interdependent-coorigination," "relational causation," the way of causal interconnection and co-arisal of all conditioned entities, and specially said of the twelve links of the <u>bhava-cakra</u> (wheel of existence).
pp. 93, 96-98, 103, 191

<u>pratyaya</u>
Remote, subordinate causal condition, as distinguished from <u>hetu</u>, contextualy used as meaning principal, proximate causal conditions. (see <u>ṣaḍ-hetavaḥ</u>).
pp. 40, 70-71, 76-78, 111-12, 117

<u>pravacana</u>
The "spoken word" or preaching of the Dharma.
pp. 4

<u>prayoga-mārga</u>
The "preparative" or "application" (mundane) Path (see <u>laukikamārga</u>).
pp. 146

<u>prāyogika-bīja-s</u>
Wholesome karmic "seeds" produced by the "application" (<u>prayoga</u>) of the will when opposing evil passions and proclivities.
pp. 85

<u>preta-s</u>
"Hungry" spirits or beings living in a level of retribution below the level of the humans.
pp. 137, 156

<u>prīti(-saumanasya)</u>
Exalted feeling of joy experienced in the early stages of the <u>rūpa</u>- (form-) concentration.
pp. 165-66, 199

<u>pṛthagjana</u>
A "common person" or "outsider" to the Buddhist Path.
pp. 157, 197

<u>pṛthivī</u>
Soil- or earth-element, one of the four primary elements of materiality, as characterized by "solidity" and "repulsion."
pp. 23

<u>puṃindriya</u>
Male sex organ.
pp. 38

<u>puruṣa-sabhāgatā</u>
The specific nature shared by rational or personal beings.
pp. 110

<u>Pūrvavideha</u>
The continent at the East of the central mount Meru, one of the four <u>dvīpa-s</u> or earthly continents.
pp. 196

<u>rāga</u>
Passionate, inordinate love.
pp. 45

<u>raṇa</u>
Turbulence, trouble, fight (see <u>saraṇa</u>, <u>araṇa</u>).
pp. 17

<u>rūpa</u>
Factors of materiality, one of the Five Divisions of <u>dharmas</u> (see <u>skandha</u>-s).
pp. 20, 33, 36-37, 56-58, 60-64, 72, 86, 110, 140, 147-50, 152-54, 156, 158, 162, 165, 169-70, 176-80, 194, 199

<u>rūpa-bīja-s</u>
Material "seeds" as deposited by "verbal" and "corporeal" human action (<u>karma</u>) and constituting the <u>avijñapti-rūpa</u>.
pp. 86

rūpa-dhātu
The "realm of Form," one of three psycho-cosmic spheres of existence (see kāma- and ārūpya-dhātu).
pp. 56-57, 64, 132, 141, 147, 151-52, 155, 158-60, 162, 166-67, 170, 173, 197, 199

rūpa-loka-s
Cosmic, rebirth levels of the Realm of Form.
pp. 57, 110, 189

rūpāṇi
Visible sense-matters as colors (varṇa) and shapes (saṃsthāna).
pp. 28-29, 131

rūpāvacara-devas
"Gods" (or superior beings) inhabiting the cosmic plains (bhūmiloka-s) of the Realm of Form (rūpa-dhātu).
pp. 171, 173

sabhāga
"Shared" allotment (or specific traits) as said of the similarity among individuals of the same species.
pp. 77-78, 85, 106, 113, 116, 123

sabhāgatā
See nikāya-sabhāga.
pp. 68, 73, 75, 109-111, 191

sabhāga-hetu
The "co-sharing" or "homogeneous" cause which transmits a "community of nature" (nikāya-sabhāga) from generator to generated.
pp. 73-77, 79, 108-113, 115, 148, 192

ṣaḍ-āyatana
The six "basis" or faculties of awareness, the mind and five sense-organs.
pp. 95, 98

sa-ādhāraṇa-bījas
"Common," "universal seeds" as "sown" by universal karma and producing universally shared effects, such as a "community of specific nature" and the "world-receptacle" or external Universe (bhājana-loka).
pp. 111, 123, 183

sadṛśa
Similar, same-looking.
pp. 191

sahabhū-hetu
Mutuality cause as principle of concausation or causal interdependency, one of six root-conditions (ṣaḍ-hetavaḥ).
pp. 73-74, 76

sahetuka-phala
Causal effect or "fruition" effected by generative causes.
pp. 144

śaikṣa
The novice or beginner in the practice of the Path.
pp. 18, 146-47, 150, 163, 197

sakṛd-āgāmin
The one who still is "to return once" to the kāma-dhātu level of the humans before becoming an ānāgamin or "non-returner" to the kāma-dhātu (Realm of Desire).
pp. 158

samādhi
Mental state of concentration or trance induced by the practice of meditation.
pp. 45, 140, 163, 167-68

samāpatti
"Attainment" as said of the higher states of concentration (see samādhi).
pp. 158, 166, 169, 172-174, 197

<u>samānabhāgya</u>
"Shared" sameness as this affects living beings of the same species (see <u>nikāya-sabhāga</u>).
pp. 68

<u>saṃcita</u>
Conglomeration, aggregation, said of the atoms of materiality.
pp. 9, 21, 27, 187

<u>saṃgha</u>
The Buddhist community or congregation.
pp. 5, 146, 179

<u>saṃghāta</u>
Conglomeration (of atoms of materiality). (See <u>saṃcita</u>).
pp. 9, 15, 21

<u>saṃgraha</u>
Seizing, grasping, com-prehending, as said of the mental activities.
pp. 6, 42

<u>saṃgrahaṇa</u>
Mental and perceptional "com-prehension."
pp. 42, 51, 53, 99, 188

<u>saṃjñā</u>
Perception and notion (co-gnition) as deriving from multiple sensations (<u>vedanā</u>), third of the Five Divisions of dharma-s (<u>pañcaskandhāḥ</u>).
pp. 20, 41-43, 49-50, 55, 59-64, 73-75, 99, 108, 181, 188-89, 191

<u>saṃprayuktaka-hetu</u>
"Association-by-reliance" cause, the concausation effected by some causal conditions as these commonly rely (<u>samāśraya</u>) upon another principal root-condition; one of the six <u>hetu</u>-s (<u>ṣaḍhetavaḥ</u>).
pp. 74-75, 97

<u>saṃpraharṣa</u>
Exultant joy
pp. 159

<u>saṃsāra</u>
"Mundane existence" as subject to the karmic cycle of birth-death-rebirth.
pp. 12

<u>saṃsarga</u>
"Co-emission," simultaneous co-discharge of momentary dharmas (see <u>kṣaṇika-saṃsarga</u>).
pp. 17

<u>saṃskāra-s</u>
Volitive forces and proclivities, fourth of the Five Divisions of <u>dharma-s</u> (<u>pañcaskandhāḥ</u>).
pp. 20-21, 42-49, 57, 62, 64, 73, 95-99, 101, 104, 173, 198

<u>saṃskṛta-dharma-s</u>
"Conditioned,: "co-produced" factors of existence, as said of the Five <u>skandhas</u>, or divisions of <u>dharma-s</u>.
pp. 73, 130-133, 145, 181

<u>saṃsthāna</u>
External, bodily shape.
pp. 21, 29

<u>saṃtāna</u>
Serial, continuing, as said of the flux of momentary existence-factors.
pp. 45, 86, 191

<u>saṃtīraṇa</u>
Function of predicative judgment.
pp. 150-51, 156, 161, 165

<u>samudaya</u>
The origin (of suffering), the second of Four Noble Truths.
pp. 4, 18

<u>samutpāda</u>
Causal "co-arisal" whereby all twelve links of the wheel of existence are said to be the <u>cause</u> of one another.
pp. 4, 18, 93, 96

<u>samutpanna</u>
Causal "co-arisal" whereby all twelve links of the wheel of existence are said to be the <u>effect</u> of one another.
pp. 93, 96

<u>samyaktva</u>
Absolute perfection (<u>summum bonum</u>).
pp. 153, 175, 181

<u>śānta</u>
Peace, calmness.
pp. 166

<u>saraṇa</u>
Restless, turbulent, "with trouble."
pp. 17

<u>śarīraceṣṭā</u>
Gesture, gesticulation, as external intimation (see <u>vijñapti</u>).
pp. 187

<u>sarvasaṃjñāvedayita-nirodha</u>
Cessation or halting to all perception and sensation.
pp. 169, 174

<u>sarvatraga-hetu</u>
The "all-pervading" cause as said of "ignorance," last of the six hetu-s (<u>ṣaḍhetavaḥ</u>).
pp. 75, 96

<u>sāsrava</u>
Soiled, tinged with passions (<u>anuśaya-s</u>), as said of the impure <u>dharma-s</u>.
pp. 17-18, 21

<u>sattva-loka</u>
World of sentient beings.
pp. 119

<u>sattva-sabhāgatā</u>
Generic share of nature among all a sentient beings.
pp. 110

<u>saumanasya</u>
Emotion of exultant joy (see <u>saṃpraharṣa</u>, <u>prīti-saumanasya</u>).
pp. 159

<u>savastuka</u>
Having a "causal" basis.
pp. 19

<u>savicikitsā</u>
"With doubt," state of uncertainty.
pp. 151

<u>skandha-s</u>
"Heaps" or "divisions" (assortments) of dharmas (see <u>rūpa</u>-, <u>vedanā</u>-, <u>saṃjñā</u>, <u>saṃskāra</u>- and <u>vijñānaskandha</u>, <u>pañcaskandhāḥ</u>).
pp. 2, 49, 181

<u>smṛti</u>
Mindfulness, memory.
pp. 45, 151

<u>sneha</u>
"Cohesion," characteristic of the state of liquidity pertaining to the water-element (<u>āp</u>).
pp. 23

<u>sopadhiśeṣanirvāṇa</u>
<u>Nirvāṇa</u> with "adjuncts" or karmic residues; incomplete, partial <u>nirvāna</u> (see <u>nirupadhiśeṣanir-vāṇa</u>
pp. 143, 156, 161

<u>sparśa</u>
Contact, said mainly of the subjective faculties or organs with their corresponding objects.
pp. 38-42, 49, 53, 55, 59, 95, 98, 100, 188

<u>sparśāyatāṇi</u>
Basis of contact (between subject and object) as said of the five sense-organs.
pp. 39

<u>spraṣṭavya-dravya</u>
Tangible entity.
pp. 33

<u>spraṣṭavya-viṣaya</u>
Tactile sense-matter, the immediate object of the touch-organ.
pp. 38

<u>srotāpannārya</u>
The noble man who has joined the stream (of the followers of the Path).
pp. 146-47, 150-51, 158, 197

<u>śrotra-indriya</u>
Auditory faculty or sound-organ.
pp. 25

<u>sthiti</u>
"Subsistence," as said of the moment of the <u>dharma</u>'s existence or manifestation in the present, prior to its extinction (<u>anityatā</u>).
pp. 46, 48

<u>strīndriya</u>
Sex organ of the female.
pp. 38

<u>styāna</u>
Indolence, lazyness.
pp. 45

<u>śubha</u>
"Excellent," "blessing," as said of good, wholesome (<u>kuśala</u>) actions and karmic "seeds" (<u>śubha-bīja-s</u>).
pp. 46

<u>Śubhakṛtsna-loka</u>
Plain of the beings of "pure fixation," fourth cosmic level of the Realm of Form (<u>rūpa-dhātu</u>).
pp. 159, 172

<u>śuddhāvāsa-kāyika-devas</u>
"Pure abode, bodily gods," the superior beings who stay "equally young" in the <u>Akaniṣṭha</u> heaven.
pp. 173

<u>sukha</u>
Pleasure, aggreeability.
pp. 166

svalakṣaṇa
Apparent, phenomenal manifestation (of the factors of existence) in the present, as distinguished from *svabhāva*, or their "noumenal" givenness in the past and future.
pp. 8, 17

tathāgata
The "Thus-come and/or thus gone," an appelative of the Buddha.
pp. 183-84

tathāgata-garbha
The "womb of the thus-come," said of the potentiality to enlightenment and Buddhahood in the individual mind, and also applied later to the potentiality of *tathatā* (Thusness) to bring forth the Universe.
pp. 184

tathatā
Thusness, the primal and ultimate "ground" of Reality, according to *Mahāyāna* literature.
pp. 184, 201

tejas
The "fire-element" one of the four primary elements (*mahābhūtas*).
pp. 23

triadhvanaḥ
The "Three Roads" of time (future, present, past).
pp. 16

tṛṣṇā
Craving, desire, appetite.
pp. 21, 95, 99

upādāna
Clinging, attachment.
pp. 21, 67, 95, 99

upādāya-rūpa-s
See *bhautika-rūpa*
pp. 22-25, 37

<u>upadhi</u>
"Adjunt" or "remnant" as said of the still remaining karmic "seeds" in the still incomplete or partial <u>nirvāṇa</u> and <u>visaṃyoga</u> (disjunction).
pp. 69, 104, 121, 143, 166, 172, 178, 200

<u>upekṣā</u>
Mental state of aquanimity.
pp. 166-73, 178-80, 200

<u>upalabdhi</u>
Pure subjective function of "apprehension" as exercised by <u>vijñāna</u> (subjective "holding" on the part of the subject's awareness).
pp. 52

<u>uṣṇata</u>, <u>uṣṇatva</u>
"Heat," the characteristic of the "fire-element" (<u>tejas</u>).
pp. 23

<u>utsarga</u>
Ejection, emission (see <u>saṃsarga</u>).
pp. 17

<u>Uttarakuru</u>
The Superior continent, North of the mount Meru, one of the four <u>dvīpa-s</u> or continents. Said also of the inhabitants of this continent.
pp. 157, 196

<u>vācika-karma</u>
"Verbal" <u>karma</u> as distinguished from the "mental" (<u>mano-</u>) and "corporeal" (<u>kāyika-</u>) human action.
pp. 36, 69-70, 80-82, 180

<u>vedanā</u>
Sensation, feeling, second of the Five Divisions of <u>dharma-s</u> (<u>skandha-s</u>).
pp. 20, 39-43, 58-59, 62, 64, 67, 73-75, 95, 99, 181, 188-89, 191

<u>vāg-</u> (or <u>vācika-</u>) <u>vijñapti</u>
"Verbal intimation" of a mental intention which results in the positing of <u>vācika-karma</u>.
pp. 35-36, 69, 187

varṇa
Color
pp. 21, 28

vāsanā-s (vāsanāḥ)
"Perfumes," as said of passive karma as this impregnates the passive, cumulative mind (citta). Used very often as synonimous with bījas (karmic "seeds").
pp. 37, 82, 89-92

vastu
"Basis" of things, real object, substance.
pp. 19, 194

vastumātragrahaṇa
Basic and simple apprehension of something.
pp. 189

vāyu
The air-element, one of the Four primary elements or mahābhūtas.
pp. 23

vicāra
"Searching thought," as distinguished from vitarka ("sustained thought").
pp. 45, 159, 165, 178, 197-98

vicikitsā
Doubt, hesitation.
pp. 196

vighna
Obstruction, impediment, prevention.
pp. 135-41, 145

vihāṇi
"Abandonment" or "avoidance" of future destinations due to wholesome causes other than "wisdom-knowledge" (jñāna).
pp. 139, 142, 145

vijñāna
Discriminative consciousness, pure subject-awareness exerting the function of comprehension and abstraction (saṃgrahaṇa, udgrahaṇa). It con-

stitutes the mind in both its active (manas) and cumulative aspects (citta). Last of the Five Skandha-s.
pp. 20-21, 24-25, 36-37, 41, 43, 49-58, 62, 64, 77, 83, 95, 98, 108, 173, 181

vijñānānantyāyatana
The mental stage in which the "infinity of consciousness" is experienced.
pp. 167, 173

vijñānavāda
"Cognitionism," the doctrine of Buddhist idealism.
pp. 35, 125

vijñapti
External "intimation" or expression of a mental intention, whether it be verbal (vācika-) or corporeal (kāyika-).
pp. 34-36, 52, 82, 187

vijñaptimātratā
"Consciousness-(projection-)only," the doctrine of Buddhist idealism.
pp. 35

vikalpa
Mental discourse, carrying the connotation of "indecisive," "hesitating," "fanciful," not accompanied by certitude.
pp. 42, 151, 165, 189

vimokṣa-s
The gradual liberations or emancipations of the different levels of existence as deriving from the acquisition of the "wisdom-knowledges" (jñānas).
pp. 156

vimukti-mārga
The Path of seven "wisdom-knowledges" (jñānas) within the darśana-mārga (Path of Seeing).
pp. 147-49, 150-151, 154, 160

vinivartanīya
"Relapsing" into lower levels of existence.
pp. 169

vipāka-hetu
The "maturation" cause, the form of causation proper to the individual karma-process, one of the six hetu-s or principal root-, causal conditions (ṣaḍ-hetavaḥ).
pp. 76-80, 83, 87-90, 93, 101-5, 107-8, 116, 121, 126, 191

vipāka-phala
The effects or fruition from individual karma as resulting through the vipāka-hetu form of causation.
pp. 88-92, 114, 117, 144, 186

vīrya
(Psychic) energy.
pp. 174

visaṃyoga
"Disjunction" from karmic levels of existence as gradually effected by the acquisition of ten "wisdom-knowledges" (jñānas). A correlate to the pratisaṃkhyā-nirodha or extinction "through wisdom-knowledge".
pp. 75, 131, 141-42, 144-45, 149, 153-54, 156, 160-62, 170, 179-80, 195

viṣaya-s (viṣayaḥ)
The sense-matters or stimuli of the five sense-organs.
pp. 25, 28-34, 54, 58-60

viṣayālambana
Gross material object of perception.
pp. 188

viṣayanimittagrahaṇa (or viṣayaviśeṣarūpagraha)
Apprehension of material characters or determinations.
pp. 42

viṣayapratighāta
The "collision" of any sense-organ with its corresponding "sense-matter."
pp. 191

viṣayaviśeṣasaṃgrahaṇa
(See viṣayanimittagrahaṇa)
pp. 49

viśeṣa
Differentiation, variation.
pp. 42

viśeṣabhāgya
"Disparity" of karmic allotment as affecting different individuals.
pp. 68

visuddha
Pure, purified (visuddhi: purification).
pp. 49

vitarka
"Sustained thought," a function of the mind (see vicāra).
pp. 45, 159, 165-66, 178, 198

vṛddhi
Growth, development.
pp. 23

vṛtti
Activity, function, modification of the mind or will.
pp. 22, 26

vyākṛta
Morally "defined" either as good or evil (as distinguished from avyākṛta: morally neutral).
pp. 46, 80, 84, 188